Cosmopolitanism and International Relations Theory

To the memory of my beloved father

Neville Fogg Beardsworth

1924–2007

Cosmopolitanism and International Relations Theory

Richard Beardsworth

polity

First published in 2011 by Polity Press

Polity Press
65 Bridge Street
Cambridge CB2 1UR, UK

Polity Press
350 Main Street
Malden, MA 02148, USA

ISBN-13: 978-0-7456-4323-6
ISBN-13: 978-0-7456-4324-3(pb)

A catalogue record for this book is available from the British Library.

Typeset in 10.5 on 12 pt Times New Roman
by Toppan Best-set Premedia Limited
Printed and bound in Great Britain by MPG Books Group Limited, Bodmin, Cornwall

The publisher has used its best endeavours to ensure that the URLs for external websites referred to in this book are correct and active at the time of going to press. However, the publisher has no responsibility for the websites and can make no guarantee that a site will remain live or that the content is or will remain appropriate.

Every effort has been made to trace all copyright holders, but if any have been inadvertently overlooked the publisher will be pleased to include any necessary credits in any subsequent reprint or edition.

For further information on Polity, visit our website: www.politybooks.com

Contents

Acknowledgements

My thanks to Stephen Barker, Seyla Benhabib, Garrett Brown, Michael Dorsch, Robert Fine, Philip Golub, Daniel Gunn, Peter Hägel, Patrick Hayden, Christian Joppke, Seán Molloy, Scott Nelson, Patricia Owens, Ali Rahnema, Leif Wenar and Michael Williams for comments on the book or discussions around it. Some of the ideas in this book were rehearsed recently in various academic venues: my particular thanks to Anne-Marie Le Gloannec and Ariel Colonomos, Sci. Po., Paris, to graduate students in the Yale Political Theory group, especially Lucas and Louis, and to past and present undergraduate and graduate students at the American University of Paris. I also thank the two anonymous reviewers for very helpful comments on the original manuscript, as well as the editorial and production teams at Polity for their speed and grace. My research assistant, Tyler Shenk-Boright, was more than productive in the last year retrieving and checking statistical information: a large thanks to him.

My final thanks to Brooke, who has always offered careful advice and patiently awaited the end of the manuscript. I dedicate this book to my father, a man who understood, with deep joy, the risk of political construction.

Introduction

The aim of this book is to relate the concerns of cosmopolitanism to the discipline of International Relations and its field, international relations and world politics.[1] The principles of cosmopolitanism – together with the cosmopolitan disposition towards international relations to which they lead – are often referred to or discussed in IR literature (earlier examples are Bull, 1977; Carr, 2001; Morgenthau, 2004; more recent examples flourish: for example, C. Brown, 1992 and 2002; Keohane and Nye, 2003; Linklater, 1998; Ruggie, 2003). Equally, both moral and political philosophy and political theory increasingly refer to international relations and the literature of IR (for example: Beitz, 1999a, 1999b, 1999c; Brock and Brighouse, 2005; Caney, 2005; Erskine, 2008a; Held, 1995a; Nussbaum, 1998). Given deepening dependence between states, between peoples and between individuals, it is understandable that there is this parallel growth in interdisciplinary reference between philosophy, political theory and IR.[2]

Since specific problems facing actors in the field of world politics are of an increasingly global nature, and since the solutions to them call for both global cooperation and global vision, the relations between the constructs of cosmopolitanism and those of IR need, however, to be explored more systematically. What are feasible cosmopolitan commitments in world politics? What are the important and effective agents for these commitments in this field? How does one respond to the persistent IR charge that cosmopolitan commitments are well-intentioned, but idealistic, if not dangerous? How does one respond to the similar charge that, when pitched pragmatically, they are ultimately complicit with liberal hegemony or with global liberal governance, and that cosmopolitan behaviour in the field of international relations must lead to elitism? These types of question need to be squarely addressed by creating a reflective space of debate between cosmopolitanism and IR. The moral and political philosophy of cosmopolitanism is fairly secured, although there are distinct positions assumed within it. What is not secured is the *relation* between the constructs of cosmopolitanism and those of international relations in a globalizing world. For this, more interdisciplinary dialogue between cosmopolitanism and the theory orienting IR thinking and research is required. Such dialogue is the subject of this book.

To orchestrate this dialogue, I have made several assumptions and one decision. Before turning to the substantive content of the book, I wish to rehearse them.[3]

(1) This book is theoretical and is theoretical on several levels. In considering the relation between cosmopolitanism and international relations, I turn to specific schools of IR theory and debate the ways in which these schools frame international relations and the way in which cosmopolitan thought can effectively respond to these framings. To make this step, I assume that theory is vital to cognition in the first place, and that, despite constituting distinct ways of theorizing the world, cosmopolitanism and IR theory are necessarily talking to each other because they are both constructs *of* the world. Cosmopolitan theory and IR theory are distinct from each other in one simple sense: the first is more normatively minded (moral framing of what should be the case); the second more empirically minded (explanatory framing of what is the case). Normative IR theory has worked with this normative/empirical distinction in recent years from within IR theory (Beitz, 1999a, 1999b, 1999c; C. Brown, 1992 and 2002; Erskine, 2008a; Frost, 1996). The assumption of the book is the following in this context: in a world of growing interdependence, the theoretical constructs of cosmopolitanism have increasing purchase on empirical reality with regard to a *specific* range of issues: international security, international human rights, financial and economic regulation, climate change mitigation, development, health and sustainability, and intercultural dialogue. Consequently, while the difference between normative theory and empirical theory remains ever-important, the actual distinction between the normative and the empirical in the domain of world politics is becoming blurred. Thus, *qua* constructs of the world within growing empirical interdependence, the moral and political thought of cosmopolitanism and IR theory are necessarily ever-more related to each other. The fact that there is an increasing volume of books on cosmopolitanism (see Brown and

Held, 2010) and that students of IR appear increasingly interested in cosmopolitan responses to international conflict and cooperation would seem to testify to this convergence of levels of interest, even if cosmopolitanism could, and should, never become an empirical theory in the heuristic tradition of social scientific theory (see Lakatos, 1970; Keohane, 1986, pp. 1–24). Cosmopolitanism constitutes a normative theory in relation to the field of world politics, but its positions on specific areas of this field are 'empirically meaningful' (to use the language of rational choice theory) given growing dependence between states. A dialogue between contemporary cosmopolitan ideas, on the one hand, and IR theory, on the other, is thus timely and fruitful.

This first assumption on theoretical convergence can be deepened by three further theoretical remarks.

First, it is commonplace within IR theory that methodological pluralism prevails, since international political reality is too complex for one type of abstraction to have descriptive or explanatory monopoly. Unlike in the physical sciences, there is no attempt to claim a unified theory of the political real. Human society is multilayered; its agents are at the same time its observers, which renders theoretical unification a priori impossible. One's theory is thus apt to change given the nature, and limits, of the object analysed. It makes little sense, for instance, to reflect upon interstate violence in the terms of the International Criminal Court. Conversely, it makes every sense to theorize state responsibility towards other states and their citizens as well as towards its own citizens in terms of the institutional evolution of international law. As the plurality of IR theories indicates, the theoretical frame and the chosen unit of analysis must fit. Given this plurality, an articulated relation between a moral and political philosophy of the world, like cosmopolitanism, and the theorization of world politics can help one to understand *what* one is theorizing and *how* one is theorizing when framing the emerging political entity called 'global politics'.

Second, normative theory in IR since the 1990s has helped many students of IR understand the immanence of ethics to questions of power in international affairs. As dependence between states increases, the question of legitimate behaviour between states also increases (Buchanan, 2003; Clark, 2005; Lebow, 2003). Ethics and law, that is, become part and parcel of one's understanding of international politics as processes of globalization deepen. This means that the relation between morality and politics grows in intricacy, the more socially dense international relations become. I make a lot of this historico-sociological argument in the book. It was first formulated on the domestic level by the sociologist Norbert Elias (1982); it is applied to the global level by Andrew Linklater (2002, 2007a,

2007b). A mutually self-excluding distinction between the normative and the positive in social science is thereby undone. In other words, while not explanatory, normative IR theory proceeds on the basis that its reflections on the principles of political behaviour and loyalty speak to empirical reality. Without this purchase upon the latter, such reflection would simply not be made in the first place. As a normative theory, cosmopolitanism itself holds a strong place in any reflection on international and supranational terms of political legitimacy. Since political legitimacy is now an immediate concern of global power structures, cosmopolitanism has, again, empirical meaning.

Third, the normative status of cosmopolitan thought is no longer distinct from empirical political reality as such. As several cosmopolitan commentaries on international law point out (see Cabrera, 2004; Hayden, 2005; Held, 2004; Robertson, 2002), normative arguments about the basic needs and interests of human beings are embedded in the international human rights regime. Following Stephen Krasner's classic definition, an international regime is composed of a set of 'implicit or explicit principles, norms, rules and decision-making procedures around which actors' expectations converge in a given area of international relations' (1983, p. 2). The international human rights regime is one such body of norms, rules and expectations that pertain to the relations between all signatory governments and their citizens, as well as to those between these governments and international or stateless refugees. Human rights constitute a normative understanding of human relations: they posit what relations between human beings as human beings *should* be. As an international regime, this normative framework has, precisely, effects in the real, although these effects remain notoriously uneven (see C. Brown, 2002 and 2005, pp. 221–46). Despite this unevenness, it is nevertheless correct for cosmopolitans to claim that, with the rights regime, normative theory has an immanent relation to the real as such. This means again that the standard social science distinction between the normative and the empirical offers too crude a theorization of reality and that affirmation of the human rights regime places cosmopolitanism squarely *within* IR theoretical framings of twenty-first-century political reality (see, particularly, Hayden, 2005 and 2008).

By looking at the relation between cosmopolitanism and international relations through debate on their respective *theories*, this book is assuming, then, several points under my first basic assumption of theoretical convergence. These theories are framing the same complex object of international reality; they therefore provide a privileged access to mutual debate. Although they are framing it differently and/or their emphasis is different, this difference fits methodological pluralism within the discipline of IR. Given increasing dependence between states and the consequences of this interdependence (I alluded above to change in terms of political legitimacy and to the rise of international regimes), the normative status of cosmopolitan theory has growing purchase on empirical international reality. Prevalent distinctions in social science between the normative and the empirical are thereby unmade. My own use of theory, when I stage debate between cosmopolitanism and IR theory, will be varied and tiered, according to the specific object analysed within the schools of IR theory selected. For example, power, global justice, international political economy and universalism form, respectively, different types of theoretical object and require different theoretical treatments within the overarching debate between cosmopolitanism and IR as a whole. I return to this very last point later in the introduction.

(2) My second basic assumption narrows the field of debate that I seek at a second level and makes straightforward sense of my choice of IR theoretical schools elaborated in point (3) below. This book considers cosmopolitanism in relation to basic liberal tenets and therefore rehearses cosmopolitan concerns as a whole in the context of modern liberalism and its avatars. This will seem to some a rather arbitrary, indeed violent circumscription. For diverse, if not opposing reasons, many theorists are today concerned to widen critical debate around a common humanity *beyond* liberal tenets (for example: Appiah, 2006; Dallmayr, 2004 and 2010; Walker, 2010). Furthermore, as Simon Caney rightly notes in *Justice Beyond Borders*, there are a series of reasons why cosmopolitanism and liberalism cannot be aligned (2005, pp. 4–6). Cosmopolitan tenets can be found in many religions; the philosophy of cosmopolitanism has a long intellectual history that well pre-dates liberalism; some committed to liberal principles (in particular, the outstanding worth of the individual) are not cosmopolitan (John Rawls, for example), while cosmopolitan understanding in Buddhism or Confucianism is not liberal. There are thus 'both non-liberal cosmopolitans and non-cosmopolitan liberals' (ibid., p. 6). These reminders regarding the complexity of cosmopolitan discourse are important, especially for cross-cultural dialogue in a globalized world (see Dallmayr, 2002; Held and Moore, 2008). The recent escalation of violence between aggressive universalism and Islamic fundamentalism is testament to the importance of cross-cultural and interreligious exchange in world politics (Dallmayr, 2004). It is also important to emphasize, in this context of bringing together cosmopolitanism and liberalism, the critical distinction between 'weak' and 'strong' cosmopolitanism.[4]

Weak cosmopolitans, like David Miller and Thomas Nagel, do not consider that rights pertaining to the dignity of moral personhood can be universalized since some of them are specific to liberal communities. That said, rights pertaining to the lower (liberal and non-liberal) threshold of the dignity of life can be (Nagel, 2005; Miller, 2007a and 2007b). Strong cosmopolitans, like Simon Caney and Thomas Pogge, consider, on the contrary, that the universalization of the rights pertaining to moral autonomy is, theoretically and ethically, the only consistent cosmopolitan position (Caney, 2005; Pogge, 1992). This distinction is important for IR not only because it concerns the contours of just war, of the rights and responsibilities of intervention, and the global reaches (or not) of economic and social justice. It is also important for deciding what *agents*, in the field of world politics, can have what *responsibilities*. One major thread of this book will be, for example, that leading states should aim for minimal cosmopolitan responsibilities given the need to solve global collective action problems, while transnational civil actors and international organizations may continue to work with, and look to, a larger pool of rights and responsibilities for humanity and the planet as a whole.

The above said, my basic claim is nevertheless the following at this stage of the argument. Although cosmopolitanism, as a loose philosophy of the universal *polis,* is larger than liberalism, contemporary cosmopolitan argument constitutes, broadly speaking, an 'offshoot' of Enlightenment liberal thought. Whether one is a weak cosmopolitan or a strong one, arguments around the extent and purpose of cosmopolitan concerns for the world as a whole are working from out of the background of liberalism. For, only with this background does one decide, to begin with, what is universalizable about the liberal subject or not. This background entails the following major attributes: separation of morality from religion; separation of the state from religion and civil society; thick civil life and market independence; moral constraints on law; individual freedom; political self-determination and political community (see the collection of writings in Rosen and Wolff, 1999). Since there are necessary trade-offs between these various attributes, liberalism has various political and economic forms through which these attributes are assumed: libertarian, neo-liberal, social or social-democratic, republican, progressive. I do not address these forms yet in the context of the international. My present concern is much more basic: when working within the contemporary fields of political thought and IR, the ideas of cosmopolitanism and liberalism are necessarily linked in some constellation or other. Given its object, world politics, this book works throughout with this link between the two.

The latter remark leads to my third decision concerning the parameters of a discussion between cosmopolitanism and international relations.

(3) The book focuses on three schools of thought within IR theory: Realism, Marxism and its avatars, and postmodernism.[5] This focus is given for strategic reasons: each school offers, from out of its intellectual identity within IR, a critique of universalism, in general, and of liberalism, in particular. Since contemporary cosmopolitanism constitutes, in the main, an offshoot of Enlightenment liberal thought, these schools' constitutive critiques of liberal universalism in the IR context of international liberalism necessarily puncture the ambitions of cosmopolitan thinking. In other words, I confront contemporary cosmopolitanism with three schools of IR theory that are most critical of cosmopolitan ideas given their innate scepticism towards liberal forms of universalism either in the international field alone (Realism) or in both the domestic and international fields (Marxism and postmodernism).

This book does not consider at length approaches to world politics in IR theory that are either methodologically individualist (rational choice theory) or methodologically insistent on a hard distinction between national and international community (certain versions of international liberalism). Although the contemporary form of international liberalism is referred to at length in chapter 1 and recurrently through the book, and although rational choice theory is used within my exposition of the realist critique of cosmopolitanism (chapter 2), this book does not give these schools of IR thought independent attention. It focuses, rather, on those theories that are constitutively critical of universalism in the international domain, and that allow me to exposit through a set of theoretical dialogues where, and how, borders fall; and where, and how, borders remain necessary. I intend to give specific attention to the minimal universalisms of international liberalism, weak cosmopolitanism, and cosmopolitan Realism in a separate book.

I turn now from these three assumptions and decisions, regarding the overall parameters of the book, to the reasons for these dialogues or debates. There are, to my mind, five major reasons for setting up these dialogues between cosmopolitanism, on the one hand, and Realism, Marxism and postmodernism, on the other.

The first reason, of which I have already spoken, is because each school of thought in IR explicitly conceives of itself as a critique of liberalism at the international level: the schools constitute themselves through their opposition to liberal thought as such. Given my claim that contemporary cosmopolitanism constitutes an offshoot of Enlightenment liberal thought in the global domain, their critiques are important. As an avatar of Enlightenment liberalism, contemporary cosmopolitanism must respond to them if it wishes to work consistently and effectively with IR. Since this claim provides the major theoretical rationale for the book and for its method, let me detail it further before turning to the other reasons.

The school of Realism was born of the failure of international liberalism and more cosmopolitan aspirations between the two world wars. Its attack on liberal universalist thought in the international domain ensues from realistic appraisal of the effect of plurality and force in world politics. With international terrorism, consistent problems besetting humanitarian intervention, the second Iraq war debacle, and the renewed insurgency in Afghanistan, principles of Realism have returned quickly to the forefront of IR thinking after the initial idealism of post-Cold War globalization theories. In the contemporary context of international terrorism, 'Great Power' nemesis, charges of liberal imperialism and global governance concerns, a prolonged dialogue between IR Realism and cosmopolitanism would be fruitful. As a result of this dialogue: (i) careful distinctions can be made between particularist and universalist claims in, and for, a globalizing world (particularly with regard to interventionism); (ii) focus can be placed on the changing dynamics of power and interest in structural interdependence, and argument can be made for a rethinking of 'national interest' in the light of this interdependence; and (iii) in the context of Realist concerns with states and with a limited ethics of statesmanship and prudence, a cosmopolitan *political ethics* of state responsibility can be delimited and rehearsed.[6] This cosmopolitan political ethics is important given the structural and historical need for state-led global leadership. In distinction to cosmopolitan literature that disowns Realism, I will therefore argue (iv) for a 'cosmopolitan realism' that considers, at this moment in history, states to be the major agents of change for cosmopolitan commitments.

Classical Marxist thought emerged as a critique of liberal thought and practice during nineteenth-century European capitalism and colonialism. It established the tenets of historical materialism, the dynamics of capitalism, and class interest and class conflict within those dynamics. Marxism, as a school of thought in IR theory, transposes this critique to the world economy and to false distinctions within liberalism between international politics and international economics. With recent accusations against Northwestern imperialism (from the 'no alternative to liberal democracy' to economic and political interventionism) and, in the context of the present financial and economic global crisis, this type of critique has an important place in political sociology, political theory, and IR (for a recent overview, see B. Cohen, 2008). The relative absence of Marxist analysis in US economic and political educational programmes remains in this light regrettable. A dialogue between Marxism and cosmopolitanism is important for at least three reasons: (i) because of the need to consider relations of power in economic terms; (ii) because of Marxist and cosmopolitan attention to the systemic inequalities of the capitalist system and to respective ways of addressing them;[7] and (iii) because of the materialist critique of liberal universalism, in general, and of the recent domestic and international practices of neo-liberalism, in particular. These three concerns are highly interrelated, but my cosmopolitan response to Marxism will increasingly foreground the third. For, in the dialogue between Marxism and contemporary cosmopolitanism, I argue the importance of discussing the normative and the empirical together: how, that is, cosmopolitanism endorses global capitalism, what type of universalism cosmopolitanism advocates in distinction to neo-liberal prescriptions and to global liberal governance, and how it frames institutional arrangements regarding the world economy in a globalized world. In other words, given fears of capitalist homogeneity and calls to local and regional resistance to it, important distinctions need to be made concerning *why* and *how* one posits the universal in global conditions of economic interdependence. A specific dialogue between Marxism in IR and cosmopolitanism is theoretically and empirically of value in this context. It allows one to appreciate, first, how differentiated cosmopolitan universalism is in distinction to recent neo-liberal universalism and, second, how what I call a 'progressive liberal cosmopolitanism' can begin to be thought in global terms.[8] These theoretical engagements are, accordingly, different in type from those with Realism and with postmodernism since they are concerned as much with the grounds of policy as they are with principled argument.[9]

Postmodernism in IR theory is not mainstream. It is nevertheless acquiring more attention in the field (see, for example, Edkins and Zehfuss, 2008). It constitutes a set of alternative frameworks for those dissatisfied with the assumptions and limits of empirical theory and embraces within IR explicitly interdisciplinary, rather than multidisciplinary, perspectives. With its stress on multiple subjectivities, it also constitutes an intellectual haven for those on the Left who have lost faith in the practical dimension to Marxism. My concern with this body of theory is here specific. Born out of the non-Marxist, French critiques of liberalism and liberal governance in the second half of the twentieth century – the thought of Michel Foucault, Jacques Derrida and others – postmodernism in IR theory considers liberal normative rule as an exercise of domination and looks, consequently, to a *non-normative* ethics as opposed to a cosmopolitan norm. It sets itself up, therefore, as a critical theory of the present terms of globalization and governance, of the expansion of modernity and modernization processes, and of liberal forms of violence in general, reserving in the field of IR some of its strongest intellectual disquiet for the concept and practice of 'humanitarian intervention'. A dialogue between postmodernism and cosmopolitanism is valuable here because a great deal of critical IR theory assumes, to a lesser or greater extent, postmodern attitudes and is critical of liberal cosmopolitanism (see, most recently, Edkins and

Vaughan-Williams, 2009). It is therefore important at this moment of historical change to clarify the stakes in IR thinking around: (i) liberal universalism and the illiberal consequences of liberalism; (ii) the function of liberal law and its tendency to dominate or to empower; and (iii) the nature and demands of ethico-political responsibility in the international political domain. My claim is that, despite telling critiques, postmodernism fails to address the requirements of the political domain and, therefore, the way to think ethically within it. My cosmopolitan response to postmodernism dovetails with conclusions to the debate between Realism and cosmopolitanism – specifically with regard to a political ethics of the lesser violence that affirms, *contra* postmodern IR thought, the *productive* power of limitation and limits in the political field.

Each engagement between cosmopolitanism and the schools of Realism, Marxism and postmodernism concerns explicit critiques of liberal universalism in its various guises – political, legal, economic, historical and ideological – and the need to specify what modality of cosmopolitanism and what type of universalism informs an effective cosmopolitan response to it. This is the first and major reason for my choice of schools.

The second reason for my choice concerns the topics covered by these schools. As a global ideology in a globalized world, cosmopolitanism has a very large agenda that works on several theoretical levels. It addresses, at the very least, the intellectual traditions of liberalism, global justice, international law, international and global political economy and environmental issues. In a globalized world, these issues and problems are inextricably interrelated: some sort of global vision for them (however minimal, however articulated), together with a set of goals and institutions underpinning this vision, are increasingly considered of import in spite of social science professionalization and specialization. In their critiques of liberalism, each school attends to at least one of the above issues. To discuss these issues in terms of a theoretical debate between a moral and political philosophy that has global pretensions, and IR schools of thought, which are constitutively nervous of liberalism and these pretensions, gives me a focal point (contemporary cosmopolitanism and its critiques) by which to address vision and goal for the twenty-first century at an appropriately abstract level, but in the context of interrelated sets of concrete concerns.

The third reason follows on from the first two and is both methodological and substantive. By placing IR critiques of universalism against contemporary cosmopolitan ideas, and responding to each critique in turn under an interrelated set of concerns, I can make a dual theoretical move. I can claim that, in the dialogue between IR and cosmopolitanism, the cosmopolitan universalism that responds best to IR theory must be either fairly *weak* and/or expressly *differentiated*. For example, in direct response to

Realism's concerns with the reality of international relations, cosmopolitanism needs to be both (a) feasible and (b) pitched at several levels. It needs (a) to work out of the practical reality of the system of states and look to cosmopolitan state-leadership. This cosmopolitanism can only be minimal, since it must remain compatible with (a nevertheless expanding) national interest, and since its issues must be concentrated enough to permit success at the intergovernmental level of negotiation. It needs (b) to conceive of its concerns with post-national democratic legitimacy in explicitly differentiated terms so that it is not branded holistic (one type of democracy for all) or idealistic (world democracy as such). My cosmopolitan response to Realism attempts to do both these things and, thereby, offers a varied, context-based understanding of contemporary cosmopolitanism. Given the pressing need for global leadership, cosmopolitanism should focus on the positive role of states in world politics and argue for state-led minimal cosmopolitan commitments. In the context of the emerging architecture of global governance, it should *at the same time* argue for a wider understanding of commitment that advocates how the political principle of self-determination can be reinvented at post-national levels.

My various responses to IR critiques of cosmopolitanism suggest therefore a mixed approach to contemporary cosmopolitan ideas. As opposed to strong cosmopolitanism (as defined earlier), I do not argue for a comprehensive liberal cosmopolitanism. Such a comprehensive theory is analytically beautiful (as in Thomas Pogge's and Simon Caney's works), but I believe that such comprehensiveness is of neither theoretical nor empirical use when confronting the reality of international relations with cosmopolitan ideas. A more minimal universalism is more effective. Since international relations essentially involve relations of power, the previous comment is not simply instrumental or pragmatic; it is also ontological. This is not to say, however, that cosmopolitans should not, at the same time, reason more comprehensively. International institutions like the UN and the World Bank require cosmopolitan moral arguments that frame each human being's right to a sustainable life in the context of global warming and climate change mitigation (see Caney, 2009a). Such sustainability, as strong cosmopolitans like Simon Caney claim, requires consideration of conditions that exceed respect for a minimally decent life (the universal right to asylum, for example). I do not think the two different arguments are, however, theoretically inconsistent: they work at different levels of reasoning and in different contexts. The obligations of the UN or of an ethically motivated NGO are not the same as those of a state. Just as neither position should be ignored when analysing world politics, so equally there is no synthesis of both. A multilayered analysis of cosmopolitan commitments is therefore appropriate. My three responses to IR critiques of contemporary cosmopolitanism work within this overall framework of theoretical flexibility. The book argues, accordingly, for both a cosmopolitan realism in the context of Realist and postmodernist critiques and a modest, 'progressive liberal' cosmopolitanism in the context of Marxist and postmodernist critiques.

The fourth reason for these specific dialogues is particular to this book, and I can be brief thereupon. These dialogues bring up important moments of theoretical clarity. Errors of argument or ambiguity of analysis can be carefully addressed through outlining respective positions. At the same time, areas of persistent theoretical difficulty come to light that require further and deeper exploration. The specific engagements of the book lead, consequently, to a set of research questions and agendas that would, I claim, enhance and refine the relevance of cosmopolitanism to the theorization of world politics.

The fifth and final reason for setting up these dialogues is more pragmatic and historically situated. In the broad context of recent American economic and military power, and in the specific context of 9/11 and its aftermath, there is a certain amount of conflation in IR theorizing between the ends and means of neo-conservatism and of neo-liberalism and those of cosmopolitan liberalism (these arguments are presented in chapters 2, 4 and 6). All lead, it is argued, to either the 'moralization' or the 'economization' of politics, processes that prove politically counter-effective. The era of George W. Bush's neo-conservative presidency has now passed. Neo-liberalism is reorganizing its ideological foundations, and the international community is preparing for the emergence of China as a great power. Although both the Bush administration and neo-liberalism have left a large legacy in international relations, the world has quickly entered a new era of power politics and of global responsibility. At this historical juncture, I consider it theoretically important to separate the fates of a modest, progressive cosmopolitan liberalism from those of neo-conservative American exceptionalism (nationalist universalism) and neo-liberal formalism (market fundamentalism). The coming generation of political leadership needs to demarcate itself from the recriminations of the previous two decades concerning political, military and economic interventionism in order to conceive appropriately its responsibilities in the next era of globalization. Theoretical distinctions, rather than conflations, can help this process. It is doubtful that the coming decades will open up an era of progressive global politics given the present economic crisis, the political uncertainty ensuing from the ongoing shift of power to Asia, and the recurrent problem of interstate coordination under conditions of resource-scarcity and climate change. It is nevertheless critical for the promise of such a political stance to demarcate cosmopolitan political judgement from somewhat aggressive forms of political and economic 'universalism'. It is, in other words, important to clear the theoretical air: these 'dialogues' or 'debates' also work towards this end.[10]

The overall argument that emerges from these debates is the following. Contemporary cosmopolitan thought constitutes an intellectual framework within which problems directly and indirectly affecting the human species can be laid out in a way that gradually promotes reciprocal behaviour between nations, international organizations (public and private), and individuals. This framework is, firstly, *moral*. All human beings are moral individuals and, as moral individuals, carry, minimally, the dignity of life, or, maximally, that of moral personhood (autonomy). This framework makes questions of humanity and justice a primary focus of political thought. It is, secondly, *normative*. With regard to the field of world politics, it promotes an ethical horizon which seeks, normatively, to guide political principle, interest and agency. While cosmopolitanism is not explanatory per se, its normative status is not, however, simply prescriptive. With regard to the human rights regime, the emerging international regimes of global public goods and strong need for global leadership, I claim that cosmopolitan normative principles of human dignity, human reciprocity and human solidarity are empirically meaningful and are slowly changing the nature of national interest. Power-politics should therefore begin to negotiate under more cosmopolitan terms of institutional and political legitimacy; and, as Daniele Archibugi (2008) has argued, democratic states should take the lead. The cosmopolitan framework offers principles of legitimacy according to which problems with a global dimension can begin to be worked out. In these three respects, cosmopolitan's normative status has strong *legal*, *institutional* and *political* implications. International regimes anticipate more rule-bound legal behaviour on the part of states and markets. Despite the weak force of international law and the asymmetries of international power, legal cosmopolitanism makes, therefore, a historically effective argument for the transformation of moral questions of justice into legal questions of posited law. But such transformation requires commitment to global institution-building. The present international system is still heavily tipped in favour of the former Great Powers. Given the rapid rise of the emerging economies, the absence in global leadership in the first decade of the century, followed by the economic crisis, together with the global nature of an increasing set of international problems, this system is under permanent structural change. The temptation of economic and political regionalization is evident to all, especially with a Chinese regional hegemon. Effective global cooperation is nevertheless critical to the resolution of global problems and must work with new strategies of state-localization. I claim that such cooperation requires enlightened, differentiated terms of institutional and political vision. While the institution of world government is undesirable in centralized form, world governance of some kind is necessary. Although its terms remain very unclear, it is important to prepare for it intellectually both at the level of nation-state behaviour and at the level of regional and global governance. The cosmopolitan argument becomes, accordingly, an *institutional* cosmopolitanism and a *political* cosmopolitanism in this context, and it is important to work out why and how.

Contra cosmopolitan positions that remain exclusively of one kind (moral, normative, legal, institutional or political), I argue, consequently, that contemporary cosmopolitanism should embrace the complementarity between the moral, normative, legal, institutional and political aspects of its own disposition. I argue this point in two ways: (i) in the sense that moral and legal cosmopolitan positions or legal and political cosmopolitan positions need increasingly to reinforce each other; and (ii) in the sense that different positions towards world politics need to be assumed depending upon the agent and its limits (whether it be the state or international organization, whether this organization be private or public, etc.). While flexible and pitched at several levels, this overall cosmopolitan disposition remains naive: it retains a straightforward optimism of the will. Naivety is, I believe, a good companion of moral and political prudence. As classical Realism teaches, idealism and realism must work together for effective progressive change to be possible. At the same time, cosmopolitanism should not be 'infantile' (in the Freudian sense of the term). It should not disavow the real, opposing the latter with idealistic constructions that are immediately undone by realities on the ground. Such rhetoric is, I believe, counter-effective to the cause of cosmopolitanism in the field of IR. Even if nations are moving towards regional blocs, I would prefer not to argue that the foremost regional bloc, the European Union, is 'cosmopolitan' (see, for example, Beck, 2006; compare Habermas, 2006; Rumford, 2007). Its juridical order (the European Convention on Human Rights, the European Court of Justice) certainly contains cosmopolitan elements in it. European immigration policies immediately preclude it, however, from being cosmopolitan. Similar preclusions apply to the old and new rhetoric of 'global cosmopolitan citizens' and 'cosmopolitan global cities'. Being idealist, cosmopolitanism needs, at one and the same time, to work from within the parameters of geographical, functional and political differentiation. Its cause in IR will be the better served if it does: hence the book's emphasis on *various forms of cosmopolitanism*, on *the complementarity of these forms*, but on *their different contextual usage*.

This argument requires a particular method. Let me conclude this introduction with how I conduct it. Chapter 1 defines cosmopolitanism. In the light of the above, it offers a spectrum of cosmopolitan positions that move from its weak cultural variant to its strong political variant. Following standard distinctions within cosmopolitan scholarship, I argue that these positions are important for understanding what I call 'the cosmopolitan disposition'. I also argue, however, that movement from one position to another is necessary, if problematic. The chapters following proceed within the framework of these distinctions and complementarities. Chapter 2 considers the Realist critique of cosmopolitanism. Since, as with Marxism and postmodernism, there is not a great deal of literature within IR theory explicitly concerned with this critique, my method of dialogue is one of extrapolation. I consider, first, the major tenets of Realism, and, second, from out of these tenets, pursue its critique of cosmopolitanism within selected current literature. Chapter 3 gives, as far as this author sees it, a cosmopolitan response to these criticisms and suggests where outstanding problems remain for a cosmopolitan argument that takes into account the Realist perspective. Several research questions are formulated that could orient further pursuit of these problems. Chapters 4 and 5 and chapters 6 and 7 follow this same procedure for Marxism and postmodernism, respectively. My readings are selective, but they try and bring out essential arguments, as far as I understand them. The conclusion brings together the important traits that inform the three debates as a whole. It argues (i) for cosmopolitan realism and state-led global leadership on specific global governance issues; (ii) in different institutional form, for a modest, progressive liberal cosmopolitan politics in the realm of the world economy and its regulation; (iii) for cosmopolitan political judgement, whatever instance is judging, and whatever context this instance is judging from. My overall claim is that these three arguments show the way in which a sophisticated cosmopolitan liberalism can be defended and articulated in the field of world politics.

Although the world political future is very uncertain, effective cooperation between nation-states, regional powers and private and public international organizations is increasingly vital. Sophisticated cosmopolitan argument can be persuasive in underlining the need for such cooperation. And, if effective cooperation begins, a new type of global politics – one in which states with cosmopolitan commitments lead; one in which national sovereignty is ceded to supranational organization on specific issues – will emerge, to which cosmopolitanism can make a large contribution from within IR.

Let me begin, first, with an initial discussion of cosmopolitanism and contemporary cosmopolitan ideas.

1
The Spectrum
of Cosmopolitanism

This chapter serves the following three functions:

1 It provides a philosophical introduction to basic cosmopolitan ideas.
2 It underlines the differences within contemporary cosmopolitan thought, differences of modality (moral, normative or institutional cosmopolitanism, for example) that express a range of positions concerning international and global political reality.
3 It shows that these different positions are also mutually reinforcing and should be considered and theorized as complementary.

Following these three goals, this chapter presents, therefore, a spectrum of cosmopolitan positions, within which important differences and complementarities can be analysed with precision and clarity. The assumption of different positions is commonplace in contemporary cosmopolitan literature (see Benhabib, 2009; G. W. Brown, 2009; Cabrera, 2004; Caney, 2005; Heater, 1996 and 2002; Miller, 2007a; Pogge, 1992); the emphasis on complementarity in the context of IR is mine.[1] This chapter thereby frames the following dialogues between IR theory and cosmopolitanism by providing a conceptual set of distinctions.

The chapter contains two sections. The first provides a short narrative of the historical background to what I call the 'cosmopolitan disposition' in general. In the second section, I give an exposition of the spectrum of cosmopolitan differences and complementarities, in order of increasing determinateness, cultural, moral, normative, institutional, legal and political modalities of cosmopolitanism. I note, finally, that my readings are selective, but fairly comprehensive in substance and that several arguments within the exposition of different cosmopolitanisms are particular to me, but make sense of later discussion.

1 The Historical Background to the Cosmopolitan Disposition

There are three major moments of cosmopolitan thought prior to recent and current re-engagement with its problematic and disposition. The first is the Stoic moment, the second that of natural law theory, the third that of European Enlightenment thought, in general, and Kantian cosmopolitanism, in particular.

As a specific way of thinking the world as a *polis* (literally, a city-state or polity), cosmopolitanism emerges, from out of religious and mythical cosmology, in the Greek Stoic writings of Diogenes (c. 413–327 BCE), Zeno the Stoa (c. 334–262 BCE) and Chrysippus (c. 280–206 BCE). Diogenes the Cynic is considered the first to describe himself as 'a citizen of the world'. 'When anyone asked him what country he came from, he said, "I am a citizen of the world (*kosmopolitēs*)"', that is, a member of the *polis* of the universe (Laertius, n.d.). The self-description meant specifically, for Diogenes, that all natural or man-made borders are morally contingent. A citizen, by chance, of the Athenian *polis*, Diogenes belonged morally to the universe. The cosmopolitan disposition emerges from out of this ironic, moral outlook on the contingency of Athenian citizenship and political empire. This outlook leads to two conceptions of the *polis*: one transcendent and borderless; the other contingent and bounded. Outside the terms of myth and religion, it provides the intellectual framework that permits the normative critique of empirical politics and loyalties. For Zeno and Chrysippus, the universe constitutes a *polis* because it is organized under law in distinction to chaos (Schofield, 1991, pp. 67–86). Members of the *cosmopolis* are gods and men only insofar as they obey laws through reason. Wider citizenship requires greater rationality. In Stoic cosmopolitanism a relation of identity is thereby set up among the universe (*cosmos*), reason (*logos*), law (*nomos*) and citizenship (*cosmopolitein*). This identity, together with the moral and normative framework it endorses, is refined in Roman Stoicism at the historical moment of violent transition from the Roman republic to the Roman *imperium*, in the authorships of Cicero (106–43 BCE), Seneca (4 BCE–65 CE), and Marcus Aurelius (121–180 CE). Seneca writes for example:

> Let us embrace with our minds two commonwealths (*res publicae*): one
> great and truly common – in which gods and men are contained, in which
> we look not to this or that corner, but measure the bounds of the our state
> (*civitas*) with the sun; the other the one to which the particular circumstances
> of birth have assigned us – the commonwealth of the Athenians or the
> Carthaginians or some other city (*urbs*) which pertains not to all men but
> to a particular group of them. Some give service to both commonwealths at
> the same time – some only to the lesser, some to the greater. (Seneca, *De
> otio*, Book 4, quoted in Schofield, 1991, p. 91)

Seneca's conception of the two cities offers not only a critique of empire,
but, again, the terms within which the lesser, contingent *polis* can be
appraised through a rational understanding of humanity and a moral conception of community and solidarity. This conception ultimately places the
field of politics under the normative horizon of rational moral constraint.
The Greek and Roman variants of Stoic cosmopolitanism provide therefore
the embryonic language through which ethical behaviour is untied from
religious custom and retied to political and legal system.

With the Christianization of the Roman Empire of the fourth century
CE, the moral tenor of cosmopolitanism is resituated within the universality
of Judeo-Christian monotheism. Augustine's *The City of God*, for example,
pits the city of the Christian God and its moral duties against those of
Rome when Augustine restricts himself to the power relations between
them; when he attempts to lay out a comprehensive political theory, he
subordinates the laws of the latter to those of the former (Augustine, 1972,
Book V). With the European dissemination of Christian institutions
(dogma, diocese, church, monastery) Stoic moral cosmopolitanism fuses
with Christian universalism to forge, from the late European medieval age
through to the Renaissance, the critical language of natural law theory.
From Aquinas to important Thomists like Francisco di Vitoria (1492–1546
CE) and Francisco Suârez (1548–1617 CE), natural laws are deemed those
given to humans as rational offspring of divinely-inspired creation (Finnis,
1992). These laws are those of 'natural' justice to which positive legal laws
should bend: they are, most importantly, those of moral equality, of peaceful co-belonging, of just war (Brown et al., 2004, pp. 311–23). Natural law
theory gives rise to the notion of 'natural rights'. Despite its evident ambi-
guities and hypocrisies ensconced within the language of Christendom (to
which I return), natural law theory thereby prepares the ground for modern
political egalitarianism.

In the third moment, of European Enlightenment thought, a consequent
and more systematic cosmopolitanism emerges. I claim that it provides the
overall framework within which contemporary cosmopolitan ideas are, in
general, discussed, even if weaker forms of cosmopolitanism resist the

move to universalize moral personhood. This framework is best found in the work of Immanuel Kant and his ethical and political writings (1784, 1785, 1788, 1793, 1795, 1797). Kant constitutes such an instrumental figure in modern cosmopolitanism and its contemporary reconfigurations that this chapter returns to him several times; here I situate his thought in the context of this brief history. Indebted to the Stoics (Nussbaum, 1997), Kant aims to maintain the identity posited between human nature, reason and law *within* modernizing processes. The cosmos can no longer be placed under the rule of law. Human cognitive agents know nothing of its internal workings as a whole. Rational concepts of the world are accordingly 'speculative ideas' only: they have no relation to the empirical and cannot be verified (Kant, 1781/1929, pp. 315–26). These ideas have, conversely, speculative interest: they are thoughts of totality that testify to the rational vocation of the human species. More importantly, this interest is not only speculative, it is also practical. Reason has, for Kant, an immediate effect on the human will (1788/1956, pp. 74–91). As both rational and sensible beings, humans necessarily take a pure moral interest in the moral law. If human beings feel guilt when they believe that they have behaved wrongly, if they admire examples of virtue in both the moral and political domains, it is because they have a rational will, however overriding their inclinations to self-interest prove to be in everyday life (1785/1987, p. 55). For Kant, the existential 'fact' of the rational will places ethical motivation immediately in the empirical field. Kant then extrapolates that human beings are members of a 'kingdom of ends'. Transposed from the ethics of the New Testament – for Kant, the most moral of all religious writings – this kingdom constitutes an ethical realm in which each has an absolute worth in himself or herself (ibid., p. 56). It is this absolute worth of the individual that makes the New Testament morally outstanding. When taken as means to others' ends, individuals have a 'price'. When considered as ends in themselves – that is, autonomous givers to themselves of their own ends – they have 'value' and 'dignity' (ibid.). Bearing dignity, individuals constitute 'moral persons' with their own agency (ibid., pp. 57 and 63). Moral personality anticipates a system of universal laws in which it is both subject of, and subject to, these laws (self-determination).

Kant's moral community of ends is a direct translation of the Stoic cosmopolitan *polis*, supplemented by Christian individuality, in the context of modernity. The dignity of the moral person organizes the moral and normative critique of hierarchical societies. It leads Kant, politically, to a liberal republicanism: the political philosophy of a liberal community in which each person is free to the extent that his freedom does not harm the freedom of others under the rule of 'public law' (in Kantian terms, *das Recht*). I come back to this critical understanding of liberalism several times in my responses to IR critiques of cosmopolitanism. Morality is thus harnessed to politics through the mechanism of law (*das Recht*) (Kant, 1793 and 1795).

Kant's liberal republicanism is both consistent and systematic. If the category of moral personality is universal for all rational human beings, then, for Kant, the moral critique of empirical polity must itself be universal. The universality of personal dignity is therefore a given at all levels of political organization. In his essay 'Perpetual Peace', for example, the ideology of liberal republicanism leads Kant to posit, beyond the international laws of states' mutual obligations to each other, a cosmopolitan law (*ius cosmopoliticum*) of states *and* individuals, and a world republic in which both states and individuals achieve political personality as 'world citizens' (Kant, 1795/1991, pp. 98–104). I address the conceptual dilemmas in this argument in sections 2.3 and 2.5 below on normative and legal cosmopolitanism.

In its three major historical moments, cosmopolitan discourse posits that geographical and political borders are morally contingent. It institutes thereby a conceptual difference between the normative and the positive by distinguishing between two forms of humanity and two forms of polity: one moral, the other political; one moral and rationally necessary, the other civic and contingent. A relation between these two forms of humanity and community is upheld because humans are endowed with reason, and their reason comes to recognize what is law. In the recognition of law, contingently embedded humans move towards moral community. This relation provides a regulative framework in which empirical political systems and loyalties can be judged according to the criterion of 'natural justice'. It is only, however, in the third Kantian (liberal republican) moment that an institutional mechanism is identified that mediates between the moral and the political: the legislative domain of public law (*das Recht*), whose legitimating source is the dignity of the moral person.

These conceptual outcomes of cosmopolitan history make up the basis of what I henceforth call the 'cosmopolitan disposition'. Someone, some collectivity or, simply, some argument that has a cosmopolitan disposition embodies the following traits. First, it considers natural or artificial borders contingent and therefore focuses on a common humanity beyond ethnic, religious, class, or gender particularities. Given this contingency of borders, second, it has an overriding interest in humanity and/or in justice as the basic scheme of world society: this interest is either rooted, more weakly, on one's humanity as a human individual, or, more strongly, on one's dignity as a moral person. And, third, it looks to world-embracing institutional arrangements through rational judgement and the mechanism of public law. I now turn to contemporary engagements with this disposition

and work through a spectrum of cosmopolitan distinctions and complementarities that will be of use when confronting IR theory.

2 The Cosmopolitan Spectrum

2.1 Cultural cosmopolitanism

Although the following debates between cosmopolitanism and IR theory
do not deal specifically with the politics of culture, when I refer to the
cultural dimensions of cosmopolitanism, I have two types of argument in
mind. I take as my examples the cosmopolitan writings of the philosopher
Kwame Appiah (Appiah, 1997 and 2006), of the comparative political
theorist Fred Dallmayr (1996 and 2002), and of the sociologist Ulrich Beck
(2006).

The first type of argument is explicitly rehearsed by thinkers like Appiah
and Dallmayr, who are responding to globalization. For Appiah, economic
globalization provokes uncertainty and the loss of identity. Fundamentalist
reactions to it are therefore understandable and must be countered by a
culture of 'cosmopolitan contamination' (2006, p. 18). Arguing against
both retrenchment on given identities and a homogenous system of global
values, Appiah affirms the mixture of cultures, particular to any culture as
such, and foregrounds a 'dialectic of understanding' within which the
common space of humanity can be reflectively explored. Religious, cultural, social and political differences are, therefore, cognized and respected
within an indeterminate notion of humanity on the one condition that they
are not exclusive of other forms of difference (ibid., pp. 31, 98, 115). I
would argue that this modality of cosmopolitanism is eminently cultural
because it seeks to avoid ideology (liberal or non-liberal) and pitches itself
at the level of a widening sensibility and understanding which either avoid
or aim below determinate forms of rational argument.

Fred Dallmayr's project to open up Western forms of rationality to internal and external forms of otherness in *Beyond Orientalism* (1996), and to
promote intercultural and interreligious exchange and dialogue on common
human practices in *Dialogue Among Civilizations* (2002) and *Peace Talks*
(2004), forms part of this same cultural endeavour. In a world of interdependence, structured by forms of both liberal and non-liberal intolerance,
Dallmayr focuses on concrete modes of ethical and cultural dialogue
that 'respect otherness beyond assimilation' and resist 'melting-pot cosmopolitanism' (1996, p. xxii). He looks specifically to non-Western ethical
practices (Confucian, Buddhist, Hindu) to retrieve an experience of
the social relation that liberal individualism and liberal proceduralism

threaten (2010, pp. 169–86). For both Dallmayr and Appiah, then, any viable cosmopolitanism today must practise respect of other cultures and values on the basis of a minimal common threshold of humanity and of the social relation. This kind of philosophical and cultural position explicitly frames, I would argue, postmodern IR theory, and I consider and respond to it, at the political level, and in political terms, in chapters 6 and 7.

The other type of argument I have in mind when referring to cultural cosmopolitanism is a form of reasoning made by Ulrich Beck. In his *Cosmopolitan Vision* (2006), for example, Beck considers globalization as 'cosmopolitanization', which comprises 'the development of multiple loyalties as well as the increase in diverse transnational forms of life, the emergence of non-state political actors (from Amnesty International to the World Trade Organization), the development of global protest movements against globalism and in support of a different kind of (cosmopolitan) globalization' (2006, p. 9).[2] A cosmopolitan outlook responds reflexively to these processes. In contrast to the 'banal cosmopolitanism' of the capitalist global life-world, this outlook constitutes a reflexive affirmation of inclusive action between differences of culture and identity, one that challenges the other response to cosmopolitanization, exclusive differentiation and fundamentalism (ibid., pp. 30–3). Thus, for Beck, questions of immigration, integration and citizenship in the core liberal democracies are, above all, *cosmopolitan* questions because they can no longer be articulated within nation-state sociology. Methodological nationalism in both the soft and hard social sciences still identifies society with the nation-state and is thereby unable to conceive the national and the global together in a cosmopolitan vision (ibid., p. 49). Beck's work on 'cosmopolitisation' has been very provocative and influential (1997, 1999, 2005, 2006). I would claim, however, that it often jumps from nationalist to cosmopolitan sociology without considered reflection on national and post-national conceptual and institutional differences. For example, when Beck argues that 'the political union [of Europe] must be conceived as a cosmopolitan union of Europe, in opposition to the false normativity of the national' (2006, p. 167), economic, social and political exclusions, which constitute the union of Europe in the first place, are elided. In the abstract opposition between 'nationalist' and 'cosmopolitan', the very use of the term 'cosmopolitan' can become rhetorical. When Beck, together with those in sociology, cultural studies and international politics who have followed in his wake, make this type of intellectual move, I consider them 'cultural cosmopolitans' (compare Delanty and Rumford, 2005; Rumford, 2007). Avoiding methodologically the necessity of borders, hard analysis is replaced by normative cultural vision. The vision is imaginative and troubling, but its existential modality is probably one of a culture of inclusion alone.

Both these types of reasoning (one explicit, one unintended) suggest, together, that the cultural cosmopolitan argument is important to IR when it looks to expansive horizons of understanding in order to resolve conflict in a globalized world, but that this same argument is problematic when it comes to the necessary limits of political community. This is at least my claim. Just as liberal cosmopolitanism, following Dallmayr, needs, therefore, to be complemented by cultural flexibility and tolerance, so cultural cosmopolitanism needs to be complemented by (the affirmation of) specific structures of rule, ones that have been rightly formalized by liberalism to allow for the articulation of difference. These are freedom of expression, a right to assembly, a right to participate in the public sphere and a notion of tolerance that excludes the intolerable from the public domain (practical fundamentalisms). Contemporary forms of cultural cosmopolitanism presuppose and anticipate, consequently, more determinate moral and legal arrangements.

2.2 Moral cosmopolitanism

As the above brief history indicated, moral cosmopolitanism is at the core of cosmopolitan thought and remains central to contemporary cosmopolitan ideas. There are, that said, various strands to contemporary moral cosmopolitanism, which are important when considering cosmopolitanism in the context of IR theory and international relations in general. First, it is thought through in several distinct ways; second, as intimated in my Introduction, the distinction between weak and strong forms of cosmopolitanism, relevant to the field of world politics, turn around the exact content of its moral core. This section on the moral modality of cosmopolitanism works through these distinctions in detail. It makes use of arguments from Charles Beitz (1999a and 1999b), Simon Caney (2005), David Miller (2007a), Thomas Nagel (2005), Onora O'Neill (1975/1999), Martha Nussbaum (1994 and 1997) and Peter Singer (1972).

First, all cosmopolitan discourse is moral in that it emphasizes the morally arbitrary nature of borders. Since this is a tenet of all cosmopolitanism, I need only repeat what was said in the brief history. Cosmopolitan sentiment and reflection begins when a purely moral distinction is made between empirical demarcations and the non-empirical lack of them. With this moral distinction, each human being comes to the fore *as* a human being (distinct from their particularity), and the space of humanity is opened up (Nussbaum, 1994). In contemporary cosmopolitan literature, following liberal thinking in general, this space becomes occupied with specific entitlements (the basic needs and rights of all human beings) and duties (the basic responsibilities all human beings have to fellow human beings in need). This universality of humanity, together with its categorization in terms of moral entitlements and moral duties, leads, in turn, to three sorts of overriding moral cosmopolitan arguments: (i) focus on human beings as individuals of moral worth with general entitlements; (ii) the grounding of personal or collective behaviour by principles that include moral responsibility to humanity; and (iii) a personal ethics of responsibility to suffering fellow humans (see, most importantly, Singer, 1972). It is within these three types of argument that important differences emerge.

Let me turn first to the writings of Thomas Pogge and Simon Caney. In a now famous essay, 'Cosmopolitanism and sovereignty', Pogge writes:

> Three elements are shared by all cosmopolitan positions. First, *individualism*: the ultimate units of concern are *human beings* or *persons* – rather than, say, family lines, tribes, ethnic, cultural or religious communities, nations or states. The latter may be units of concern only indirectly, in virtue of their individual members or citizens. Second, *universality*: the status of ultimate concern attaches to *every* living human being *equally* – not merely to some subset, such as men, aristocrats, Aryans, whites, or Muslims. Third, *generality*: this special status has global force. Persons are ultimate units of concern *for everyone* – not only for their compatriots, fellow religionists, or suchlike. (Pogge, 1992, pp. 48–9)

Pogge here resurrects the Stoic ideal of cosmopolitanism in the context of liberal modernity. The moral arbitrariness of borders is articulated in terms of the Kantian dignity of moral personhood. The 'person' now prevails morally over all other forms of identity, and, for Pogge, is of universal and general import. Pogge claims two things here. First, the individual is the ultimate focus of cosmopolitan moral interest and responsibility (moral egalitarianism becomes global); second, universal moral personhood leads to the moral commitment to just conditions of individual life worldwide. Focus on the universality of moral personhood leads, therefore, to engagement with *global justice*. Just as the freedom and equality of the individual is guaranteed within the borders of the liberal nation-state, so this autonomy from biological and social dependence should be gradually guaranteed across the world. This is a necessary consequence of the incidence of universality implicit in the Kantian concept of a moral subject, one that Pogge considers absolute. For Pogge, therefore, there can be no categorical distinction, morally speaking, between domestic and foreign policy or between social and global justice (see also Beitz, 1999b). I return to the institutional consequences of this thought in section 2.4 below.

In *Justice Beyond Borders* (2005), Simon Caney systematizes further this cosmopolitan moral egalitarianism. If one affirms moral personhood as such, then an analogy between the domestic level of community and the global level of community is theoretically consistent, and autonomy (and all that it entails) should serve as a norm in the empirical international world (ibid., pp. 66, 77–8, 124). Caney argues, consequently, for a strong theory of global justice, one that requires a 'comprehensive theory' of rights and an appropriately comprehensive set of 'international duties' (ibid., p. 66). These rights would not simply allow basic human needs or interests to be fulfilled; they would, in principle, give all human beings specific economic, civil and political entitlements since the latter are, he claims, necessarily 'interconnected' (ibid., p. 85). Theories which affirm rights at one level but reject them at another are, in Caney's terms, 'incomplete' (ibid., pp. 65–6). Regarding civil and political rights, Caney accepts, for example, the claim by Andrew Kuper that freedom of expression must presuppose in some form or other democratic government (ibid., p. 83). Affirming a limited compatibility between global principles and domestic principles of distributive justice, he agrees, further, with Samuel Black that a 'distributive theory, that ascribes rights and claims on the basis of certain universal attributes of persons, cannot at the same time restrict the grounds for those claims to a person's membership or status within a given society' (quoted in ibid., p. 107). As for Pogge, questions of freedom and equality should gravitate up from domestic political theory and provide the terms for a comprehensive moral theorization of international relations precisely because one cannot reasonably draw the line – morally and normatively speaking – between different levels of personality and justice (ibid., pp. 72, 124). Unlike Pogge, however, Caney leaves the question of institutional implementation to one side of his moral justification.

Weak cosmopolitans like David Miller and Thomas Nagel do not accept these intellectual moves towards global egalitarianism (Miller, 2002, 2007a, 2007b; Nagel, 2005). Their moral theorization of international political and economic reality is, consequently, minimalist and contained within basic humanitarianism. Their moral theories are made to 'fit the world as it is' (Miller, 2007a, p. 20).

For Nagel, moral conceptions of justice at a world level can only deal with basic levels of need and, therefore, basic duties of humanity (2005, pp. 119–20). Moral cosmopolitanism concerns the 'duty of fairness that we owe to our fellow human beings, not just fellow citizens' (ibid.). The individual remains indeed the highest object of moral worth, and the moral context is larger than any political one; but it is also much more indeterminate, addressing basic levels of sustainable life alone (ibid., p. 131). The political conception of justice concerns, conversely, substantive relations of associative reciprocity and solidarity, because, in Hobbesian vein, the state requires our active cooperation (ibid., p. 128; see also Blake, 2001).

It is only on the basis of this coercive, involuntary association, to begin with, that a conception of socioeconomic justice and the value of equality can have purchase (Nagel, 2005, p. 133). Nagel writes:

> Everyone may have the right to live in a just society, but we do not have an obligation to live in a just society with everyone. The right to justice is the right that the society one lives in be justly governed. Any claims this creates against other societies and their members are distinctly secondary to those it creates against one's fellow citizens. (Ibid., p. 132)

Individuals are therefore not entitled to equal treatment individually except through the societies in which they are citizens. This means that global socioeconomic justice can be entertained as a *political* idea alone. But only once relations of reciprocity and solidarity between peoples and individuals have been achieved can this idea have any concrete meaning. Nagel asserts: '[m]ere economic interaction does not trigger the heightened standards of socioeconomic justice' (ibid., p. 138). Moral cosmopolitanism cannot therefore consider the world order from the perspective of the autonomy of moral personhood, since the institutional requirements are lacking to force collective cooperation at the global level. For Nagel, following Hobbes, personal autonomy and equality can only result from such assurance. Moral vision for the world must therefore remain at the lower threshold level of 'basic rights and duties', ones 'that *are* universal' because they are '*not* contingent on specific institutional relations between people' (ibid., p. 131, my emphasis).

David Miller's argument is similar to Nagel's, although it is made in terms of the requirements of political citizenship, not the requirements of political order. Strong cosmopolitans are right to foreground the individual as the ultimate unit of moral worth; it is a different question, however, what each of us does in response to people's harms. Each person will respond differently, for example, to a missing child, if they are a relative of the child, a fellow village member, or a concerned citizen from another community (Miller, 2002, p. 82). Miller writes:

> This is the point that ethical cosmopolitans miss when they slide from saying that every human being has equal moral worth to saying that *therefore* we are required to treat all human beings equally, in the sense that we have the same duties to each. This, as the missing child example shows, is simply a *non sequitur*. Yet it plays an important part in cosmopolitan rhetoric. (Ibid.)

For Miller, as with Nagel, we have different duties to our fellow human beings according to the context from out of which we relate to them. A clear distinction between 'social justice' and 'global justice' is therefore necessary. For the extension of the principles of social justice to the international or global level (some form of starting equality of resources, some form of equality of opportunity) would require a global community within which it would make sense for members to *compare* themselves with each other in the first place. Since, for Miller, 'justice is concerned with comparative rather than absolute outcomes' (2007b, p. 9), and no concrete comparison of justice can be made from one self-determining political community to another, a theory of 'global justice' is in fact best understood in terms of a theory of 'basic human needs' (absolute outcomes). This theory works in terms of the difference between domestic and international contexts: between rights of citizenship and basic human rights, and between responsibilities of citizenship and basic human duties (2007a, p. 22). Thus, for Miller, 'there is nothing unjust about international inequalities as such. What should concern even weak cosmopolitans are societies that cannot guarantee their members fundamental rights [to a minimally decent human life]' (1998, p. 179). Accordingly, '[p]rovided that we attach some value to the idea that, in a culturally diverse world, political communities should be able to determine their own futures, we have a good reason to allow significant departures from global equality' (2007a, p. 74).

These distinctions between strong and weak moral cosmopolitanism are important for determining the relations between ethics and international affairs, and depend on specific conceptions of political community. For both Nagel and Miller, since political community remains empirically sub-global, moral cosmopolitan vision must be minimal. For Pogge and Caney, since the moral core of liberal political community (the absolute worth of the individual) must be universalized to be consistent as such at *any* level, global justice concerns are much larger, implying socioeconomic, civil and political considerations.

That said, before turning to the next modality of normative cosmopolitanism, I wish briefly to consider an argument the value of which both Nagel and Miller appear to refuse and which is of import to me later: increasing economic interdependence creates an increasing array of moral obligations to fellow human beings (Miller, 2002, p. 82; Nagel, 2005, p. 138). For Miller and Nagel, such interdependence connotes neither the (political) interconnectedness nor the (political) cooperation and solidarity specific to the state form.

In her classic article 'Lifeboat earth' (1975/1999), Onora O'Neill considers the responsibility of persons of affluent countries towards those dying of famine in the Third World. Her thesis 'not to avoid death is in fact to kill' (ibid., p. 310) is well known. The thesis concerns me less here than its justification. O'Neill writes:

Some may object to the metaphor 'lifeboat Earth'. A lifeboat is small; all have equal claims to be there and to share equally in the provisions. Whereas . . . the starving millions are far away and have no right to what is owned by affluent individuals or nations, even if it could prevent their deaths. . . . I think that this could reasonably have been said in times past. The poverty and consequent deaths of far-off persons were something which the affluent might perhaps have done something to prevent, but which they had often done nothing to bring about. Hence they had not violated the right not to be killed of those living far off. But the economic and technological interdependence of today alters this situation. Sometimes deaths are produced by some persons or groups in distant, usually affluent nations. . . . Only if we knew that we were not part of any system of activities causing unjustifiable deaths could we have no duties to support policies which seek to avoid such deaths. Modern economic chains are so complex that it is likely that only those who are economically isolated and self-sufficient could know that they are part of no such system of activities. (Ibid., pp. 310, 313)

I have quoted O'Neill at length because I wish to be clear that minimal cosmopolitans have internalized her thesis: not to avoid death is to kill; we therefore have a duty to protect and sustain the life of our fellow human beings. That said, there is a historico-sociological logic to O'Neill's argument that goes beyond Miller's and Nagel's clear-cut distinctions between economic interdependence and political interconnectedness and, therefore, troubles a *categorical* distinction between strong and weak forms of cosmopolitanism. This argument is important to me in the respective cosmopolitan responses to Realism and Marxism. For O'Neill, increasing economic interdependence entails increasing responsibility towards those who are harmed either directly or indirectly by our actions. The possibility of moral conscience towards other lives in other parts of the planet deepens as we become more aware of the long-distance causality between seemingly independent human actions. The cognitive consequences that ensue from a materially evermore interdependent world, together with the human ability to *react* to them, foster, that is, a cosmopolitan disposition to international events. As Friedrich Nietzsche (1887/1994) was the first to argue consistently, *morality evolves materially*. This means, following the sociology of Norbert Elias (1982), that the more socially dense interdependence becomes, the deeper and wider our sense of obligation becomes.[3] This, after all, is how national loyalty also emerged after the dissipation of feudalism. Post-national loyalties *are* emerging in the wake of new forms of social density: through world events that affect all human beings, global communication of these events, sports events, transnational civil activism, regional associations, international summits, and so forth. These forms of reciprocity remain, of course, very thin, as my comments on the cultural dimension to Beck's 'cosmopolitanizing' sociology assume. They do, however, entail that the tenets of moral cosmopolitanism are *already* in the process of becoming embedded at more than the national level of the state or political community. Although enforced global collective cooperation is non-existent (see Blake, 2001; Risse, 2005, pp. 100–1), although the post-national political community of the EU is thin and singular, an emerging political dimension to these forms of reciprocity cannot be theoretically ignored. Miller's and Nagel's respective theories of political cooperative conditionality and political coercive conditionality ignore them. This point will frame one set of responses to the Realist critique of cosmopolitanism and inform my particular understanding of the weak, but existent thrust of progressive cosmopolitan liberalism.

2.3 Normative cosmopolitanism

As the Introduction to this book discussed, the normative modality of cosmopolitanism is quite complex. If, following the last section, all cosmopolitan thought is moral, all cosmopolitan thought is also normative. Morality and normativity are, however, not equivalent. I wish to argue this point in three ways. (i) Moral principles of human behaviour are grounded normatively; (ii) behaviour is normatively constrained; and (iii) norms have a horizonal character and hold a specific relation to history. I emphasize the last trait, looking at length at the normative aspect of Kant's and Jürgen Habermas's cosmopolitan political thought. The normative theorization of international relations is often underestimated by empirically minded IR theory, despite the importance of recent normative IR theory (Brown, 1992; Frost, 1996; Erskine, 2008a, 2008b; Lebow, 2003). My most important claim in this section is the following, and, as argued in my Introduction, I make use of it a lot in this book's responses to IR critiques of cosmopolitanism. Understood as a constraint on political behaviour, norms are not simply rules prescribing or deterring action. In a world of interdependence, they increasingly 'hover' between the prescriptive and the empirical. This 'hovering' makes their exact ontological status difficult to circumscribe; the point emphasizes, however, their purchase on empirical reality in resistance to the prevalent distinction in social science between the normative and the empirical.

The first definition of the normative dimension of cosmopolitanism is commonsensical and informs normative political theory as such. In the last section, we saw that Thomas Pogge and Simon Caney advocated the extension of liberal principles of moral egalitarianism to the international and global levels and, therefore, claimed the existence of global principles of civil, political and socioeconomic justice. Normative theory justifies this claim (see Caney, 2005, pp. 1–7). Caney argues that global use of these principles is compatible with domestic use of them because, otherwise, their universal value at a domestic level is inconsistent (compare Beitz 1999a, 1999b, 1999c; Nussbaum, 1994; Erskine 2008a, 2008b). Jürgen Habermas's discourse-theoretic justification of the extension of legal principles is normative in another meta-theoretical manner (Habermas, 1997, pp. 118–30). For Habermas, intersubjective recognition between participating parties in the empirical field requires generally accepted validity claims. These claims, achieved through rational argumentation, ground the moral principles of public legality, which, in turn, fixes the relations of mutual obligation in posited law (ibid., pp. 118–19). Normative cosmopolitanism is thus firstly about deducing, as far as possible, one's moral claims so that these claims are rationally accounted for, and not simply opined.

The second meaning of normative cosmopolitanism concerns the manner in which behaviour is constrained through moral rules. Moral cosmopolitanism is normative in the sense that it looks to the submission of power-politics to a moral vision and to a set of moral rules (Beitz, 1999a; G. W. Brown, 2009; Falk, 2004; Habermas, 1996; Held, 2005a; Pogge, 2008). A general argument made by Patrick Hayden in his *Cosmopolitan Global Politics* (2005) adds a further observation to this kind of reasoning that I underlined in my initial comments on theory in the Introduction. Hayden emphasizes that moral cosmopolitanism is not just normative in critical opposition to empirical political reality. It is already 'embedded' in the international human rights regime (ibid., p. 11). At international and national constitutional levels, the normative principles of human rights translate, in other words, an emerging reality at all levels of governance (ibid., pp. 11–37). The cosmopolitan focus on the moral rights and interests of individuals, as opposed to those of states, has therefore an increasingly institutional reality, one that gradually locks-in domestic, regional and global rights regimes (ibid., pp. 71, 96, 122). The section on legal cosmopolitanism considers this point again from the problematic angle of international law and its enforcement. Here I simply underscore the point that an international regime like that of human rights embeds strong normative cosmopolitan claims (the dignity of moral personhood) in empirical international reality.

The third meaning of normative pinpoints both the prescriptive and the horizonal aspects of principles that seek to underpin the organization of world politics. This third use of the term is complex, and Kant's cosmopolitan political writings offer, I believe, one of the clearest examples of this normative complexity. In his essays 'Idea for a universal history with a cosmopolitan purpose', 'This may be true in theory . . .' and 'Perpetual peace' (Kant, 1784, 1793 and 1795), Kant conceives of the liberal republican norm of personal autonomy on a domestic and an international level. Domestically, all political societies should aspire to a republican constitution, since it is within such a regime that the freedom of the moral person can be politically attained in relation to the freedoms of others under general law (1793/1991, pp. 73–4). Internationally, this freedom can only be guaranteed by cosmopolitan law that takes as its object both states and individuals (1795/1991, pp. 98–9, n.1). Since, however, cosmopolitan law can only be guaranteed as *public* law by the force of a world republican state, freedom is endangered by the very instance that provides it (ibid., pp. 90–2). A world republic thus runs the risk of dominating the geographical, cultural and linguistic plurality of the world and of contradicting, more importantly politically, acting states' own principles of coercive right (ibid., p. 104; see Habermas, 1997, p. 128). The norm of republicanism works, therefore, empirically at the domestic level given the closeness of government to the people in a geographically delimited space. But it does not work empirically *as* a norm at the global level. Political virtue (world republicanism) inverts, ironically, into political vice (monarchic despotism). As is well known, Kant does not theorize this tragic contradiction or aporia, but opts for a second-best federation of like-minded republican states to uphold peace through self-obligating 'public laws' (ibid.). I return to this important legal inconsistency later. Here I use this example of normative reasoning in order to stress the complexity of normative cosmopolitan thinking. For, it is the case that all contemporary cosmopolitan discourse is sensitive to the Kantian aporia of a universal state.

The complexity of normative cosmopolitanism, concerned with principle in the international domain, can be seen through Kant's argument. It is seen:

1 in the moral horizon that has claims on politics (liberal republicanism);
2 in the institutionalization of this horizon through the gradual construction of international federalism and basic cosmopolitan rights (to begin with, for Kant, the cosmopolitan right to 'hospitality'); and
3 in the contradictory horizon of a world republican state of law that would guarantee the function of cosmopolitan rights, while at the same time risking their validity.

In Kant's political writings, the normative is upheld as an immanent historical possibility towards which humans can aspire and as a self-contradictory, unrealizable idea.

Now, critics of cosmopolitanism tend to place normative cosmopolitanism in (3): the normative horizon is politically unrealistic, moreover impractical. I wish to argue, however, that all three positions are, together, of intellectual interest. Point (3) – the norm of pure practical reason in the field of world politics – is by itself a non-starter: the norm's horizon does not work institutionally. Pure practical reason in the political field contradicts itself (it may promote despotism, not republicanism). But point (1) – the general idea of a legal community of rational beings – provides an ideational framework within which *historical possibility* can be thought. And point (2) – the institutional arrangements of federalism – gives that framework unverifiable, but plausible concrete content (to be tested over time). Therefore, points (1), (2) and (3) suggest, *together*, something like a 'horizonal space' of legal and political invention in which different types of legality and polity, at different but interrelated levels of community, may be rehearsed. This complex horizonal space is, I would argue, what makes Kant of such interest to international relations thought since it cannot be contained within the opposition between Kantian idealism and Kantian pragmatism (on this opposition in Kant's political writings, see Ellis, 2005).

Following Kant and his aporia of world government in his 'Perpetual peace' essay, I would argue, then, that normative cosmopolitanism asserts an understanding of the relation between past, present and future. Once a progressive norm of human thought begins to open up a domain of political invention within history, this norm tends to have cumulative effects in the world, however institutionally inadequate and reversible these effects are. The idea and regime of human rights have been one feasible, if partial, alternative to other normative organizations of human identity. This idea offers a normative horizon for ethico-political behaviour in the sense that the *impossibility* of an enacted set of global rights and duties (world republicanism) nevertheless motivates more sophisticated legal and political invention.

The work of Jürgen Habermas provides a good example of this approach, although there are problems in his analysis which I address in section 2.5. Well aware of the aporia of world government, Habermas focuses on aligning domestic and international law under the general norm of a world community of law (Habermas, 1997 and 2006). His normative focus rests, therefore, on the increasing importance of documents of international law since Wilson's 1918 Fourteen Points on national self-determination: to run through them, the charter of the League of Nations, the UN Charter, the Universal Declaration of Human Rights (1948), the Geneva conventions on genocide and the rules of war, the subsequent covenants on civil and political rights and economic and social rights (1976–7), the Vienna conference of 1993 on human rights, the various 1990s documents on women, children and minority rights, and the 2002 institution of the International Criminal Court (ICC). These international articles are all historical events that point, for Habermas, to a slow, reversible, but histori- cally inevitable 'juridification' of international relations through which state power is made increasingly subordinate to universal principles of validity (1997, pp. 128–9; 2006, pp. 147–50). For Habermas, massive qualifications to either the universality or the generality of the international human rights regime (double standards, selectivity) do not muddy, there- fore, their essential normative point. For Habermas, the above collection of articles have, on average, increasingly oriented state behaviour and given substantial content to converging values of the international com- munity. The ICC is therefore unthinkable *without* the prior failure of the League of Nations. The ICC is presently beset by institutional and political problems: it is not independent of world executive power (the UN Security Council – UNSC) and its attempt to pursue heads of state, accused of crimes against humanity, is easily instrumentalized by either side of a conflict or remains dead letter. Despite these serious problems (of immedi- ate concern to empirical political analysis), Habermas would still claim a certain direction to history, one working with the power of institutional value and legal norm (2006, pp. 173–4). His emphasis on the gradual juridification of international relations anticipates, in this sense, a morally mediated thin political community at the global level.

Let me summarize this argument. Following the work of Jürgen Habermas, I suggest that normative cosmopolitanism has effects in the real as an ideational guide to human behaviour, as embedded in normative regimes that set standards and rules (the human rights regime), and as a prescription of what 'should' be the case that constitutes, once posited within history, an irreducible accomplishment of progress, launching politi- cal invention. I am further emphasizing (beyond Habermas's own language) that *empirically impossible or not, and/or empirically ignored or not, this prescription forms a norm for future historical behaviour and institution- building.* Normative cosmopolitanism is therefore far from being only a non-explanatory justification of moral commitments or an ethical idealist framework within which to think political reality. On both registers of embedding in international regimes and of complex horizonal anticipation, it 'hovers' between the empirical and the non-empirical. And, as a complex horizon of prescriptive impossibility *and* possibility, it responds, within given historical dynamics, to the openness of the future. My claim is that normative uses of cosmopolitanism distinguish themselves most from moral cosmopolitanism by this complex relation to history. My cosmopolitan response to the Realist critique of cosmopolitanism (see chapter 3) makes much of this argument.[4]

2.4 Institutional cosmopolitanism

The institutional modality of cosmopolitanism addresses the need to move from theoretical or purely moral cosmopolitan considerations to collective practical solutions. It therefore emphasizes institutional arrangements over cultural, moral or normative arguments. This is often a purely analytical distinction, but it brings into its own the side to contemporary cosmopolitan literature that wishes to tackle systemic global problems or wishes to tackle such problems itself systematically. I address the specificity of institutional cosmopolitanism by focusing again on Thomas Pogge (2008) and the difference between his position on global justice and that of John Rawls (Rawls, 1971, 1993, 1999). Section 2.2 on moral cosmopolitanism has already rehearsed some of the philosophical arguments of import to this difference, so this section proceeds quite quickly.

Like Miller and Nagel, John Rawls is a minimalist when it comes to questions of justice beyond the borders of the nation-state. As is well known, *A Theory of Justice* maintains that principles of justice are 'those of fairness of cooperation between members of the same society' (1971, p. 11). Rawls elaborates first-order and second-order principles of justice: a political community should, first, hold to basic individual liberties (civil and political) and grant impartially fundamental opportunities of choice (to health, housing, education, employment). Second, it should only allow economic advantage insofar as such advantage also advantages the most disadvantaged of society (the 'difference principle') (ibid., pp. 60–83). According to Rawls, this society is closed (ibid., p. 8); as for Nagel and Miller, justice can only work within a system of cooperation. International principles of justice are those that apply to both liberal and non-liberal societies (at least those that are well-ordered). A global culture underpinning these principles therefore redounds, for Rawls, to the following: non-aggression, popular consent to the terms of governance and a basic set of Lockean-type rights: life, liberty and property (1999, pp. 85–8). The international society at play between societies and peoples excludes the first-order liberties associated with liberal political and civil rights and the second-order principle of global distributive justice (ibid., pp. 37–8, 115–19). Consequently, for Rawls, the extension of domestic principles of justice to the global level is both politically unrealistic and moralizing towards other cultures which embody the will of their people, but hold non-liberal values (ibid., pp. 34–6). Rawls agrees that natural and man-made borders are historically arbitrary; but, in a non-ideal theoretical set-up, these borders, together with the different values expressed on each side of them, constitute the *starting-point* from out of which a tolerant global family of political concepts can slowly grow (1993, p. 56).

Now, for Thomas Pogge, the problem with this weak cosmopolitanism is as much the fact that it fails to address the structural causes of world poverty as it is a question of internal philosophical inconsistency (compare Caney, 2005, pp. 65–6; Pogge, 2008, pp. 97–123). Regarding the latter, the universality and generality of moral personhood implies, for Pogge, that wealthy societies have duties to both the poor and the suffering because the definition of arbitrary borders includes the *arbitrary distribution of natural resources*. That some countries have more or fewer natural resources than others is, from the moral standpoint, as arbitrary as any other form of particularity (race, class, nation, gender). Pogge looks, accordingly, for 'a single universal criterion of justice at the global level' and finds it, *contra* Rawls, in Rawls's 'difference principle' (Pogge, 2008, p. 145): global economic advantage is just as long as it also advantages the most disadvantaged. Pogge turns, second, to the empirical world as it is and notes the 2004 World Bank data on measures of disparity of wealth between the developed and developing world (ibid., p. 2). These data have not changed substantially in the last few years. According to 2007 calculations, there were well over a billion people under the absolute poverty line (calculated at less than $1 a day, PPP), and fewer than one half of the world's population live on less than $2 a day (World Bank, 2007). A billion people in the industrialized countries live on an average of $82 a day, PPP, without taking into account their immobile and mobile assets (real estate, stocks, investments, pensions): together this billion people control about 80% of the global product, while the poorest billion control under 0.3% of the global product (ibid.). Such comparative statistics of world wealth and the radically uneven distribution of this wealth prompt two conclusions from Pogge. Both absolute world poverty and overall world inequality are *structurally pervasive* and *systemic.* They constitute a necessary effect of (i) the history of Western colonialism and (ii) the basic ground rules of national polities and international institutions like the IMF, the World Bank and the WTO (Pogge, 2008, pp. 202–10). Rawls's weak cosmopolitanism simply fails to address this systemic causality. For Pogge, therefore, international institutions need to be reformed so that a more equitable global economic order is possible, an order within which world poverty and severe world imbalances of wealth can be effectively addressed (ibid., pp. 203–5).

To this end, Pogge has proposed a Global Resources Tax or Dividend (2005, pp. 105–8). A property rights tax, fixed at 1%, would fall on the owners of natural resources at the moment of extraction and on the receivers at the moment of consumption. He calculates that in one year the tax would raise approximately \$320 billion (ibid., p. 105). This sum is much less than 1% of the total global product, but 55 times the amount presently given to development aid for social services (ibid.). These figures are telling. Practicalities of implementation aside, this tax presents an institutional corrective to a shared institutional order that 'foreseeably and avoidably reproduces radical inequality' (ibid., p. 101). For Pogge, a consequent liberalism at the domestic level and moral cosmopolitan awareness of the causality of harm lead to institutional liberal cosmopolitanism.[5]

The Rawls/Pogge difference neatly highlights, within the general problematic of weak and strong cosmopolitanism, the difference between non-institutional and institutional modalities of cosmopolitanism. For a weak cosmopolitan liberal like Rawls, institutional cosmopolitanism is both impractical and potentially intolerant in the non-ideal domain of world politics. For a strong cosmopolitan liberal like Pogge, the very lack of institution-building on cosmopolitan principle is both inconsistent with liberal moral analysis per se, leading to the political hypocrisy of liberal 'double standards' (Pogge 2008, pp. 112–14) and it also fails to address the systemic outcomes of global capitalism. Both these double-standards and this failure have given rise to alienation from Western-conceived models of political and social justice.[6] Given the economic system and its alienating geopolitical consequences, it is consequently both idealistic *and* realistic, for institutional cosmopolitans like Pogge, that world injustice is tackled where it is structurally pervasive and avoidable: in *institutions* of *global rule-making*.

Following my comments on O'Neill in section 2.2, I assume the structural and institutional parts of Pogge's argument in my cosmopolitan response to the Marxist critique of cosmopolitanism. I am unsure, however, that a 'single universal criterion of justice' (Pogge, 2008, p. 145) should mean more in world politics than the idea that global rules and institutions are put in place that permit, in the first place, local determinations of justice and community which fit a world of economic interdependence. My argument is for a differentiated universalism that affirms global principle, global rule and global institution, but for the sake of endogenous development.

2.5 Legal cosmopolitanism

Legal cosmopolitanism is a form of institutional cosmopolitanism and is committed to the complementarity between moral rights and legal entitlement. It aims to provide basic moral rights with international/global legal status and international law with moral foundation (Buchanan, 2003). In this section, I focus on the human rights regime, although legal cosmopolitans are concerned with the contractarian grounds of international regimes as a whole (G. W. Brown, 2009). I wish to give theoretical context to this liberal regime since it is important for an understanding of this regime's complex nature: I therefore return to the liberal republican analyses by Kant and by Habermas on law (Kant, 1793, 1795, 1797; Habermas, 1996, 1997, 2006). The general claim of this section is that legal cosmopolitanism requires a differentiated analysis of law to be persuasive and that it should be complemented by political cosmopolitan judgement and leadership.

Following Kantian political thought, we have seen that the institutional bridge between morality and politics is public law (*das Recht*). In criticism of natural law theory, which posits divinely endowed 'natural justice' and 'natural rights', Kant (1793) is the first to argue consistently within liberalism that justice and rights can only be guaranteed through the coercion of law. For the modern values of justice and freedom to be enacted, they depend on the force of law. The freedom of each is only possible in a social environment if it is compatible with the freedom of all. This compatibility requires external obligation and, therefore, public laws. In contrast to moral rights, the domain of 'Right' is consequently only to be understood in the context of personal self-limitation through external force. Law realizes right through external constraint; it also lends it social legitimacy as the statement of public will through parliamentary assembly. The institutional bridge between morality and politics is one of law, but law also involves public debate: its source is therefore both moral principle and public legislation. In Habermasian terms rights have 'validity', but they also have 'function' (Habermas, 1996).

As we have also seen, this precise understanding of right leads to an irreducible dilemma as one moves, legally, from the domestic to the international sphere with the ethical compass of individual moral worth. In 'Idea for a universal history with a cosmopolitan purpose' (1784) and 'Perpetual peace' (1795), Kant takes the notion of civic freedom beyond the borders of the nation-state. The domain of international right involves the rights of states in their legal relations with each other (legal obligation based on treaty and custom). The domain of cosmopolitan right (in general) involves the rights of states and individuals in their legal relations to each other under cosmopolitan law. In an 'Idea for a universal history' Kant is the first to pursue in the liberal tradition a rigorous analogy between domestic law and global law based on the self-limiting concept of civic freedom. Just as the rights of the individual are secured in a republican commonwealth, so the rights of individuals and states can only be guaranteed in a universal state of world citizenship (a world republic). World citizens can only be such under the coercion of universal law (compare Nagel's argument, outlined above in section 2.2). If, in other words, the domain of right can levitate up to the global level, unlike the international domain of right, then right must be secured through hard law (law with the backing of force). Kant's above-mentioned retreat from a world republic is, in essence, the *dilemma* of global right: coercive law at the world level runs the risk of domination and conflict, given both the geographic, cultural and linguistic diversity of the world and the integrity of the domestic sphere of civic freedom (individuals' domestic freedoms are secured through the indivisible power of nation-state law). As Kant puts it:

> While natural rights allow us to say of men living in a lawless condition that they ought to abandon it, the right of nations does not allow us to say the same of states. For as states, they *already* have a lawful internal constitution, and have thus outgrown the coercive right of others to subject them to a wider legal constitution in accordance with their conception of right. (Kant, 1795/1991, p. 104, my emphasis)

Kant's negative substitute, a lawful federation of nation-states, counts on the 'soft law' rules of international right given the republican principles of their own internal constitution. His way out of the dilemma of the *function* of cosmopolitan right is to opt, therefore, for a federal assembly of 'self-obligating' republics and for the gradual elimination of conflict and war through the dissemination of republican example. 'One powerful state will provide a focal point for federal association among other states. These will join up with the first one, thus securing the freedom of each state with the idea of international right, and the whole will gradually spread further and further' (ibid.). Kant's legal republicanism at the cosmopolitan level requires, in other words, the world politics of republican state leadership.

The lesser bad of a federal association of republican states means that both state and individual rights are cut loose from their lawful condition. Kant's attempt to provide – over the top of weak international law – an analogy between strong domestic law and strong cosmopolitan law fails in its own terms. Now, this leaves the functional concept of extensive rights, pertaining to all human beings as moral persons, unfulfilled. I wish to claim here that *the practice of legal cosmopolitanism can do nothing but invent within these conceptual dilemmas of cosmopolitan liberal theory*. Rights need force to be right. A rigorous analogy between domestic and cosmopolitan law is therefore appropriate. At the global level, however, such analogy runs the risk of substantially curtailing domestic civic freedom.

Therefore, similarity and difference of 'public law' at each level of community in a globalized world becomes necessary in order for complementarity between morality and law to be sustained. Theoretically, legal cosmopolitanism must countenance a *differentiated universalism*, which invents in loose analogy with domestic law. It depends furthermore on political judgement and political leadership. As the following chapters argue at several junctures, relations between legitimacy, law and force must be practised in a variety of ways for legal cosmopolitanism to be consistent.

Before I turn to political cosmopolitanism, let me reinforce these last points with the problematic invention of Jürgen Habermas within these equivocations of law.

Habermas has argued consistently since the 1990s that the Kantian dilemma of supranational government, in the context of rights, can be rethought if it is given a different institutional form (Habermas, 1997, p. 127; 2006, p. 136). This form is that of 'juridifying' international relations in exclusive terms of giving legal rights to individual citizens at the world level. The state, state-sovereignty, and their problematic subsumption under a world republic must be 'by-passed'. As noted above in section 2.3 on normative cosmopolitanism, international legal documents that lead from the UN Charter to the constitutive articles of the ICC testify, for Habermas, to the 'quasi-*constitutionalization*' of international relations (2006, pp. 159–63). This process places states' responsibilities towards their peoples under juridical procedure. Arbitrary behaviour by states towards their own peoples (crimes against 'humanity') and/or states' exceptionalism (the terms of intervention of the second Iraq War) will thereby be reduced. For Habermas, if intervention in another state can follow, for instance, the quasi-impartiality of international juridical process – where human rights acquire legal status and procedure – intervention can acquire global legitimacy and follow functional protocol (ibid., pp. 169–73). To argue for the juridification of international relations is therefore to insist, following the spirit of Kantian legalism, that human rights find legal entitlement, that they be embedded as coherently as possible in the texts of international law and that they foster legal procedure according to norms of universality, generality and impartiality. Only on the basis of this quasi-legal impartiality will *all* state behaviour become gradually consistent with the cosmopolitan dimensions of the UN Charter and the UN Declaration of Human Rights. This is one of the most consistent arguments to date for legal cosmopolitanism in the domain of international relations.

That said, the argument cannot avert, I would claim, the Kantian dilemma of cosmopolitan law. Although Habermas focuses on the compelling need for greater juridification of international relations, the dilemma makes two additional arguments necessary. First, legal cosmopolitanism should fore-ground/invent varying relations between law and force in the domain of legal rights so as to eschew critiques of formal universalism. Second, legal cosmopolitanism must entertain a relation with power-politics, political judgement and political leadership. At the cosmopolitan level, a straight-forward 'domestic' separation of judicial and executive powers is both necessary (for impartiality of legal procedure) and unwanted (global lead-ership is critical to its realization). Both arguments make, in different ways, the domain of cosmopolitan legality also a political project. Just as moral rights and legal entitlement are rightly considered under the logic of com-plementarity (Buchanan, 2003), so, equally, I argue, legal and political cosmopolitanisms constitute complementary parts of a cosmopolitan outlook on world politics. My responses to Realism and postmodernism make much of this point.

2.6 Political cosmopolitanism

I understand political cosmopolitanism in two senses. The first is the well-known project of 'cosmopolitan democracy', first advocated by Daniele Archibugi and David Held in the mid-1990s as a critical response to the victory of nation-state liberal democracy over communism (Archibugi and Held, 1995). This political project is theoretically rigorous, but lacking in feasibility when confronting international relations with cosmopolitanism. I nevertheless expound the project in detail here: partly because of its own conceptual rigour and partly because I reconfigure it in chapter 3 (to respond to Realist criticisms of cosmopolitanism) and use it loosely in chapter 5 to respond to the Marxist critique of 'Third Way' social demo-cratic thinking. An appreciation of this project is therefore important to the book's engagements. I understand political cosmopolitanism in a second more prosaic sense: the importance of cosmopolitan political argument and cosmopolitan political judgement. This second sense has been recently, if briefly, rehearsed by Robert Fine (2007, pp. 93–5) and William Smith (2007, pp. 84–6), but it clearly addresses an urgent, feasible need in world politics: that of supplementing cosmopolitan moral and legal principle with political advocacy, political judgement and political leadership. Several comments on this second understanding follow my exposition of the project of cosmopolitan democracy: it is specifically taken up when I rehearse a cosmopolitan political ethics of limitation in response to Realism and to postmodernism (chapters 3 and 7).

The two proponents of cosmopolitan democracy are – following the insights of Jürgen Habermas – David Held and Daniele Archibugi (especially Held, 2004; Archibugi, 2008). Their general argument is the following: critical of the 'democracy talk' of the 1990s, political cosmopolitans must (i) tie the cosmopolitan disposition to a theory and practice of democracy, (ii) curtail the international hypocrisy of democratic nation-states, and (iii) show that democracy, to be true to its name ('the rule of the people'), should be thought and practised in a globalized world at as many levels of governance as possible. Given the effects of globalization, the nation-state no longer has a monopoly over its borders. Since this monopoly was made legitimate through increasingly democratic forms of government from the eighteenth to twentieth centuries, the loss of monopoly entails the loss of democracy for those represented by their governments. Issues of global proportion that affect all citizens of nations, directly or indirectly, can no longer be addressed by states alone. Democratic states stand, therefore, in contradiction with their own principles of rule (Held, 1995a, pp. 267–78; 1995b, pp. 97–103). The 'democratic deficit' that accompanies globalization means that both the irreducible principles and the institutions of democracy need to be carried over into the international system. Without this 'extension' of democracy, democratic states become both domestically and internationally 'hypocritical'. Domestic democracies can, domestically, no longer provide national public goods in isolation from the turbulence of the world economy. Global regulation is therefore a prerequisite of the maintenance of domestic democracy. Leading democratic states have, internationally, refused to align their practices of foreign policy with those of domestic policy, maintaining hard Realist distinctions between the international and the national. Transcending this 'democratic schizophrenia' between domestic and foreign policy requires both democratic example in the international field and cosmopolitan governance (Archibugi, 2008, p. 7). Unlike the other modalities of cosmopolitanism, these two mutually reinforcing arguments on democratic deficit entail the following political focus.

While deeply engaged in the international human rights regime, the political project of cosmopolitan democracy highlights the need to 'enact' rights, that is, to create procedures of will-formation and political participation that give legal rights political validity and functionality. The project cannot remain satisfied, normatively, with the historical evolution of democratic polities towards some form of federation of democracies (Kant's negative substitute for a world republican state). Where international community exists and where, for cosmopolitans, it is irreducible, this community must be gradually transformed into a global political community by being itself 'democratized'. This political norm does not return, however, to the Kantian logic of world statehood: the project entails the invention of new institutional forms of democratic transparency and accountability and the 'locking-in' of supranational models of governance with national models of government. I wish to suggest, therefore, that the notion of democratic *invention* rather than that of *extension* is perhaps more appropriate when considering the project of cosmopolitan democracy (and I will argue so further in chapter 3). Cosmopolitan democracy does not envisage the end of the nation-state; it foregrounds regional and global supplements to it, so that national democracies can reorganize their principles of power and legitimacy in a tiered, integrated structure of democratic decision-making. Only then will those affected by decisions – however distant the instance of decision lies from the affected in a globalized world – begin to participate in the process that leads to these decisions. The extraordinary ambition of this political cosmopolitanism ensues from its politico-theoretical completeness.

For Held and Archibugi this ambition gives rise in turn to three major agendas. (i) Conceptualization of what democracy irreducibly entails; (ii) formulation of what the principles of cosmopolitan democratic law and a cosmopolitan democratic order entail; (iii) appreciation of how power and authority can be organized, in global terms, such that these promote cooperation between global, regional and national instances. This cooperation will mitigate the top-down centralism of global elites. I will briefly work through each point, amalgamating comments from the various articles and books of each author.

Held and Archibugi emphasize different aspects of democracy, but both work with a fundamental set of thoughts. Modern democracy concerns collective and individual autonomy. It is embodied in the concept of popular sovereignty, representative government, the separation of powers, and the constitutional framework of rights. Applied supra-nationally, these meta-principles of autonomy give rise to a set of second-order principles that underpin political response to the connectedness of action, issue and outcome. These are:

1 The principle of *moral egalitarianism* (dignity of the person).
2 The principle of *self-affection*: those significantly affected by processes and decisions should participate in the decision-making procedures by which such processes are addressed and such decisions are made.
3 The principle of *subsidiarity*: the making and implementation of decisions belong to the level of political order – municipal, national, regional, global – at which both effectiveness and legitimacy are achieved together (see also Cabrera, 2004).
4 The principles of *symmetry* and *reciprocity*: all behaviour and action between agents (at whatever level) work on the basis of the symmetry of decision-makers and the reciprocity of responsibilities and duties.

5 The principle of *sustainability*: the present moral duty towards future generations to provide them with a planet upon which they can achieve dignity of life.

These second-order principles catch the overall requirement of legitimacy that the reinvention of democracy at a world level would entail. If irreducibly global issues such as pollution, terrorism, nuclear proliferation, migration movements and excessive capital accumulation can only be effectively addressed in global terms, then the decision, taken at the global level, should be made accountable to those whom it significantly affects. The principle of subsidiarity seems especially crucial to this democratic reinvention of nation-state democracy, as I argue in chapter 3. The challenge of democracy in a globalized world is one of instituting these principles in what Held calls 'an interconnected series of power and authority centers' (Held, 2003, p. 176). These integrated, but decentralized power structures will gradually give political legitimacy to cosmopolitan legality and international law and diplomacy. The preceding principles must be thought not only across world space, but also across time (the future of a sustainable planet). Since the mid-1990s, both Held and Archibugi have argued consistently for reforms in the light of these comments (see table 1.1; also see Archibugi, 1995, 2003, 2008; Archibugi and Held, 1995; Held, 1995a, 1995b, 2003, 2004).

The charted suggestions given in table 1.1 may come across a little like a 'shopping-list', reminiscent of Kantian formalism. Proposals of reform are listed; they are not worked up from out of empirical givens (compare Hegel's critique of Kant: Hegel, 1807/1977, Preface, §§47, 59). From this perspective, these reforms all remain prescriptive 'shoulds', eminent, but not immanent ways of thinking forward. There is perhaps some truth to this criticism. That said, the project of cosmopolitan democracy does speak immediately, in critical normative vein, to the failings of empirical reality. Democratic control of capital accumulation and volatility requires, for instance, national fiscal sovereignty and global financial regulation. Such regulation should be made, at some point, as democratically accountable as possible, if the ideology of democracy is to remain the best normative way of conceptually framing political organization. Since no better alternative has emerged, the cosmopolitan democrat might argue, it is incumbent upon theorists and practitioners to invent the mechanisms whereby state sovereignty merges with institutional mechanisms of subsidiarity. The peoples of the world are still governed on matters of global security and peace by the victory powers of the Second World War (with the exception of China). The General Assembly of the United Nations has a purely consultative role in the UN system, which means that the executive power of

Table 1.1

Short/mid-term reforms	Long-term reforms
Enlargement of the UNSC (regional representation, change of veto system)	Clear separation of powers at international and supranational levels; single persons recognized as ultimate source of political authority
Institution of a World Parliament, second chamber of general world assembly	Public funding of global deliberative processes, electoral processes, and global public policy; global taxation schemes
Institution of an Economic, Social and Environmental Security Council within the UN system	Locking-in of rights and duties across political, civic, social and economic fields
Effective coordination between the Bretton Woods institutions and the UN assemblies and councils (committee accountability)	
Compulsory jurisdiction before the ICC (individuals as subjects of international law) and the International Court of Justice (states as subjects of international law)	Locking-in of rights and duties between national, regional and global polities
Effective supranational military force (a UN-led small standing army and/or rapid deployment force)	Shift of coercive capacities from national to regional and global instances

the UNSC has appropriated legislative power. The judiciary is either marginal (the International Court of Justice – ICJ) or has as yet little independence from the executive branch and the vetoes of the permanent five (the ICC): there is therefore no institution perceived to fulfil the judicial vocation of impartiality. Without tough terms of engagement and the logistical ability to deploy force rapidly, the UN is unable to prevent conflict and can arrive too late in reaction to one. UN non-aggressive peacekeeping of borders becomes quickly blunted or instrumentalized by the conflict parties (as in the cases of Bosnia, Somalia and East Timor). It is commonsense, for political cosmopolitans like Held and Archibugi, that if the representative body of the UNSC was widened to represent the configuration of world powers, and if the veto was restricted to justifiable concerns of national self-interest, the UN would become more impartial and more legitimate worldwide. Such reform begins, for the cosmopolitan democrat, a due process of democratization at the international level, the end term of which would be the radical overhaul of the UN system according to the democratic principle of the separation of powers.

A cosmopolitan democrat, like Held or Archibugi, responds, therefore, to the failings of international political reality by holding to the analogy between domestic democracy and cosmopolitan democracy. It should nevertheless be clear from my account that the principle of subsidiarity (*qua* a democratic counter-principle to exclusive modes of state sovereignty) requires new forms of democratic *invention* within and between national, regional and global institutions. The project of cosmopolitan democracy is both straightforwardly modernist and necessarily open to new forms of democratic polity in a globalized world. The complex, impractical nature of many of the above-listed reforms does not, therefore, detract from this form of political cosmopolitanism: in response to both the irreducible dynamic of interdependence and its disempowering effects at all levels of social life, it expounds the conditions of democratic renewal. In this sense, at the precise moment that it theoretically resolves the dilemma of legal cosmopolitanism, its modality of discourse reverts to the normative. The price of politico-theoretical rigour is immediate realism. It offers, nevertheless, a normative framework within which to think and practise more democratic appropriations of globalization that refuse particularism (and I loosely use this framework in chapter 5).

Political cosmopolitanism should also be understood in another, more simple sense. I end this section on this second use of the term. The need for 'cosmopolitan political argument', following Robert Fine (2007, pp. 93–5), can be considered a form of political cosmopolitanism. This need occurs in the *gap* between principle and experience. In his excellent reading of cosmopolitanism, Fine refers to this gap in the context of Habermas's legal cosmopolitanism: the juridification of international relations. As I will detail in chapter 3, he argues that juridification risks proceduralism and avoids the requirement of political judgement. To argue why and when a military intervention should take place lies to one side of the automatic application of international rules. Argument and judgement of a political nature are needed. As Fine wittily puts it, 'the unkindest image I sometimes have of legal cosmopolitanism is that we can have the same politicians in power in Western states but that we should go to war for humanitarian reasons because a group of judges say we should' (ibid., p. 95). The political supplement to legal cosmopolitanism involves, again, the enactment of rights. This enactment involves here, however, much less a long-term project of cosmopolitan democracy than the short-term risk of political discrimination and the responsibility of political decision in specific contexts. This form of cosmopolitan political judgement is well argued by William Smith (2007). Since the same principles are ultimately at stake, what distinguishes these two forms of political cosmopolitanism are moment and emphasis. As my responses to Realism and to postmodernism argue, this difference is important, since it allows one to think and practise cosmopolitan ideas within a political ethics of limitation and trade-offs. This second understanding of political cosmopolitanism will be more acceptable to many in IR since it is empirically concrete and dovetails with a political theory of prudence and world statesmanship. I use both understandings in the following chapters according to context.

3 Conclusion

This long chapter has fulfilled several goals. First, it has given a broad, but precise exposition of contemporary cosmopolitan ideas with a background history. I hope that, in making this exposition, I have made clear, on several levels, the powerful relation in contemporary cosmopolitan thought between cosmopolitanism and liberalism. Second, it has given definitions to the most important modalities of cosmopolitanism and has shown the pertinence of the differences within each modality and from one modality to another. Distinctions, for example, between weak and strong cosmopolitanism, between institutional and non-institutional cosmopolitanism, or between moral and legal cosmopolitanism are important when confronting IR with cosmopolitan ideas. Third, with such distinctions one can make different arguments for the relevance of cosmopolitanism to IR on the basis of different agents and different responsibilities. These different arguments allow a *flexible* set of responses to IR critiques of universalism in the field of world politics. Fourth, the spectrum of contemporary cosmopolitan positions allows one, consequently, to see that these different positions are also mutually self-reinforcing or complementary. Legal cosmopolitanism needs, for example, political argument and political leadership to be effective in world politics. The role of states in the promotion of global rules is critical. An understanding of practical cosmopolitanism in the field of international relations requires, accordingly, a theory of state responsibility to weak cosmopolitan commitments. But this does not prevent stronger commitments being theorized, morally, normatively and institutionally, at the level of civic engagement and international organization under conditions of interdependence. The complementarity of cosmopolitan positions makes the cosmopolitan disposition towards international relations agile and flexible, while remaining ontologically consistent. Fifth, the foregoing spectrum has therefore offered a series of arguments that can help frame specific debates with IR critiques of universalism.

International relations grew into a specific discipline through the Realist attack on international liberalism between the two world wars. In the United States, working with rational choice theory, the school of Realism remains preponderant. I turn to it first.

2

The Realist Critique
of Cosmopolitanism

The theoretical status of the Realist school in IR pertains in part to its ability to work from out of a long tradition of realist thought (Williams, 2005, p. 3). The security dilemma rehearsed by John Herz is, for instance, formulated on the back of Thucydides' observations in *History of the Peloponnesian Wars* (Herz, 1950). Out of fear that the Athenians would expand, the Spartans consider themselves forced to engage in war with them (Thucydides, 1954, Introduction). The very means by which one state intends to maintain its own security presents a necessary threat to another state, which in turn responds by arming itself: the dilemma explains arms' escalation. Herz's Realist observation that conflict is a consequence of the radically uncertain structure of plurality is thus endorsed by Thucydides. The implicit suggestion is that historical precedent makes this dilemma a fundamental truth of politics. Unlike any other school in IR, Realism works with these permanent, structural truths of history, secured by a tradition of hard-headed thinkers. Thucydides, Aristotle, Machiavelli, Hobbes, Spinoza, Hegel, Nietzsche and Max Weber have become, retroactively, the philosophical foundation of the Realist outlook. This retroactively organized sense of tradition is important. The Realist school stands on major precedent: it is unwise to ignore the fundamental lessons of history. In this chapter I expound the major tenets of the school of Realism and then consider, from out of these tenets, what the brunt of its criticisms of cosmopolitanism amounts to. Since Realism in IR constitutes itself through its critique of international liberalism between the wars, and since, as I have argued, contemporary cosmopolitan tenets are liberal (in a wide sense) in inspiration, I move from the Realist critique of idealism and liberal universalism as such to recent Realist critiques of cosmopolitanism.[1]

As is well known, there are important variants of the school: the 'classical Realism' of Edward Carr (2001), Hans Morgenthau (1946, 1952 and 2005), George Kennan (1984) and Reinhold Niebuhr (2008); the 'structural Realism' of Kenneth Waltz (1954 and 1979); the 'hard Realism' of John Mearsheimer (2001); and the 'neo-Realism' of Waltz's followers like Stephen Krasner (1983 and 1992) and Robert Jervis (1998 and 1999). Each variant emphasizes a different aspect of power and interest and/or a different approach to them: the distinction between classical Realism and the other forms of Realism will be important to me later in this chapter and the next. The school can nevertheless be identified by a set of common traits; it is this set of traits – in response to liberalism's general effects in the domain of international politics – that concerns me first.

1 The Major Tenets of Realism

I will argue that there are five major constants within Realist analysis. I set them out individually for the sake of analytical clarity and in order of importance; they are nevertheless mutually complementary points.

(1) When it comes to political organization, *questions of order precede those of justice*. It is usually to Hobbes that Realist literature refers on this point. As Hobbes writes in the profound thirteenth chapter of the *Leviathan*, no law between persons can be made 'till agreement upon the person that make it' (Hobbes, 1651/1982, I, xiii, p. 185). A power in common, to which all have traded their own (right to) force for the promise of security, is necessary for legislation to be possible in the first place. Power is the condition of law in the precise sense that security and order precede the very possibility of legislation. The contemporary Realist, Robert Kagan, repeats the Hobbesian point at an international level when he argues in *Paradise and Power* that both the normative and legal dimensions to European integration and polity depend in the first place on post-World War II US power (Kagan, 2003, pp. 14–27). Without this precondition of power, contemporary European affirmation of law over force would not be possible. For Kagan, recent European slowness at forming a common defence policy proves how blind post-Second World War European liberals remain to this '*fundamental historical* insight' (ibid., p. 18, my emphasis). Despite the lessons of Nazi appeasement, Europeans 'took the end of the Cold War as a holiday from strategy [and capability]' (ibid., p. 25). The

liberal desire to subordinate power to law avoids, in Machiavellian language, the 'founding violence' of any political organization. For Machiavelli, a new political order requires violence to be instituted as such: it is through this founding violence alone that a break with the forces of past and present interests and the forging of new polities are made possible (Machiavelli, 1532/1983, I, ix). For, individuals in a state of radical uncertainty must first transfer their forces and fears towards an individual monopoly of force and fear before either social behaviour or a moral 'sense of the just and the unjust' are possible (Hobbes, 1651/1982, I, xiii, p. 188). There is a further point here. Structurally prior to law and justice, this founding violence of polity re-emerges each time the borders of a political community are (re-)secured against virtual or actual aggressors. For Realists, the forceful preconditions of political community reappear, in other words, each time security comes forward as a predominant domestic and/or international issue (the dilemma of nation-building in Afghanistan would be a good example of this point).

(2) *Power is the irreducible trait of politics.* Whatever else politics is, power remains central to political behaviour and political analysis. The liberal desire to reduce power to law misunderstands, therefore, the enduring structures of political behaviour. In the Realist tradition, this behaviour is thought either psychologically (Niebuhr, 2002 and 2008; Morgenthau, 1946 and 2005) or systemically (Waltz, 1979). For classical Realists, following Machiavelli and Nietzsche, power constitutes the end of political action. Whether described in terms of naked will or national interest, power cannot be subordinated to moral or legal obligation. Rather, morality and law constitute themselves in the international sphere *as* configurations of power. They clothe particular interest in the formal terms of moral or legal equality. As Edward Carr famously put it with regard to international ethics:

> Theories of international morality are the product of dominant nations or groups of nations. For the past hundred years, and more especially since 1781, the English-speaking peoples have formed the dominant group in the world; and current theories of international morality have been designed to perpetuate their supremacy and expressed in the idiom particular to them. . . . Both the view that the English-speaking peoples are monopolists of international morality and the view that they are consummate international hypocrites may be reduced to the plain fact that the current canons of international virtue have, by a natural and inevitable process, been mainly created by them. (2001, pp. 187–8)

For structural Realists, this anthropology of power is too dependent on human psychology (see Waltz, 1979, pp. 79–102). Rather, power is irreducible in the political domain for structural reasons: the condition of 'anarchy'. International anarchy describes the fact that there is no monopoly of violence at the international level. Because of the lack of a global 'power in common' (Waltz, 1954, p. 222), states behave in structural uncertainty with regard to each other. This structural uncertainty takes the form of power politics between autonomous players. In other words, power is nothing more, but nothing less, than the consequence of plurality (or, 'anarchy'). Realism's 'state-centrism' (Krasner, 1992, p. 39) is therefore systemic, not substantive. From this perspective cosmopolitans are wrong to pursue Realism for being state-centric and over-concerned with national interest in an age of globalization (see, for example, Hayden, 2005, pp. 1, 9, 67–9, 108). States are simply the major units between which plurality works in the modern world. That world has not yet been left. When it is left, Realism will focus on the next units under the general limits of anarchy or interest: power between regions and/or power between nations, regions and global institutions (see Carr, 2001, p. 140; Morgenthau, 2005, p. 12; Niebuhr, 2008, 147–8; Waltz, 1954, p. 180). In a finite world of plurality (structural realism) or passion (classical realism), borders and power are irreducible. Whatever the particular variant of Realism, the relation between morality and politics must consequently *begin* with this first-order premise. Point (5) returns to this conclusion.

(3) Realism accuses international liberalism of making *a category error* in the international domain, an error of thought resulting in the *'legalistic-moralistic fallacy'* that power can be subordinated to morality and law (Carr, 2001, pp. 160–88; Kennan, 1984, pp. 95–104; Morgenthau, 1946, p. 50; 2005, pp. 3–16). Kant's legal cosmopolitanism and its contemporary legacy commit, for example, the fallacy in the following manner: just as individuals assemble to form a social contract upon which domestic law is grounded, so states assemble to form a federal league upon which international and cosmopolitan legislation can be grounded (see Kant, 1784/1991). Since the legitimacy of legality is in turn rooted in moral principle, the suggestion is that international power-politics can be gradually subordinated to moral law *by analogy* with domestic public law. Principles of morality and legality, particular to the individual and domestic domains of personal and legal obligation, can be extended, in other words, to the international sphere. For Realism, this normative argument of extension carries an invalid inference. In Kennan's and Morgenthau's terms, the 'legalistic-moralistic fallacy' ensues from use of the 'domestic analogy'. This concept is critical to Realist judgement. It consists in the belief either that relations between state-units can be thought *as if* they were relations between individuals within states or that states can be thought of as if they were individuals on a wider (moral) scale (see

Bull, 1977, pp. 40–2; Kennan, 1984, p. 95; Morgenthau, 1946, pp. 43, 50–1). The invalid nature of this inference destroys a priori, for Realists, the normative horizon of liberalism and its variants in the international field – in particular, the reduction of international violence through law and the cession of national interest to supranational concern (Morgenthau, 1971, pp. 222–4).

The Realist assumption of this 'category error' (Krasner, 1992; Jervis 1998) does scant justice to Kant's aporia of the universal state and the subsequent Kantian distinctions between domestic, international and cosmopolitan law in his essay 'Perpetual peace' (1795/1991; see above, chapter 1, section 2.5). I come back to this point at length in the next chapter. The argument is nevertheless telling. Normative liberal thought rides free of the specificity of the international political domain: interest, anarchy and their consequences. As a result, extension of principles of individual and domestic morality and legality to the international sphere is fallacious. The Realist solution to international 'anarchy' can only be world government (Morgenthau, 2005, Part 6). Monopolizing violence worldwide, it would put an end, in both Hobbesian-psychological and Waltzian-systemic terms, to the radical uncertainty, pertaining to relations between states, that makes them permanently 'disposed to war' (Hobbes, 1651/1982, p. 187). It would equally institute a world order upon which questions of global justice and legislation could properly function. The weak moral cosmopolitanism of Thomas Nagel (see above, chapter 1, section 2.2) is close to this position. Since, for Realists, however, world government is both impractical and potentially tyrannous, plurality and power are givens of the international order. Questions of global justice and law remain, therefore, second-order considerations. This is the Realist version of the Kantian aporia of a universal state. It makes the Realist a sceptical proponent of world government, but for non-cosmopolitan reasons.

(4) The liberal extension of morality and legality to the international domain is not an error of thought alone; *it leads to the 'moralization' of politics*. This moralization produces counter-effective consequences in the international political realm. I understand by this term, here, the propensity to fashion foreign policy in moral or moral/legal terms (Bacevich, 2008, p. 81; Morgenthau, 1971, p. 11; Niebuhr, 2008, pp. 91, 133). US presidencies' inclinations to conceive of foreign policy in terms of the defence of freedom and democracy are well known in this regard, from Woodrow Wilson to George W. Bush (see an excellent Realist summary in T. Smith, 2010). The category error of moral and judicial thinking in the latter realm can result in more violence than that contested. Since law's intent is to end violence in the public sphere, both moral and judicial thinking in interna-

tional politics may result in the exact opposite of what they intend. This ironic inversion of political moralization can take place in several ways (see Bacevich, 2008, pp. 171–7; Morgenthau, 1946, pp. 50–1; Niebuhr, 2008, pp. 153–4); I foreground two ironies within international liberalism. The first is the liberal refusal to see the necessity of violence in the international domain. As Morgenthau comments on Wilsonian foreign policy:

> Liberalism detached the specific techniques it had developed as instruments of its domestic domination, such as legal pledges, judicial machinery, economic transactions, from their political substratum and transferred them as self-sufficient entities, devoid of their original political function, to the international sphere. . . . This application . . . led to catastrophic results. Liberals brought themselves to see in violence the absolute evil and were thus prevented by their moral convictions from using violence where the use of violence was required by the rules of the game. (1946, p. 51)

The primary need for international political order is lost under domestically inspired justice claims, leading to the actual increase in violence and war. The second is the more subtle irony of moral purpose in the international realm. Since international liberals seek peace through law (rather than through diplomacy), law is proposed in the normative name of peace, justice, human rights or democracy. As a result, justice determines the end of liberal politics as such. Political violence comes thereby to be *justified*, in moral terms, as the necessary means to the end of liberal polity (for an excellent discussion of the moral justification of political means, see Morgenthau, 1946, pp. 180–7). Since no theoretical limits constrain this goal, such justification risks becoming boundless, as can the violence that it underpins. This risk unfolds the ironic structure of liberal imperialism. For Realism, liberal imperialism furthers the hypocrisy of which the subordination of politics to morality originally smacks. Realism argues, ethically therefore, against any moral or moral-legal form of exceptionalism or universalism shaping international politics (Donnelly, 2008; Lieven and Hulsman, 2006; Wohlforth, 2008).

(5) Given both the irreducibility of power (point 2) and the above liberal illusion and *hubris* (point 4), Realism advocates *the political virtue of prudence*. Harder versions of Realism turn to Machiavelli's *The Prince* to discuss this virtue of the political (Kissinger, 1994). The prince must maintain himself in existent relations between republics and principalities. In this context, 'a man who wishes to profess virtue at all times will come to ruin among so many who are not virtuous' (Machiavelli, 1531/2005, XV, p. 53). Principled action, in the force-field of international politics, becomes self-destructive. One must therefore learn 'not to be virtuous'

(ibid.). States must sometimes do what is morally wrong out of necessity (the 'reason of state' position of Henry Kissinger and Richard Nixon regarding Vietnam). Machiavelli's secularization of medieval political thought constitutes a brilliant radicalization of Aristotle's exposition of prudence. It is nevertheless worth turning to Aristotle's *Nicomachean Ethics* to understand the argument more substantively since such argument underscores the political ethics of realism (Aristotle, 1984a, VI, 5–9; compare Weber, 1968, IV).

For Aristotle, prudence is the virtue of deliberation and choice in a contingent world. Wisdom is achieved through the knowledge of universal rule in particulars; prudence is gained through the exercise of judgement between norm and experience. It is the disposition to choose and act regarding 'what is in our power to do and not to do' (1984a, III, 7). Prudence is therefore a specific take on the relation between means and ends. For moral idealism (Plato, Kant, Gandhi), political means should either be subordinated to moral ends (the good, the moral law) or indeed consonant with them (the politics of non-violence). For Aristotle, conversely, means must be adapted to ends, but ends must *also* be adapted to means. One must choose an end consonant with one's means. As Krasner remarks in the context of Realist policy prescription, 'states must equate their commitments with their capabilities. . . . The two great mistakes in the conduct of foreign policy are doing too little and doing too much' (1992, p. 42). Or, as Morgenthau remarks, 'scientific analysis has the urgent task of pruning down national objectives to the measure of available resources in order to make their pursuit compatible with national survival' (1971, p. 224). Prudence is therefore neither idealist nor opportunist ('the power for power's sake' argument of Machiavelli's *The Prince*). There is no prudence without moral virtue. But humans are not gods in the specific sense that their will is not independent of time, action, circumstance, and resource. As a result, the means we choose to achieve a certain good has 'an efficient causality' of its own (Aristotle, 1984a, VI, 8–9). This *autonomy* of the means must be taken into account both in the choice of the means to achieve a certain end and in the choice of an achievable end itself (ibid., III, 4). Prudence constitutes, therefore, a practical virtue of deliberation and choice, matching at one and the same time means to ends and ends to means. The conclusion to be drawn from Aristotle – as done by Machiavelli and Max Weber – is that ethics wills the good, but politics must will the 'best possible', the 'relative good', or in terms of limitation, the 'lesser bad' or the 'least worst'.[2] This lesser bad is not ethically lesser in the essentially tragic domain of action (compare Morgenthau, 1946; Niebuhr, 2008; see, most recently, Molloy, 2009, esp. pp. 99ff). On the contrary, for Aristotle, it is easy to will the good: intentional rectitude is the child's game of the wise. It is far less easy to will and to choose together: to choose, that is, at the right moment (*kairos*) the right means, with regard to an achievable end, under circumstances of plurality and time. Aristotelian prudence becomes a political virtue of self-constrained risk as much as one of decision. This notion of political risk is recounted historically by Machiavelli's *Discourses* on the founding and decay of the Roman republic (Machiavelli, 1532/1983). Political judgement consists in the seizing of *fortuna*, to pursue through chosen means an achievable end that is, as far as possible, related to the independence of one's people. This judgement enacts a 'political ethics' of the 'lesser bad'.

Finally, since, for Aristotle, prudence is not the object of a science and cannot be taught, one only sees political virtue *in act*. Prudence is not a theoretical object; it translates in conceptual terms the behaviour of prudent men and women. As Nietzsche argued (*contra* Kant), it is not the will and its intentions that concerns politics, but their 'embodiment' (Nietzsche, 1887/1994, §§1–2). Prudence does not exist; only prudent people and prudent acts do.

In Aristotelian terms, then, political realism as prudence – the matching of means to ends and of ends to means – is the very condition of ethics, not its abolition. The IR school of Realism makes this political virtue of prudence its own in the amoral, 'non-legal' field of international plurality and finite national resources. As a contemporary classical Realist puts it, 'reducing the world to an expression of theoretical models, political platforms or ideological programmes, [one] fails to engage with reality and . . . avoids the process of reflection at the heart of responsibility. By contrast, Realist objectivity engages with this intractable "object" [of the autonomy of means], that is not reducible to one's will, as a necessary condition of ethical engagement' (Williams, 2005, p. 175).

Realism holds, I argue, these five constants above all variation. Let me summarize them:

1 The primacy of order makes law and justice secondary concerns.
2 The field of the political is structured through power (its equilibriums and disequilibriums) given the irreducibility of interest and the condition of anarchy. The imposition of law – however 'universal' – is always a specific configuration of power and interest: it is this configuration of interest that has to be tracked, not the intention of the will as such.
3 Anarchy at the international level undercuts, from the beginning, valid use of the domestic analogy: the fallacious attempt to extend categories, pertinent to the domestic sphere of political action and behaviour, to the international sphere. This extension constitutes a legalistic-moralistic error of thought.

4 The danger of this error is the moralization of politics, which can lead, paradoxically or ironically, to the escalation of violence rather than its reduction.

5 Political virtue is therefore that of prudence: the ability to separate the achievable from the desirable and choose, with plausible chance of success, the lesser bad or the least worst.

These tenets of Realism apply immediately to cosmopolitanism as an extended form of liberal universalism that responds to increasing dependence between states. Realists may well have deep sympathies with the disposition of moral cosmopolitanism. However, as soon as the moral principles of cosmopolitanism cross over into the domain of international politics, Realist operative concepts – order, power and interest, anarchy, abuse of the domestic analogy, category errors, interrelation of means and ends, and prudence – bite. The next section shows how this 'bite' works within a representative group of contemporary Realist authors. Section 2.1 examines points (1) to (4) through the Realist approach to international law and its implications for cosmopolitanism; section 2.2 considers points (3) and (4) through the complicity between contemporary cosmopolitanism and liberal imperialism; sections 2.3 and 2.4 examine points (4) and (5) by expositing cosmopolitan humanitarian intervention and its terms of imprudence.

2 Critique of Cosmopolitanism

2.1 The Realist approach to international law

Jack Goldsmith and Eric Posner's *The Limits of International Law* (2005) comprises an empirical approach to international law that foregrounds Realism and a state-centred rational choice theory to understand the customary nature of international law. It is an appropriate work to examine in the context of a theoretical debate between Realism and cosmopolitanism because of the clarity of its systematic use of the fore-mentioned tenets: in particular, the irreducibility of power and interest, the category errors of liberalism in general and misuse of the domestic analogy. Since their precise theoretical argument against international legalism and cosmopolitan liberal theory is applicable to all modalities of cosmopolitanism, I consider their work emblematic in the larger context.

Critical of notions of either moral or legal obligation at the interstate level, Goldsmith and Posner consider international law and treaty as the reflection alone of balance of interests and power concerns. International law does not, therefore, change state behaviour. They write: 'International law emerges from the states' pursuit of self-interested policies on the international stage. International law is, in this sense, *endogenous* to state interests. It is not a check on state self-interest; it is a product of state-interest' (2005, p. 13). The assumption that states comply with international law for non-instrumental reasons (because it is either morally or legally the legitimate thing to do) constitutes, precisely, the liberal 'category error' of which cosmopolitan argument is the contemporary exponent (ibid., p. 185). Motivation is always interested, never altruistic. The analogies between individual and state obligation and between liberal democracy and global democratic governance are consequently cognitive fallacies (ibid., pp. 205–23). States will never act to promote the good of all individuals in the world, but act only in the interest of their own citizens (or rather, groups thereof) and only engage in cooperation between states when it lies in these interests. If multilateral treaties exist and function, this is due, following the assumptions of rational choice theory and institutionalism, either to coincidence of interest or to coercion (ibid., pp. 27–35). Normative theories of international law hold, consequently, no *explanatory* purchase on international legal reality: they are prescriptive only. The implications for moral, normative, legal and political modalities of cosmopolitanism in the field of IR are clear. Let me turn to the legal level first: consistency of state behaviour with international legal rules.

According to Goldsmith and Posner, consistency of much state action with international human rights law simply means, regarding liberal democratic governments, coherence between domestic and international law. Democratic governments value civil and political liberties more than authoritarian governments do. 'By the second half of the twentieth century, most liberal democracies could comply with most aspects of the modern human rights treaties *without changing their behaviour*' (ibid., p. 111, my emphasis). Where, conversely, authoritarian governments comply with the 1951 Convention on the Crime of Genocide or customary international law prohibition on war crimes and crimes against humanity, it is in their interest to do so – for self-evident moral, social and economic reasons. These reasons are, however, independent of human rights law since the law 'does not supply the motivation' (ibid., p. 111).

Where an international treaty does demand change in behaviour on the part of liberal democracies or authoritarian regimes, these states radically qualify the force of the treaty to which they sign up. In the ratification of the International Covenant on Civil and Political Rights (ICCPR) – entering into force in 1976, with 78% of UN members ratifying it (ibid., p. 108) – more than one-third of the signatory parties have negotiated reservations, understandings and future default rules (RUDs) that let them out of certain clauses of the covenant (ibid., p. 112). The US declined consent to the covenant's capital punishment limitations and to its ban on treating juveniles as adults. The UK opted out of certain immigration restrictions and marriage rights contrary to UK domestic law. France ensured that the covenant's strictures on military discipline and certain minority rights were no stricter than existing French law (ibid., pp. 110–12). The authors conclude from these test cases:

> RUDs permit liberal democracies to conform ICCPR obligations to the contours of extant domestic law, permitting compliance without any change of behaviour . . . thereby continuing to follow domestic practices all the while signing up to the international human rights regime. (Ibid., pp. 112, 128)

Respectively, authoritarian governments can sign up to the ICCPR in the knowledge that its commitment to human rights is externally unenforceable and that the Human Rights Commission of the UN is unable to secure effective monitoring and evaluation. Hence, they too 'suffer little cost from . . . noncompliance' (ibid.). From a Realist perspective, the authors emphasize that the only resolution to legal anomaly at the international level would be coercive global force of law. Strengthening the UN towards centralized coercion is, however, structurally impractical given the diverse and radically skewed interests of its members. 'Like all collective security schemes, the United Nations depends wholly on member states' self-interested (and thus uneven) acts for coercion' (ibid., p. 224). It is highly implausible, therefore, that militarily powerful states would agree to any other scheme of enforcement, since 'they have no interest in sacrificing their military interests for others' (ibid.). Furthermore, international or global governance can 'never work like domestic government' due to the 'lack of incentives on a global scale' (ibid., p. 226). This Realist argument undermines a priori the first meaning of political cosmopolitanism: the project of cosmopolitan democracy.

Liberal use of the domestic analogy between national and international law is wrong-headed. Domestic law works on contract and statute (ibid., p. 90). International agreements are formal, non-legal forms of agreement based on a three-step process of intent, formalized by treaty and institutional agreements (protocols, etc.). These steps are coincidence of interest, negotiation of common terms, and mutually beneficial action through common compliance (ibid., pp. 86–90). If cooperation by states on mitigating abuse of human rights law exists, it is only due, for the authors, to increasing cooperative symmetries between states. These symmetries stabilize state behaviour towards its peoples and minorities. The institution of the European Union is the clearest example of this process so far. Lack of symmetry in Central Africa presents negative proof of the exactitude of this process. Another reason for symmetry would be the coercion exercised by a leading state. Goldsmith and Posner here use hegemonic stability theory in IR and dwell on the example of Great Britain ending the slave trade after it stopped trading itself in 1807 (ibid., pp. 114–15).

Between 1807 and the 1860s Spain, Portugal and Brazil all agreed to abolish the slave trade in exchange for economic benefits. But where compliance did not hold, the threat of retaliation or force itself (the burning of Portuguese and Brazilian ships by the British in the 1830s) was used (ibid., p. 116). 'British coercion, often in violation of international law, made possible compliance with this new rule of international law' (ibid., p. 114). British interest in acting as the hegemon for the abolition of the slave trade lay in competitive interest in universal application *once* it had itself unilaterally resolved to give up its own advantage. For the authors, Britain's original intent (whether religiously motivated or economic) is 'of no relevance' to their own focus on the motivation behind the gradual application of international law (ibid.). The very last point is not convincing; the authors are on more solid ground with regard to selectivity.

For Goldsmith and Posner, 'human rights' selectivity indicates that interest always trumps moral or legal obligation. The fact that contemporary human rights violations are not met by systematic and uniform application of force signals necessarily the particularist slant to moral universalism in the international domain. Human rights enforcement is for instance costly, and enforcement mechanisms necessarily involve militarily powerful states. It is therefore necessary that such enforcement directly or indirectly dovetails with powerful security and/or economic interests. They conclude: 'Coercion is applied episodically and inconsistently [and depends on] the economic and political interests of the enforcing state[s] and the costs of enforcement' (ibid., p. 117). The selective pattern of recent US human rights' enforcement provides ample evidence for this argument.

The US government was committed to redress human rights violation in Kosovo in 1999. It acted as the leader to cut through the collective action problem in the UNSC (Chinese and Russian vetoes) and mobilized the NATO alliance to intervene. Independent of human rights concerns (which were genuine), the US had, argue Goldsmith and Posner, 'a strategic interest in preventing central European conflict and resolving NATO's post-Cold War crisis of credibility and purpose' (ibid.). Throughout the 1990s the US had obvious strategic and geopolitical interests in Iraq (ibid., p. 203). The intervention in Haiti was in the US's interest because massive domestic unrest was creating a domestic crisis in Florida. When and where the US did not intervene is for similar, if inverse, reasons of interest. Lack of US-led intervention in Africa (Central African states, of which Rwanda remains the outstanding example) was not simply due to the failure of the US 1992 intervention in Somalia. US strategic interests in Africa were not considered strong enough to override that failure, leaving China an open door to the sub-Saharan continent. Possible intervention after heavy sanctions has never been on the table regarding Egypt, Saudi Arabia, Russia and Chechnya, or China and Tibet. A utilitarian cost-benefit analysis explains why. In the case of strategic allies or powerful states 'strategic interests conflict with the enforcement of the human rights agenda, and . . . costs of enforcement [would always be] significantly higher' (ibid., pp. 117–18).

The episodic nature of coercion explains the strategic nature of state behaviour regarding humanitarian intervention. Human rights treaties and international law themselves are not, therefore, the explanatory factor. Against the legalistic-moralistic category error of legal cosmopolitanism, Goldsmith and Posner argue that the status of international customary law creates obligation and consent through mechanisms of interstate cooperation and coercion alone. Since there will never be a world government, international law cannot have the moral or legal status of domestic law: that is, democratic legitimacy and coercive force of law. The ultimate extension of cosmopolitan duty to state actors inverts the direction of causality. What appears as obligation is in fact mitigated interest of state parties. This rational choice outlook explains, again, the permanent selectivity of humanitarian intervention. *International law is neither morality nor law, but politics.*

Having criticized the cognitive error of moral and legal obligation arguments in the sphere of cosmopolitan international law, Goldsmith and Posner then debunk cosmopolitan uses of the domestic analogy. In chapter 1 (section 2.4), I argued that, given the implausibility of individual moral action, institutional cosmopolitanism takes over the burden of conscience and moral scruple from individuals. For Goldsmith and Posner the ascription of cosmopolitan duties to political institutions like liberal democracies as a whole confronts, however, the same 'plausibility constraints' (2005, p. 209). Because of the variety of interests that they represent states cannot commit to cosmopolitan acts of charity. This inability to commit is very different from the ready commitment made by NGOs that are focused on particular issues (Human Rights Watch, Amnesty International, Oxfam International, the International Red Cross, etc.). States are much more complex institutions, whose overall end, in the normative case of democracies, is to promote the mutual benefits of their citizens. Foreign policy must consequently be tailored to the welfare of the national interest (however this is defined non-ideally). For Goldsmith and Posner, widespread cosmopolitan sentiment does not exist to change the state's understanding of solidarity (ibid., p. 212). Democratic state agents (leaders) are beholden to their principals (the voters). Given this agency-principal problem, democratic institutions cannot easily engage in cosmopolitan action. Americans are not willing, for example, to accept the costs of blood and wealth for humanitarian interventions if they are not perceived to be in the national interest. The long delay on intervention in Bosnia in 1995, together with the eventual decision to do so only with high-altitude bombing (reducing US casualties, but amplifying the probability of civilian loss of life), indicate how difficult it is for democracies to work for the international human rights regime. According to Goldsmith and Posner, the 'absence of democratic support [remains] a fundamental check on humanitarian intervention' (ibid., p. 214). Samantha Power's well-known critique of the US failure to intervene in order to stop genocides ignores this point (Power, 2002). Cosmopolitan action by a liberal democracy 'is [necessarily] bounded by constituent preferences' (Goldsmith and Posner, 2005, p. 219). Given the structural constraints of domestic democracy, states do not have, and cannot enact, duties to strong cosmopolitan commitments. The Kantian extension of liberal republicanism is in this sense facile and, again, wrongheaded. Following rational choice assumptions, Goldsmith and Posner maintain, rather, that the constituents of liberal democracies will ultimately tend to resist such extensions. Present reserve regarding the maintenance of NATO troops in Afghanistan would bear this Realist observation out (Goldgeier, 2010).

The above debunking of the domestic analogy underpins two final arguments in Goldsmith and Posner's *The Limits of International Law*. First, the disanalogy between domestic democracy and global governance is irreducible not only because of the impracticality of world government (we recall, the sacrifice of state military power for it to be possible is implausible). The disanalogy is also irreducible because of the very nature of nation-state democracies and their constituent interests. If democracies are to function well at the domestic level, they cannot be cosmopolitan in purpose (Goldsmith and Posner, 2005, p. 223). In line with communitarian postulates, the authors argue that well-functioning democracies require loyalty and a sense of civic solidarity that are undermined by cosmopolitan sentiment and commitment (ibid., pp. 208–20). Moral cosmopolitanism's widening circle of human sensibility – from the family through the polity to humanity as a whole – constitutes an intellectual illusion. *Loyalties are mutually self-exclusive and require hard trade-offs*. The prosperous collective life of a democratic state implies, inversely, weak global governance; strong global governance indicates, inversely, the end of national democratic life. Democratic extension is not a 'win–win' situation. From this perspective, my first definition of political cosmopolitanism, the project of cosmopolitan democracy, fails at a fundamental level to understand concrete causes of motivation.

This last point can be pushed further than Goldsmith and Posner's own comments. Legal cosmopolitanism looks for exogenous constraints on state behaviour, but these constraints are the result of endogenous state interest and coercion. It therefore inverts the direction of motivation. The democratic variant of political cosmopolitanism seeks a widening of democratic sentiment and commitment beyond the national level; but such sentiment and commitment can only function properly *within* delimited communities (compare David Miller's weak cosmopolitanism outlined in chapter 1, section 2.2). It therefore inverts the direction of democratic motivation. In the realm of institutional analysis both legal and political cosmopolitanisms commit fundamental 'category errors'.

Second, and consequently, many global issues are intrinsically unsolvable in political terms (ibid., p. 203). Because of (i) the lack of civil solidarity at the global level, (ii) the lack of institutional enforcement mechanisms, and (iii) the impossibility of solving the democratic deficit associated with ever-broadening global institutions, the solution to global issues will perforce remain at the level of state-interest coordination. In this context the EU does not present, for Goldsmith and Posner, a 'model' of future global governance. Reflecting state-building with a common heritage, endowments and similar interests, it cannot provide 'a map for global government of peoples of radically different cultures, histories and endowments' (ibid., p. 224). The normative cosmopolitan argument concerning the EU generalizes, wrongly, the particularism of the European predicament. For Goldsmith and Posner, this argument can be better explained by interest (ibid., pp. 221–3): international concerns with cosmopolitan law constitute the discourse of the 'middle powers'. The weak seek power to be independent from existent powers; the strong have no need to attend to law unless it is in their interest to do so; but neither the weak nor the strong must focus on non-politico-military issues that gain them the most influence in the international field. Cosmopolitanism tends, therefore, to be the discourse of middle powers like Sweden and Norway. One can again push Goldsmith and Posner's structural explanation of cosmopolitan duty further here. In Nietzschean terms, cosmopolitanism constitutes *the* discourse of declining/decadent powers. Emerging global powers like China and India may have little truck with it, especially given their colonized histories under Western power.

The Limits of International Law harnesses Realist and rational choice theory in order to make a set of telling and consistent criticisms of normative, legal, institutional and political modalities of cosmopolitanism. Its overall critique of international legalism puts pay to one of the basic insights of normative cosmopolitanism, as expounded in chapter 1 (section 2.3). Normative international legal argument has no purchase on the explanation of state behaviour. It therefore remains theoretically abstract and only rides empirical counter-evidence *through* postulating a normative horizon in distinction to empirical life. This postulate is, however, a priori undone by the politics of power and interest that pertain to a world under conditions of anarchy. The social science distinction between normative and positive theories remains, consequently, valid.

Rational choice/Realist explanations of world politics focus on the amoral nature of state behaviour. The remaining sections of this chapter concentrate on the Realist response to the fate of universal moral principles in world politics and to the type of means-ends thinking that tempts this fate. In the context of Realism's five constants, they focus on the moralization of international politics, its fate and the consequent imprudence of universal concerns in the international political realm.

2.2 Cosmopolitan 'domination'

For political cosmopolitans like David Held and Daniele Archibugi, the project of cosmopolitan democracy entails impartial institutions at the global level. The building of meta-state institutions would follow domestic democratic example. Regarding radical reform of the UN, the executive decisions of the UNSC would be mandated by the legislative assembly of a World Parliament, and reform of the judicial structure of the United Nations (both the ICJ and the the ICC), together with the creation of a UN rapid deployment police force, would allow for judgements that are both more independent of the will of the Great Powers and less marginal, more effective. In the context of humanitarian intervention, these reforms would legitimize the procedures by which the international community decides to intervene within the sovereignty of particular states (Archibugi, 2003, pp. 1–15). In direct response to Archibugi's commitments, Geoffrey Hawthorn argues in 'Running the world through windows' (2003) that cosmopolitan legitimacy in world politics is an unfeasible, misplaced and dangerous idea.[3]

For Hawthorn, following Realist literature, democratic legitimation can only work at a domestic level, at best at a regional level given community of interests (as in the European Parliament). Meta-state institutions at a higher level can only work through 'delegated accountability' (compare Keohane and Nye, 2003). Such delegation invites, structurally, capture by particular interests: power and interest will therefore always remain the irreducible traits of world politics (Hawthorn, 2003, p. 21). Following

Hobbes's precedence of order over justice, intervention in the name of humanity or democracy fails unless security and order are guaranteed first. Without these guarantees, that require local legitimation, military and humanitarian interventions pursued under moral ends may lead to the very opposite of what is originally intended: that is, less humanity and less democracy (ibid., pp. 22–3). Hence, for Hawthorn, the moralization of political motivation in the international sphere leads to an escalation in violence, not its reduction. In the name of democracy – in part, the abolition of violence from the public sphere – international democratic policy, as advocated by Daniele Archibugi, will lead to more violence in the public sphere, not less (ibid., pp. 23–4). In an age of international neo-liberal doctrine, Hawthorn agrees with Archibugi and Held that more politics is required. Political cosmopolitan analysis inverts, however, 'the picture of politics' needed (ibid., p. 26). It is political government, not ethico-political orientation that is called for. This inversion constitutes, in the terms of this chapter, another liberal 'category error', one that risks making political power at an international level unaccountable. It also scuppers the chance of an achievable goal: the reduction of violence in specific conflict-ridden areas of international concern. For Hawthorn, following Reinhold Niebuhr, the IR school of Realism theorizes this cruel paradox (Niebuhr, 2008, pp. 154–5). As an intensification of liberal internationalist concerns with the promotion of democracy, cosmopolitan liberal idealism ignores this paradox at other peoples' peril. However progressive legal cosmopolitanism and the political project of cosmopolitan democracy wish to be, they unwittingly remain ethical discourses complicit with political domination.

Danilo Zolo's *Cosmopolis: Prospects for World Government* (1997) makes this paradox more explicit. The book's basic argument is that global ethics is incommensurate with the functional requirements of international politics (ibid., pp. 69–75). The division of labour and of legitimacy between international organization and states rests on the functional constraint that the state must protect its own members first and that this protection depends on a hierarchy of the use of force. This hierarchy of force cannot be displaced upward without undermining the *raison d'être* of the state in the first place (ibid.). Zolo comments: 'Only by observing this twofold functional logic of exclusion and subordination can the state grant its citizens a selective regulation of social risk and a corresponding "reduction of fear" (ibid., pp. 69–70). Given this functional constraint, the moralization of international politics is bound to end up prescriptive and dominating, *however* impartial the initial moral vision and intention are. The moral law may have immediate effect on the human will (in Kantian language), but the empirical outcome of moral intent is structurally perverse in a system of states. Let me turn here, more directly, to the problematic of humanitarian intervention.

For Zolo, humanitarian intervention, together with subsequent democratically oriented state-building, will be necessarily perceived on the ground as the imposition of values by those who carry coercive force at the international level. Since it is the Western powers that still hold this force, intervention and democratization amount to an imposition of Western values upon the rest of the world (ibid., pp. 83–4). From the first Iraq War of 1991 to intervention in Bosnia in 1995, one is witness to attempts to control areas of the world subjected to previous Arab and Russian influence. Humanitarian intervention and democratization cannot be perceived, accordingly, as anything but international acts of 'Westernization' and, at worst, the continuation of *pax Americana* by other means (ibid., p. 79). In the historical context of the functional constraint of state sovereignty, cosmopolitan calls for legitimacy cannot avoid being complicit with imperialist modes of domination. I return at length to this thesis in the chapters on Marxism and postmodernism, since it typifies responses on the Left to legal and political cosmopolitan moves. Here, I emphasize Zolo's furtherance of Hawthorn's paradox. Use of the domestic analogy in the international sphere leads to a moralization of politics, which incites, in turn, an increase in violence and the perception of domination. In the historical context of functional constraints, this moralization inverts into another form of imperial power for two reasons: (i) Western values are being naturally imposed by the still dominant nations of the international scene (see Carr, quoted above); and (ii) given the structural arrangements of post-Second World War sovereign equality (UN Charter, Article 2, 1), intervention with ethico-political concerns risks ending up as an illegitimate form of domination (compare Jean Cohen, 2004).

The recent fates of intervention in Kosovo (1999), Afghanistan (2002) and the second Iraq war of (2003) make these two Realist arguments of the late 1990s the more compelling. I would claim that a precipitate amalgamation of cosmopolitan liberalism and of neo-conservative ideology is made here. Realists consider universal claims on the part of a leading democratic state like the USA a form of 'exceptionalism' – particular to its virtuous foundations – and of imperial overreach that mismatches moralizing political ends with economic means (Bacevich, 2008; Desch, 2007; Lieven and Hulsman, 2006; Reilly, 2009; Snyder, 1991). For Realists, the neo-conservative foreign policy of George W. Bush actually pushes this American exceptionalism/Wilsonian liberal internationalism to its limit (Smith, 2009 and 2010). In this particular context and in the more general context of political responses to increasing state interdependence, it is important to understand and untangle this amalgamation of cosmopolitan liberalism and neo-conservative foreign policy. Accordingly, I advance the Realist case regarding intervention and prudence in the next section and then respond to it in chapter 3. I focus on two explicitly theoretical arguments: one by Patricia Owens (2007); the other by Michael Williams (2005 and 2007). While Owens is not a Realist as such, her political realism uses the conceptual tools of Realist argument effectively to prosecute her case. Both think from out of the context of Bush's post-9/11 moralization of international politics, although their theoretical arguments concern political moralism as such in state-led global leadership.[4]

2.3 Humanitarian intervention and political moralism

Patricia Owens's work *Between War and Politics* considers the relation between morality, politics and violence. Persuasively bringing the thought of Hannah Arendt into IR theory through consideration of this relation, she makes three clear Realist proposals:

1 High moral theory is dangerous for foreign policy.
2 If the end of political action lies outside politics, as is the case for the moral ends of 'justice' or 'humanity', violence becomes justified.
3 Such justification leads to the escalation of violence, not its reduction.

The particularity of Owens's book lies in its elaboration of these theses through the political thought of Arendt; it allows her to propose an alternative to Realism based on the 'non-violence' of the interhuman political world of speech and construction. I do not consider this alternative here. Despite her recognition of the differences between neo-conservatism and legal and political cosmopolitanism, Owens does not see the 'normative critical theory' of Jürgen Habermas as offering an alternative to neo-conservatism. They remain, rather, in the same cognitive paradigm because they both subordinate the political means of war to a moral end. With this moral justification of violence, violence becomes potentially limitless. In order to understand Owens's own version of this Realist logic, we need to return to Habermas's legal cosmopolitan argument (Habermas, 1997 and 2006).

Within the Kantian aporia of a world republic, Habermas's legal cosmopolitanism emphasizes less the dissemination of republican example than the emergence of cosmopolitan law for states and individuals. The juridification or quasi-constitutionalization of international relations will prevent, in other words, the arbitrary use of power at the global level. In *The Divided West*, written during the onset of the second Iraq war, Habermas conceives this process of juridification as the only alternative to neo-conservatism (2006, pp. 179–85). The neo-conservative project was explicitly put in place during the 1990s by advocates of the 'New American Century', a tight group of radical intellectuals and politicians who, as Michael Williams puts it, were able to 'locate issues of security and foreign policy within a broader field of political culture' (2007, p. 93). The key to this culture was, as Irving Kristol wished since the 1970s, the recovery of republican virtue within the liberal order of political and economic modernity (compare Fukuyama 2007, pp. 12–65). Neo-conservatism's achievement at the end of the twentieth century was to reorganize American liberal power into a nationalist universalism: that is, 'an outwardly looking nationalist politics embodying universal principles' (Williams, 2007, p. 104). This reorganization became policy with George Bush's post-9/11 shift in foreign policy. For Habermas, more simply, this politics constitutes 'the project of a new liberal world order under the banner of *pax Americana*' (2006, p. 106).

Normative and legal cosmopolitanism provide exclusive answers to it because they offer the only remedy to nationalist power politics in a globalized world. For Habermas, neo-conservatives are the ones who moralize politics because a global sovereign decree becomes the monopoly of US exceptionalism (outward-turned republican virtue). The US government has thereby instrumentalized the universal vocation of international law for its own ends (2006, p. 150). Conversely, to place superpower under the constraints of global legal procedure *reduces* the possibility of the moralization of politics. The gesture maintains, all the while, a global moral politics by insisting on legal conditions of universality, generality and impartiality. The republican virtue of leading democratic states becomes, in Kantian liberal vein, legal self-constraint under international law.

> The Kantian conception of international law [in contrast to the idea that 'relations of power provide the ultimate hermeneutic key to legal relations'] allows for the possibility that a superpower, assuming it has a democratic constitution and acts with foresight and prudence, will not always instrumentalize international law for its own ends but can promote a project that ends up tying its own hands. (Ibid., p. 150; compare pp. 173–9)

Contra neo-conservatives, on the one hand, and Carl Schmitt and the Realists, on the other, Habermas argues that universalism, properly institutionalized, can give account: (i) through the increasing establishment of global law; and (ii) through the gradual widening of global public debate and world public opinion (the formation of a global 'public sphere'). The first point turns the choices of international politics into vetted procedure;

the second gives legitimacy to such choices while proper legislative process waits its day at the United Nations (Habermas, 2006, esp. pp. 173–6).

For Owens, Habermas's position does not constitute a competing theory against neo-conservatism; it enacts, rather, a similar logic of political moralization (Owens, 2007, pp. 132–5). Neo-conservatism distinguishes itself by embracing violence at the level of US foreign policy to effect political change. From the first Iraq war, Bosnia, Haiti and Kosovo, through to Afghanistan and the second Iraq war (1991–2003), neo-conservatism has succeeded in recasting American exceptionalism as an aggressive international project, subordinating international politics to 'American values' of universal reach. Increasing resistance to this subordination is a necessary consequence of this missionary exemplarity in the international sphere. The cosmopolitan liberal response (juridification of international relations; foregrounding of world public opinion against the 2003 Iraq war) fails, however, to be a radical alternative because it uses the *same* means-end argument, embracing violence as an effective means 'to produce world obligations' (ibid., p. 144). Owens' argument is subtle (ibid., pp. 133–47).

While Habermas's legal and institutional cosmopolitanism looks to legitimate military intervention in world terms, it is in fact the intervention that 'makes' the legitimacy of the 'global public' in the first place. Habermas inverts the order of causality. What can only crystallize as 'world public opinion' and as 'global public law' as a result of intervention is placed prior to intervention *qua* its legitimating condition. In Nietzschean language, this reversal of cause and effect mistakes the consequence for the cause. Idealist thought is characterized by this 'error' (Nietzsche, 1888/1988): in Realist terms, it is another 'category error'. How is this reversal a legitimate reading of Habermas given the millions of demonstrators against the Iraq war across the planet in February 2003, prior to the US–UK invasion in March? Since, for Owens, the global world republic (or some such non-hierarchized equivalent) is not in place, and since, therefore, coercive law does not exist at the global level, Habermas is in a 'dilemma' (Owens, 2007, pp. 130–1). One has to act, writes Habermas, 'as if a completely institutionalized cosmopolitan condition already existed, the achievement of which is supposed to be promoted' (2000, quoted in Owens, 2007, p. 131). For Owens, following Arendt, this dilemma is particular to the *political act of founding*. The paradox of founding is 'resolved' precisely through violence (ibid). Habermas's public of 'world citizens' *requires* violent mobilization in the first place, if it is to be produced as a social entity. In the effort to 'make' a global public, Owens argues, 'we are seeing an explicit justification of "humanitarian" war in [this kind of] normative international theory' (ibid., p. 131).

For Habermas, recent 'humanitarian' wars are read as occasions in which violence is legitimated by the conscience of a global public. The move of public opinion against the second Iraq war proved the illegitimacy of US and UK interests. This illegitimacy was ratified *post factum* by the UN secretary-general's September 2004 declaration that the war was illegal. For Owens, conversely:

> It is possible that to come into existence, a global public sphere, like the publics of nation-states before them, may *depend* upon violence. Civic patriotism in a global context might not only be the outcome of a sense of obligation to others. . . . It is possible that such obligations are produced *through* the use of violence. . . . You cannot 'make' a global public sphere, as Arendt might put it, without killing people. (Ibid., p. 144)

Analogously, Owens criticizes Habermas's earlier theorization of the bourgeois public sphere (Habermas, 1991) because it does not link the domestic emergence of universal liberal norms *with* the expansion of colonialism and imperialist aggression. Now, given this dilemma of founding through violence, normative thought cannot separate the universal from the particular, the ethical from empirical violence. In this sense, such violence is not simply empirical; *it is structural to the moral end of politics*. This structural violence is, however, not theorized by liberal thought, given its overt wish to distinguish itself from other political philosophies by its reduction of violence in the public realm. For Owens, the eighteenth and nineteenth centuries' emergent liberal democracies projected this structural violence out into Africa and Asia in order to secure 'the nation's indivisibility', 'security' and 'peace' at home. In Schmittian terms, a global public sphere of humanity does not have, conversely, an 'enemy' through which it can identify itself politically (compare Schmitt, 1927/2007, pp. 49, 54). And yet, differentiation remains necessary in the political domain. For Owens, the intensification of difference that pertains to the political takes place today through, precisely, the violence of what is called 'humanitarian intervention'. Humanitarian war is consequently justified 'to "make" a global public realm' (ibid., p. 135); it is, in other words, the means by which a cosmopolitan politics of peace is possible in the first place.

Within this tight means-ends argument, Habermas is unable to distinguish his thinking from the Bush doctrine of 'the axis of evil' and 'failed states'. This is a large irony given his explicit concern to demoralize politics through the juridification of international relations. Following Hannah Arendt's critical position on stateless human rights (Arendt, 1968, pp. 265–302), the irony ultimately emerges, for Owens, from the fact that rights and duties are only functional in circumscribed political form.

Bounded by the limits of political community that is empowered to negotiate conflict between antagonists, rights only have meaning *qua* civic rights within the *polis* (ibid., p. 296; compare Miller, 2007b). Since such limitation is absent at the global level without a world republic, human rights can never become juridical prerogatives of effective citizenship – except at the price of a world despotic order. Juridification of international relations reverts, therefore, to their moralization.

Owens does not wish to abandon all cosmopolitan projects of global political reform; she is a weak cosmopolitan (compare Owens, 2009a). She is, nevertheless, suspicious that the global regulation of military power would in fact 'replicate sovereign domination (control over "legitimate" violence) at the highest level of abstraction' (2007, p. 145). Short-term use of violence for ending genocide and other massive crimes against humanity is justifiable and important. Anything wider, in the name of 'freedom' or 'democracy', may lead to imperialist violence. At the very least, humanitarian wars should not be pursued in order to *find out* what the global legitimation of force might entail. Consequently, the excessive way in which Habermas reflects upon the emergence of both global law and the global public sphere does not constitute a legitimate alternative to the American unilateralism of the George W. Bush period of government. Both neo-conservatism and normative and legal cosmopolitanism end up in political moralism: namely, distinct from Kantian categorization, the imprudent subordination of political means (instrumental violence) to moral ends (democracy promotion). Neo-conservatism has consequently only been defeated by the stubbornness of facts; not, ideologically, by a better competing theory.

2.4 Towards a prudent politics of limits

Hans Morgenthau argued in his *In Defense of the National Interest* that realistic analysis of the political field is the condition of ethico-political responsibility. Analysis enables one to distinguish between what is desirable and what is possible; such distinctions essentially limit the normative horizon of practice since they allow the statesman 'to foresee the political consequences of seemingly moral action' (Morgenthau, 1952, p. 132). Following Aristotle, Machiavelli and Max Weber, Morgenthau concludes that one seeks the 'lesser bad', not the 'good' (compare Morgenthau, 1971, p. 205). This Realist politics of ethico-political responsibility is well rehearsed by Michael Williams in his *The Realist Tradition and the Limits of International Relations* (2005). I use his theoretical reading of Morgenthau's classical Realism to conclude upon the 'imprudence' of institutional and political cosmopolitanism. I also consider Williams because he too conflates the foreign policy of neo-conservatism and liberal univer-salism and opposes to both Realist prudence.[5]

For Morgenthau, amalgamating Aristotle and Weber, whoever engages in politics as a vocation must begin with the ethical paradox that the result of political action will conflict with the original intention (Morgenthau, 1952, pp. 28–39). In a world where power is backed up by violence, means and ends have their own distinct laws. If the politician must contract with violent means to achieve his or her ends, he or she is exposed to the specific consequences of the means chosen. The ethico-political responsibility of the politician lies in handling these paradoxes as carefully as possible, aware that any end may be curtailed by the *very means* chosen to achieve that end. For Williams, this ethical realism underlies Morgenthau's 'politics of limitation' (Williams, 2005, pp. 112, 118–19). Morgenthau is often cited in IR theory as the founder of the school of Realism, the theorist who, disillusioned with international liberalism between the wars and the inad-equate liberal response to Nazism and Fascism, exclusively understands international politics in terms of power. As Williams rightly stresses, this understanding is wrong. Realism is not opposed to the liberal tradition that informs the tenets of liberalism and its contemporary cosmopolitan exten-sion (ibid., pp. 120–30). But, like Carr and his *Twenty Years' Crisis*, Morgenthau intends to 'reconstruct the liberal project' *through* the analysis and limitations of international practical reality (ibid., p. 104). The liberal project is one of non-violence in the public sphere. Since judicial instances cannot resolve potential violence except through the legitimate monopoly of violence (the Realist aporia of world government), law does not present an effective means of reducing violence. For Morgenthau, foreign and international policy-makers have to find, consequently, other ways of insu-lating the political sphere from physical violence. Classical realism com-prises a strategy of peace *within* the limits of given reality and the means-end paradox. As Williams puts it, 'the ethics of responsibility involves *pru-dence*, but seeks ultimately the creation of responsible subjects within a philosophy of limits' (ibid., p. 175). Although Williams does not engage directly with cosmopolitanism in his book, the implications of Morgenthau's 'disillusioned liberalism' for the cosmopolitan disposition in IR are clear.

In contradistinction to both neo-conservatism and a cosmopolitan poli-tics founded on distinct principles of universal rationalism (moral egali-tarianism, the rule of law, consensus through reason), ethical practice in world politics requires recognition of factual resistance to the will (see ibid., pp. 119, 138, 186). This requires, in turn, recognition of others' interests as 'ends in themselves' under the general 'rule' of indeterminacy (an 'open sky' in Morgenthau's terms). It requires 'recognition of the *particularity* of *all* values' (ibid., p. 188, my emphasis) and openness to 'political debate and conflict in a plural world' (ibid., p. 194). In the light of this Weberian argument, normative, institutional and political modalities of cosmopolitanism can be considered not to accept the preliminary condition of liberal modernity: politics should not be regulated by principles transcendent to its sphere (dignity of the moral person, human rights, rational consensus).

As we have seen, Realist prudence is neither relativism nor opportunism: it entails the construction of value, freedom and non-violence through the practical and functional constraints of a plural, violent world. These constraints are not negative barriers, to be ultimately overcome down the path of history; they essentially limit political possibility. Ethical responsibility in the political domain emerges from this limitation. Ethico-political rigour cannot therefore entail the imposition of value upon these constraints: the subordination of politics to morality. It must consist in the negotiation of interests, through these constraints, towards their lesser bad. As Morgenthau remarks, 'it is not a question of imposing moral principle upon practical reality, but of deducing moral principle from practical reality' (1952, p. 140). After a lengthy deliberation in *Scientific Man versus Power Politics* on a political ethics of 'the lesser evil', he summarizes:

> We have no choice between power and the common good. To act successfully, that is according to the rules of the political art, is political wisdom. To know with despair that the political art is inevitably evil, and to act nonetheless is moral courage. To choose among several expedient actions the least evil one is moral judgement. (1946, p. 202)

As I have previously noted, I prefer to avoid the term 'evil', given its ontological assumptions, and replace it with the terms 'lesser bad', 'least bad' or 'lesser violence'. Given the paradoxes of ethics in the political sphere, the lesser violence is the 'best possible' not only because it is the least worst alternative; but because it has, in the first place, a greater chance of bringing peace than a politics *regulated by* the principle of peace. Williams's reading of classical Realist responsibility is powerful here. As we have seen through Hawthorn's, Zolo's and Owens's Realist arguments against cosmopolitan ambition, the ethics of tolerance may well breed the politics of intolerance; a cosmopolitan liberal politics, founded on the assumption of universal rational value, may well become imprudent and end up as the worst option. Williams moves logically from this irony to the point of ethico-political prudence. Non-violence in the international/ global public sphere is only achievable through a politics of limits: that is, in order to achieve peace, one may well *not* take as one's end, peace.

A small, but telling example of this Realist logic is found in the US administration's response to the June 2009 Iranian elections (I ignore here all subsequent events). The elections were, in essence, a *coup d'état* by the harder military and religious elements of the Iranian regime. The Obama administration decided not to pursue outward calls for democratic legitimacy and for the guarantee of basic civil and political rights at that moment, since its end remained the stoppage of the Iranian nuclear programme for military use. This end required, at the moment of the elections, curtailing any attempt to label American power as imperial and to justify, retroactively, the stolen election through the argument of external interference. Collective condemnation of the Iranian repression of democratic processes was therefore restricted to the civil sphere. Despite neo-conservative cries within the American polity, any moral attempt to universalize the condition of the Iranian people under the banner of 'human rights' and 'democracy' (as happened with the 1989 events of Tiananmen Square) was subordinated to a political ethics of the lesser bad. Given this politics, gradual de-nuclearization of the Middle East was considered less unlikely.

While political cosmopolitans may well be in pragmatic agreement with US foreign policy regarding Iran, the ethical foundations of cosmopolitanism still lead to the moralizing of politics in the light of this example. For, despite Habermas's legal mediations, its end is to subordinate power politics to a moral end that transcends the political realm (moral principles as such). It thereby *jumps over* the specificity of political limits in a force-field of contending parties: the political choice of specific ends given concrete circumstances of time and place; the choice of specific means; the risk that this choice may fail; and the handling of this risk. For Realists like Morgenthau, these choices and risks require the political ethics of state leadership in the international political field, divested of abstract universal moral principle (see Morgenthau, 1971, pp. 233–4).

3 Conclusion

This chapter presented, first, what I consider to be Realism's five major tenets of the Realist school – order, power, category errors, moralization of politics, and prudence. It then took specific examples of Realist literature that show how these tenets play themselves out in Realist criticisms of the cosmopolitan sophistication of liberalism. From tracking configuration of power and interest and abuses of the domestic analogy to expositing a political ethics of the lesser bad, Realism lays out an international political landscape of *cognitive and practical limits*: limits upon the aspiration to international justice and post-national democratic motivation and institution; upon category errors and the fallacious extension of domestic political reasoning to the global sphere; upon the efficient causality of means; upon the conceptualization of violence; and upon ethical action in the political sphere. For Realists, contemporary cosmopolitan ideas and practices ignore these limits at the risk of others' lives. At best, these ideas can be embodied by individual and collective civil action; at worst, they end up in state foreign policy and risk becoming imperial, given both ideological and functional differentiation in the world political field. Realism looks instead to this force-field as such, holds to the constituent elements of power and interest that make it up, and, more overtly in its classical version, looks to a political ethics of prudence that filters moral principle through the limits of circumstance. At its most ambitious, the school of Realism bends itself to the construction of a better world from within the limits of the given world. This construction excludes, however, the potential *hubris* of cosmopolitan ambition in the political domain. I now turn to what I consider the most appropriate cosmopolitan responses to this tightly-knit set of Realist criticisms.

3

A Cosmopolitan Response to Realism

The aim of this chapter is to provide a set of responses to the Realist critique of cosmopolitanism. This set of responses adds up to the following overall argument:

1 Realism's use of the empirical/normative divide and its concomitant relegation of cosmopolitan argument to the prescriptive underestimates the role of normative declaration in world politics under conditions of increasing interdependence.
2 Realist examination of liberal 'category errors' to undermine use of the domestic analogy in cosmopolitan argument underestimates the *differentiated* understanding of universalism that institutional, legal and political modalities of cosmopolitanism pursue.
3 Realism's historical focus on the state as the major agent in international relations can be effectively transformed into focus on the state as the major agent of change for minimal cosmopolitan commitments to resolve global collective action problems.

These three meta-arguments use several arguments rehearsed in chapter 1, and I will duly refer back to them in context. The most important is a flexible cosmopolitan response that argues for a weak cosmopolitanism at the state level and for stronger forms of cosmopolitanism, within the context of a differentiated universalism, at civil and post-national levels. As point (3) makes clear, my response to the Realist critique of cosmopolitanism is neither defensive nor aggressive. While cosmopolitanism gives an analysis of the real that is different from that of realism, the continuing reality of the state system means that cosmopolitanism must at the same time confront state-centrism when considering moral, normative and institutional cosmopolitan concerns. By arguing for a cosmopolitan political ethics of the lesser violence, I respond to Realism in a manner that is theoretically attuned to the school's own concerns with limitation and prudence. These three meta-arguments are filtered through the following specific responses to chapter 2.

Section 1 meets Goldsmith and Posner's Realist charge that international law does not explain state behaviour with the complex status of the normative in conditions of interdependence (compare chapter 1, section 2.3). Section 2 undermines exclusive concerns with power and interest by placing both in the context of dependence between states and the structural constraints of international legitimacy. It advocates accordingly a reconceptualization of the concept of 'national interest'. Section 3 refutes the Realist use, against liberal universalism, of (the concepts of) the 'domestic analogy', of the 'moralistic-legalistic fallacy' and of 'anarchy' by expositing a differentiated analysis of law. The argument is fairly philosophical, but is centred on Norbert Elias's sociological understanding of civilization processes (1982). Section 4 meets the Realist critique of the cosmopolitan moralization of politics on two complementary levels: with (i) insistence on the legal cosmopolitan argument for legal mediation between morality and politics; and (ii) a political cosmopolitan argument for global leadership for the lesser violence. Having elaborated a cosmopolitan political ethics of prudence in this context, I then turn back in section 5 to an analysis of the first meaning of political cosmopolitanism: the project of cosmopolitan democracy. I suggest, in response to the Realist critiques of global motivation and world government, that this project makes concrete sense in the differentiated terms of the concept of 'subsidiarity', but that it requires cosmopolitans to address the necessarily aristocratic component in democratic reinvention at the global level. My response to the Realist critique concludes with four research agendas that would pursue the terms of this initial debate.

1 The Status of the Normative in Conditions of Interdependence

I recall that Goldsmith and Posner's thesis is that international law is a product of state power and interest and of their interstate configurations (coordination, cooperation or coercion). Normative theory of international law has, accordingly, no explanatory purchase on international legal reality. Goldsmith and Posner consequently maintain a hard distinction between normative theory (prescriptive) and empirical theory (explanatory) and place all modalities of cosmopolitanism on the side of an exclusively pre-scriptive understanding of international behaviour. I suggest that this major Realist thesis is best met in two ways from a cosmopolitan perspective: first, by an analysis of the novelty of international political reality under conditions of interdependence; second, by closer examination of the status of the normative under these very conditions (chapter 1, sections 2.2 and 2.3). I address both points through David Held's normative cosmopolitan arguments concerning increasing dependence between states and peoples, with a supplement argument for the second point based on Patrick Hayden's discussion of the 'embeddedness' of the international human rights regime.

Held has stressed since the early 1990s that, with globalization pro-cesses, both domestic and international political reality is increasingly shaped by what he calls 'overlapping communities of fate' (2004, p. x). Increasing economic and technological interdependence, together with the global problems they bring about, forge new configurations of causality, determination and interest that overflow the cooperative dynamics of discrete national communities and discrete collective interest. In today's world, he writes:

> It is not only the violent exception that links people across borders; the very nature of everyday problems and processes join people in multiple ways. From the movement of ideas and cultural artefacts to the fundamental issues of genetic engineering, from the conditions of financial stability to environ-mental degradation, the fate and fortunes of each of us is thoroughly inter-twined. (Ibid.)

Few would disagree with the general outlines of this comment today; it has become a commonplace of the globalized world. But Held makes, I believe, a substantive point against Realism in this context. The reality of nation-state behaviour has become so intertwined with that of other nation-states, with transnational civil society and with international organization, that this behaviour is *qualitatively* changing. Within the terms of this qualitative change, the normative cannot be simply opposed to posited empirical fact. Rather, given the practical reality of interdependence, states require new principles of behaviour to act in the international realm, and these principles transcend national interest.

One can use Realism's attention to the real against its own exclusive focus on state-centredness here. As we saw in chapter 2, Hans Morgenthau defined 'prudence' in in these terms: 'It is not a question of imposing moral principle *upon* practical reality but deducing moral principle *from* practical reality' (Morgenthau, 1952, p. 140, my emphasis). In light of this tenet of classical Realism, Held's political cosmopolitanism can be considered a project of principle that responds to an emerging reality: the loss of self-determination at the national level given the consequences of interdependence. These consequences concern, most visibly, the following global governance issues: collective international security regimes, genocide, crimes against humanity, ethnic cleansing and war crimes, post-national financial and economic regulation, climate change mitigation, a global health order to prevent transborder pandemic, and sustainable development of countries caught in poverty traps (for the formulation of these global problems since the late 1990s, see Held et al., 1999; Held and McGrew, 2000 and 2002; Held, 1995b, 2004, 2005b). Normative cosmopolitan principle is not imposed by Held upon twenty-first-century reality (a prescriptive 'should' upon a recalcitrant 'is'); the emerging reality of interdependence calls forth the (re-)invention of national, transnational and, ultimately, supra-national political principle. The normative cosmopolitan point is, therefore, not simply that cosmopolitanism may provide the right *moral* response to the effects of globalization. Rather, the normative content of cosmopolitanism can be considered to be historically deduced *from* the complexity of interdependence. This seems, to this author at least, the strongest cosmopolitan counter-argument to the over-hard distinction between value and fact within the normative/empirical divide informing Goldsmith and Posner's arguments.

As we saw for Held in chapter 1, section 2.6, cosmopolitan values are expressed in terms of a set of principles. I emphasized those of moral egalitarianism, democratic participation in collective decision-making, inclusiveness and subsidiarity. In his 'Principles of cosmopolitan order' (Held, 2005a), these principles are formally expounded. Held provides thereby a strong cosmopolitan moral framework for 'non-coercive collective agreement and governance' (ibid., p. 13). This moral cosmopolitan oversight over world politics is important, although its exact intellectual pitch is difficult to situate with regard to the political domain: I specifically return to this question in section 5 with regard to the principle of subsidiarity. Here, however, in the context of Goldsmith and Posner's Realist critique of normative constraint on state interests, I am emphasizing the historical-normative point *behind* the moral framework. Technological, economic and communicational types of interdependence are, the cosmopolitan argues, such that normative principles begin to work *with reality*, not in abstraction *from it*. It is evident, for example, that the dignity of moral personhood is neither culturally nor politically respected in many parts of the world.

Held's point would be – if I have understood him correctly – that the moral norm of the dignity of individual life is nevertheless emerging out of complex reality *as* the most fitting norm for political self-organization (however this organization is then thought). This dignity is, in other words, not simply posited in prescriptive terms in the Universal Declaration of Human Rights and following covenants. It works, in loose terms, within the historical parameters of modernization processes. The assumption will need to be more secured at a material level when I respond to Marxist critique and discuss the individualization processes of the capitalist market system (chapter 5, section 1.2).

For many, this emphasis on the relation between norm and history will smack of both liberal teleology and Westernism, especially in the present context of an economic shift of power to Asia together with the present recrudescence of autocratic regimes (see Held's responses in his 2005b; on China, see Jacques, 2010; C. Brown, 2010). Following my historical understanding of normative cosmopolitanism, I believe that Held is nevertheless right to argue that the normative comprises a general historical *possibility* (Held, 2005b, pp. 153–5), one that can be translated politically to a lesser or greater degree. Held, for example, makes this argument concerning 1945:

> The cosmopolitan values entrenched in the UN Charter were . . . articulated in the aftermath of the Holocaust, the horrors of two world wars, and the separation and division of Europe. The values remain of enduring significance, but the geopolitical settlement of 1945 is the wrong institutional basis to makes these values count across the globe. (ibid., p. 154)

Four points of interest underlie this argument:

1 One must separate the validity of value from the latter's source (compare Caney, 2005, p. 87; Donnelly, 1989, p. 60).
2 A normative cosmopolitan framework is deduced from out of a sense that history has a general orientation (most countries are adopting some form of capitalism).
3 While this direction of history is not necessary (there are reversals, dead-ends, catastrophes), history nevertheless works within specific material constraints (economic, technical, and communicational).
4 These material constraints gradually undo *functional* constraints like state-sovereignty (compare, Zolo, 1997) and require institutional re-coordination of interest under competing ideologies (liberal democracy, social democracy, Islamic democracy, state capitalism, etc.).

I consider Held, following the sociology of Jürgen Habermas (1984), to emphasize, therefore, a *historico-sociological* point that modern history is inhabited by norms and that these norms tend to self-select themselves given material reality. Placed in the context of Goldsmith and Posner's over-neat distinction between the normative and the explanatory, this assumption has several further implications, all of which put in question a static notion of the normative.

1 The difference between norm and interest is not possible, historically speaking. Principles of behaviour are never simply formal: I focus on this implication in the next section.
2 While clear-cut distinctions between the normative and the positive, the endogenous and the exogenous can be intellectually clarifying – and often politically necessary – they are not rewarding when analysing the complex reality of interdependence. The relation between globalization processes, international law and state behaviour is one such complex reality. Prudent political decisions should be based on an awareness of this complexity, although it must simplify it.
3 The crude Realist claim, evident in Goldsmith and Posner's argument, that power and interest undermine a priori the horizon of normative thinking is too abstract: power and interest form part of complex histori-cal processes and change under normative constraints within these processes.
4 These norms – and the global rules that work with them – may have their source in the West, but they are not Western per se: they respond well to the constraints and opportunities of global reality.

Avoiding teleology, Held's above argument on 'historical possibility' is, I think, strong in this context. A general argument made by Patrick Hayden in his *Cosmopolitan Global Politics* (2005) supplements this form of reasoning. As covered in chapter 1, section 2.3 on normative cosmo-politanism, Hayden emphasizes that the cosmopolitan outlook is not just normative in critical opposition to empirical political reality: it is already 'embedded' in the international human rights regime. At international and national constitutional levels, the normative principles of human rights translate an emerging reality for all levels of political governance, which work in human and sustainable development accompanies (ibid., pp. 11–37, 71, 96, 122). For Hayden, therefore, a state-centred focus on national interest oversimplifies complex interdependence of capacity and function in an integrated world system. Its focus on state motivation is too exclusive; integration promotes, rather, increasing *inclusiveness* of agency (ibid., pp. 153–4). Realist analysis of institutional practices of globalization becomes, consequently, impertinent because its limited focus on the moment of self-interested motivation (when states, for example, defect from collective cooperation and principle) fails to note how institutionally embedded rights practices are and fails to follow how this institutional embedding changes the norms of its members' behaviour over time (ibid., pp. 46–65; see also Cabrera, 2004, pp. 105–20; Held, 2004, pp. 139–43; on the EU, see Delanty and Rumford, 2005). Hayden's critique of Realism is too sharp and underestimates the importance of state behaviour for the cosmopolitan argument: '[Realism] promotes militaristic values' and is concerned with 'the state's enhancement of power with regard to other states' (2005, p. 79 and p. 71). His constructivist and institutionalist points remain nevertheless persuasive: institutionalization without coercive force changes, over time, the *terms* of interstate obligation.

For both Held and Hayden, then, social scientific distinctions between the normative and the positive, value and fact are inappropriate in light of the normative consequences of interdependence. Norms, once posited (as in 1945–8), inhabit history and inform institutional reconfigurations. This reconfiguration is not necessary; if the norms, however, constitute an appropriate response to the emerging historical environment, their institutionalization is more rather than less likely. The normative regime of international human rights law has over the past 50 years been increasingly embedded in an incoherent, but potentially self-relating system of declaration, treaty and constitution (Cassese, 2005; Robertson, 2002). This institutional embedding necessarily informs state interest and behaviour. *Contra* Goldsmith and Posner, the international human rights regime has, in these terms, an *exogenous* effect on state interest.

2 Power, Interest and Legitimacy: A Cosmopolitan Perspective

Goldsmith and Posner's argument implies, more generally, that moral and legal duties, pertinent to individual and domestic motivation, become *category errors* at the international and global level. To respond to this criticism, this section looks at the intertwined nature of norm and interest from the perspective of the wielding of power in an interdependent world and from that of global leadership. Contemporary cosmopolitans rightly insist on the importance of the role of the state within a cosmopolitan outlook. They seek not to replace the state by world government, but to attenuate the right of national sovereignty given their ethico-political focus on human life and/or moral personhood (Archibugi, 2008; G. W. Brown,

2009; Cabrera, 2004; Hayden, 2005; Held, 2004 and 2005a). That said, both in the face of Realist critique and the present dilemmas of global collective action, cosmopolitanism should focus more on the state-function and the reconfiguration of national interest. One way to do this is through the political thought of the supposed founder of the US Realist school, Hans Morgenthau.

Jürgen Habermas gives Morgenthau short shrift in his cosmopolitan wish to subordinate power to law: 'In the view of Hans Morgenthau, the founder of the Realist school, the incessant drive for power is rooted in human nature' (Habermas, 2006, p. 167). On an initial reading of Morgenthau, it is true that 'interest is defined as power' and that power is defined as 'the lust for domination involv[ing] all men' (Morgenthau, 2005, p. 10; 1946, p. 215). As I argued in chapter 2, this second invariant trait of the Realist school appears irreducible. Morgenthau's discussions of the national interest would also appear intractable. Moral principles should not be opposed to the national interest, but these principles only have concrete meaning through the consensus achieved within national communities (1952, p. 34). In the absence of strong world government that could safeguard, by force, the interests of all nation-states without resorting to the leading nations, 'it is morally wrong to ask a nation to forego its national interests' (ibid., p. 36) and morally right both to forgo 'unfounded claims of providing moral standards for all humanity' and to defend national survival against 'usurpation by non-national interests' (ibid., p. 37). In a later essay, 'The problem of the national interest', this distinction between 'utopianism' and 'realism' becomes, however, more complicated (reprinted in Morenthau 1971, pp. 204–37).

It is no longer a question of either stressing the weakness of international institutions in a world of global threats or opposing abstract moral principle to concrete meanings of justice; but of filtering moral principles through concrete contexts, on the one hand, and of respecting the 'legitimate' interests of other nation-states, on the other (ibid., pp. 224–5). The political virtue of prudence translates, precisely, this complex work of evaluation (ibid., p. 236). Thus, speaking to nuclear disarmament, Morgenthau writes:

> The supranational control of atomic energy is today in the national interest of all nations; for while the present bipolarity of atomic power is dangerous to all nations, the acquisition of uncontrolled atomic power by an indefinite number of nations is likely to prove fatal to civilized life on this planet. In consequence, the nations of the world are faced with, and must overcome, the dilemma that the pursuit of their interests, conceived in national terms, is incompatible with modern technology, which requires supranational political organization. (Ibid., p. 219)

Material reality requires passage from national to supra-national organization given the collective and individual interests of the nation-state under
conditions of technological interdependence. I would suggest in this
context that the cosmopolitan argument of the last section straightforwardly extends this argument under conditions of intensified interdependence. The dilemmas now provoked ensue from the incompatibility
between the pursuit of national interest and the material consequences of
an integrated world. Morgenthau did not see a way out of the dilemma
of the military use of nuclear energy except through 'the mutual recognition of the national interests concerned' (ibid., p. 218). Now, this point
precisely endorses the need for leading states to be committed to resolving global collective action problems; therefore, leading states should
entertain, at the very least, minimal cosmopolitan principles such as protection of the dignity of life (see chapter 1, section 2.2 on weak moral
cosmopolitanism).

Following classic and recent rational choice literature on this subject
(Olson, 1965; Barry and Hardin, 1983; Sandler, 2004; Kaul et al., 1999
and 2003), I understand a collective action problem as one determined by
the lack of incentives – enforcement mechanisms or outstanding benefits
– to forge cooperation among individual agents in order to address a rationally understood collective problem. Nuclear disarmament, financial regulation of the world economy, and global climate change mitigation constitute
important global collective action problems today (Sandler, 2004, pp. 6–7).
Given a lack of both global coercive force and the potential for overt
hegemony, leading states must together assume responsibility in order to
overcome global collective inaction, with the expected benefit of multilateral leadership status (ibid., pp. 7–10, 39). I discuss this point in substantive detail in the context of climate change mitigation in my response
to Marxism (see chapter 5). Suffice it to say here – on the back of
Morgenthau's understanding of 'national interest' in a nuclear age – that
national interest changes qualitatively under conditions of interdependence, that such change is critical at this juncture of history for leading
state behaviour in the world and that, therefore, *international power is
increasingly mediated by collective constraints*. Given the material reality
of interdependence, Realist analysis should, consequently, move its focus
on the state to one, also, on state responsibility to supra-national concerns;
just as political cosmopolitanism should focus more on cosmopolitan
responsibility through the filter of the state.

I wish now to discuss the penultimate point on power in terms of international legitimacy. International legitimacy is an immediate concern of
the English school in IR, given the school's focus on the way international
rules shape interstate behaviour and international society (see Clark, 2005).

My argument is, however, made again through Hans Morgenthau, given the context of response to Realist critique.

Although, as Habermas argued above, Morgenthau conceives of the lust for power as an anthropological constant, his analysis of power in *Politics Among Nations* (2005) is differentiated and mediated. Assuming a degree of interdependence, it allows one to reconceive national interest in the context of international legitimacy. Power has biological, military, economic, legal, ideological and political aspects (2005, pp. 32–41): in all these aspects, it establishes the control of x over 'the minds and actions' of y (ibid., p. 30). The specificity of *political* power, for Morgenthau, as Michael Williams has argued (see chapter 2), concerns ridding the political domain of physical violence. Morgenthau's 'disillusioned liberalism' (Williams, 2005, pp. 120–7) addresses the most effective means to do this in a plural world of interests. Williams's important reading underplays, nevertheless, a critical point in Morgenthau's thought that requires further attention here in the context of interdependence and its implications for power. For Morgenthau, following Weber, if power is properly political, power must be justified (2005, p. 93). At one end of Morgenthau's continuum of power, power is pure material force: x forces y to do z. At the other end ('ideology' in the neutral sense), power signifies the capacity or opportunity on the part of x to persuade y to do z: that is, the command must be considered morally or legally justified by those it affects. The question of power, for Morgenthau, is therefore also the question of accepted principle, that is, the question of legitimacy. Power and principle become inextricably bound.

Given this analysis, as opposed to other Realists, Morgenthau was highly critical from the early 1950s onwards of American foreign policy in Southeast Asia (1952, p. 33; 2004, pp. 70–90). Morgenthau argued that American foreign policy-makers, unable to make a distinction between 'Russian imperialism' and 'genuine revolution', failed to perceive that communist political ideology in Asia 'reflects the life experience of those whom it wishes to reach' (1952, p. 212). I would argue that one should extend this classical Realist understanding of power beyond Morgenthau's own domestic/foreign policy opposition and readdress the question of legitimacy for international power-wielding today. If one does, categorial distinctions between power and justice, like those of Goldmith and Posner, become difficult. I make the argument on four scores. They concern:

1 The international perception of legitimacy.
2 International legitimacy for leading democratic states.
3 The nature of international legal duty.
4 Co-implication of national interests.

(1) If the second Iraq war is widely considered a foreign policy failure on the part of leading democratic states, one important reason is because it was *perceived* internationally as illegitimate both before and after the war (on the importance of foreign perceptions, compare Nye's analysis of soft power in Nye, 2004, p. 125). To say this does not deny the reality on the ground: it was, precisely, the lack of WMD that caused the success of the argument against the invasion in the first place.[1] That said, international perceptions played a critical role. I would argue therefore that by intensifying the speed and density of these cross-border perceptions, communicational technology is constraining the international use of power. The primary reason for regime change (WMD) was quickly seen to be trumped up by the Bush and Blair governments, and the post-conflict phase was unplanned (Pew Global Attitudes Project, 2003). The perception of illegitimacy crossed diverse and mutually antagonistic actors: from the UN, through non-party global civil opinion, state actors, to insurgency forces on the Iraqi ground. In the context of this war, I suggest that in a highly interdependent world, action on the part of powerful states must be seen as legitimate *by those it affects* if it is to meet success. Precisely put, the ideology of power – for those leading states that wield it on an international stage – has become more than national in an interdependent world. The Israeli invasion of South Lebanon in 2006 and of the Gaza strip in 2009 brought forward large international condemnation despite long-standing Western sympathy with Israeli national interests. Its disproportionate use of violence was widely considered illegitimate and, in the case of Gaza, illegal – to the extent that unconditional US support for Israel is now openly considered by leading Realists as counter to US national interest (Mearsheimer and Walt, 2008).[2] The number of civilian deaths in Afghanistan as a result of American bombing, accompanied by the perception of the Iraq war, made many reticent as to the legitimacy of the Afghan war prior to the strategic question of which enemy (Al Qaeda or the Taliban) was being combated (Rashid, 2008; Obama, 2009a). For political power and its military expression to be legitimate in a globalized world, non-national interest must increasingly be taken into account. Both these examples suggest the hypothesis that in a highly integrated world, exclusive action can be quickly perceived as illegitimate and that, at the level of ideology, this perception undermines, sooner or later, power itself.

(2) This perceived illegitimacy is obviously all the more severe for states whose domestic power rests on democratic legitimacy. Wielders of power in democratic states must be increasingly careful about the way in which they wield power beyond their borders. For, given communicational density, charges of hypocrisy and double standards can only be dodged for a limited amount of time (Keukeleire and MacNaughtan, 2008, p. 225). I would

argue, therefore, that consistent legitimate behaviour is important to the very maintenance of power in a highly integrated system. Previous distinctions between domestic and foreign policy, domestic and international legitimacy may no longer be upheld in this sense for leading democratic states. If such a state wants today to wield power globally, if it wants to assume the mantle of global leadership, it may increasingly have to build others' interests into its own, given its *own* criteria of legitimate power, under conditions of interdependence. Democratic states have, therefore, to be more consistent in their domestic and non-domestic behaviour (Falk, 2004, pp. 3–44). This new global reality is, I am claiming, confirmed by the second Iraq war. Democracy emerged in Eastern European states from 1989 and, with the backdrop of market globalization, in that same year was launched the ideology of liberal democracy throughout the world. International events between 2001 and 2005 have made it clear that this ideology of democracy can only work *both* internally *and* externally, if ever it is to become a fundamental principle of power throughout the world.

Contra Goldsmith and Posner's critique of cosmopolitan legal theory, and expanding upon Morgenthau's understanding of power, I claim that power and interest are differentiated and mediated in the context of global political realities: interest is not first individual, and, second, through coordination with others, more than individual. In the integrated system of a globalized world, *legitimate* interests increasingly involve, on issues of global reach, proactive response to others' interests. One major challenge of the future is for democratic state units to organize their power in terms that are, in principle, inseparably domestic and foreign *so that* they lead by example, not by imposition or unnecessary hypocrisy (compare K. Smith, 2008). In a multipolar world of democratic and autocratic states, such example is important. In terms of international legitimacy, Daniele Archibugi is consequently right to insist on the democratic practices of democratic states in both domestic and international arenas (Archibugi, 2008).

(3) What does this general point about the principles of power in a globalized world imply about international legal duty? First, in increasingly complex societies the separation of international questions of justice from power undercuts power (Lebow, 2003). Second, the modality of international legal duty should be clearly distinguished by Realists from that of domestic legal duty. As the English School insists, international norms, set up in international treaty and law, constrain state behaviour because, in principle, a sovereign state cannot be recognized as a sovereign member of the United Nations unless it follows a set of legal duties (Clark, 2005, pp. 180–3; Suganami, 2007). In their exposition of the motivation behind state compliance with international rules, Goldsmith and Posner are right

to emphasize that there are many state exceptions, opt-out clauses and international bureaucratic inconsistencies. At the international level, legal duty is not enforced by coercive power, unless specific crimes have been perpetrated by a particular government: international law is customary in this sense of lacking force. However, rather than thinking international legal duty, in Realist terms, as the *precipitate* of state interest in coordination with other state interests, it would, I think, be more appropriate to say that international legal duty is *structurally different* from domestic legal duty. Given this structural difference, international legal duty is closer to interest, but it has also become separate from it. *In this separation, it exercises a constraining force on power.* I consider this point with regard to EU law in a moment. I suggest, here, that this weak force becomes visible in, and through, the *perception* of legitimate and illegitimate state behaviour in the emerging global public domain. The force is weak (as for the present Israeli government), but it has independent effects. These independent effects should be delimited in reality and theoretically understood in their singularity. From this perspective of the international wielding of power, Goldsmith and Posner's thesis that international law is not explanatory of state behaviour is, again, incorrect.

(4) I return here to a historico-sociological approach to national interest and its expansion under conditions of interdependence. Alexander Wendt argues well in *Social Theory of International Relations* that interests change in interaction with other interests (1999, pp. 92–138). Coordination and cooperation between state interests produce new interest for the parties concerned, not simply the sum of, or compromise between, those interests. I wish to argue this constructivist and institutionalist point in historical terms. An example is to be found in the global response to climate change (see chapter 5, section 4, for further detail). Pollution is, formally speaking, a problem of global reach, since the environment does not have borders, and since one ton of carbon emission has the same effect on the world wherever its source of emission. It is in the interest of the richer, predominantly Western states to coordinate the reduction of CO_2 emissions between developed and developing countries. In 2050 the developing countries will probably emit 80% of the world's energy-related CO_2 (IEA, 2008, pp. 46, 417). It is therefore impossible to lower atmospheric concentrations of CO_2 without the active participation of developing and/or non-democratic countries. Realists, like Goldsmith and Posner, are correct to say that the Western states are not moral agents given the complexity of interests they represent. When Gordon Brown, ex-prime minister of the UK, advocated recently the 'moral duty' on the part of 'post-industrial countries' to clean up the planet, this duty had no concrete meaning since neither the moral agent nor the moral responsibility was clearly defined (G. Brown, 2009;

compare Erskine, 2001, 2008a, 2008b). State cooperation on climate change will be the consequence of commutative justice (the bargaining towards a collective interest). That said, with regard to a global collective action problem like climate change, it is not only a question of 'mutual recognition of interests', as Morgenthau argued above. On questions of global reach like climate change, national interest will increasingly respond to other national interests *in order to define its own interest*. Its interest will, accordingly, become more 'inclusive' of other national interests in order to be a viable interest in the first place. In a world of interdependence and emerging international social differentiation, one unit's interest is increasingly mediated by the interests of others, even if national motivation remains initially interest of self. In sum, on an array of issues that ensue from increasing interdependence, national interest can itself only be achieved *through* the satisfaction of other national interests. As a result, the *reality* of national interest has been 'sublated' (to put it in Hegelian terms) – towards what remains unclear institutionally, since what one is addressing is partial, often indirect cession of national sovereignty on a set of global governance issues. This new confluence of interests hovers between 'the national and the international' and 'the national and the supra-national'. I suggest, in response to Realist critique, that contemporary cosmopolitanism constitutes one important attempt to understand and to guide the historical direction of this ongoing qualitative change in national interest.[3]

The above conclusion does not argue that the source of motivation changes. The incompatibility between cosmopolitan motivation (moral duty) and Realist motivation (interest) still seems in this sense unbridgeable. Goldsmith and Posner's thesis would remain essentially correct: regarding CO_2 emission reduction, states are acting in a regional and global interest because *it is in their interest to do so* (coincidence of interests). The best cosmopolitan response to Goldsmith and Posner seems to me in this respect to be two-tiered. Analytically, this difference appears absolute, although analytical delimitations of state moral agency are, following Michael Walzer's emphasis on the moral significance of states, emerging (Walzer, 1977; Erskine, 2001, 2008b, 2010; Ypi, 2008). As I argued above, however, an exclusively analytical approach reduces terms of agency. Historically, the opposition between the cosmopolitan and the Realist approach is formal. Following the principles of historical sociology, individual and collective units internalize external norms over generational periods of time. What is for one generation a formal constraint becomes an internal impulse a couple of generations later. As the sociologist Norbert Elias (1982) argues, the history of 'civilization' comprises the internalization of constraint with increasing differentiation of labour and multiplication and density of social agency. Indeed, the concept of 'civilization' describes nothing, for Elias, but the internalization of external constraints, which accompanies social differentiation. Today's globalized world constitutes the beginning of a new social environment (Linklater, 2007a and 2007b). With growing transnational social differentiation (in loose analogy with domestic modernization processes), external constraints will, I would argue, gradually revert to internal norms. Or better, those constraints concerning specific issues of global reach will revert.

In the recent history of political theory, sociological observation on motivation has been sidelined from mainstream thinking for, I think, two reasons. On the one hand, from Enlightenment liberalism onwards (starting with Kantian ethics), liberals tend to give ahistorical accounts of moral motivation since this account serves the ideology of liberal individualism. On the other hand, from within the methodological individualism of rational choice theory and structural realism, Realists work with motivation of interest in terms of individual units of analysis separated from historical and social context. Motivation is, however, a historically mediated process at both individual and collective levels. Given the constraints of international collective action, it is in the mid-term interest of a nation-state to give up its national prerogative over domestic environmental policy and join supra-national participatory forms of rule-making (compare Slaughter, 2004). *Analytically*, this is a new form of interest-formation based on the invariable nature of interest. *Historically*, however, this is an evolution towards a more 'ethically- based' form of national politics. First, it includes, rather than excludes, other nations and institutions in the decision-making process, and therefore begins to adhere to David Held's wider principle of self-affection (participation in decisions that significantly affect one). Second, and more importantly, after a certain amount of time, motivation and loyalty begin *with* this participation, and not with individual interest *in* this participation. The constraint (specific market and government regulations on carbon emissions, for example) then becomes a normative form of behaviour that *fashions interest in the first place*. At a certain moment of the internalization of norms this self-binding behaviour may well be considered 'moral'. A state would act, to continue my example, for the sake of the planet, not for the sake of its own interest in saving the planet. At that point, one might conclude with Gordon Brown (2009) that states are indeed 'moral agents'.

There is no plausible argument to say that this evolution will occur, and exemplary state behaviour may be motivated, mid-term, by national pride *in* altruism. I have argued, conversely, that morality, *contra* Kantian moral idealism, is not separate from the evolution of collective and individual behaviour. One should not argue, as a consequence, that states *cannot* become moral agents. As Nietzsche (1887) demonstrated, individuals have themselves only become individual moral selves through social constraint. A 'domestic analogy' between individuals and states is therefore possible on the basis of the *material* evolution of individual and collective morality, but on this basis alone. This negative argument is enough to pursue the cosmopolitan perspective; and, again, it endorses a normative cosmopolitanism that works from *within* the dynamics of history (rather than looking to normative principles beyond them).

In conclusion to this long section, I have made several arguments, in response to Goldsmith and Posner's positivism, that emphasize the historically mediated relation between power and principle and that, in response to Realism as a whole, begin to recast the concepts of national interest and power under conditions of interdependence. These arguments allow normative, legal and political modalities of cosmopolitanism to begin to make sense of evolving practical reality. They can be briefly summarized.

In conditions of increasing interdependence, power is likely to gravitate upwards and become more ideational and principled (compare Held, 2005a), at the very least for those powers that seek global leadership. Given the growing social density of state and non-state actors on the international scene, legitimacy of power turns on the *relation* between actors, no longer on the difference between them. In an increasingly dense environment, legitimate power must internalize these relations. If power is considered in terms of interest, national interests become increasingly mediated by other interests, and a qualitative jump in the nature of national interest takes place, one that calls forth more inclusive principles of state behaviour. While accepting the difference between domestic and international modes of legislation, this new interest can be considered, loosely, to be 'legally' mediated. The counter-argument that this new interest could not become 'moral' at the state level is historically unconvincing. Emerging constituent pressure on democratic states to align the legitimacy of their foreign policy with that of domestic policy constitutes one sign of this possible evolution in state legitimacy under conditions of interdependence.

3 Category Errors: Domestic Analogy, 'Legalistic-Moralistic' Fallacy and Anarchy

The preceding two sections already imply that the three functional concepts of Realism – abuse of the domestic analogy, legalistic-moralistic fallacy and anarchy – are in theoretical difficulty. This section makes this difficulty more explicit by showing how contemporary cosmopolitanism articulates a 'differentiated universalism' (see chapter 1, section 2.5).

The last chapter pinpointed how deep the liberal abuse of the domestic analogy goes for Realists. To presume that international processes can be analysed as if they were domestic processes short-circuits the paradoxes of power, plurality and ethico-political responsibility in the international realm. Cosmopolitanism – particularly legal and political cosmopolitanism (that of the extension of democracy to the global level) – prolongs this abuse. A theoretical line must be drawn against this abuse for the sake of the lesser violence. This line of argument is problematic for several reasons.

First, Realism works itself with the domestic analogy. The Realist aporia of world government depends on an analogy with the character of domestic law. 'Anarchy' can only be resolved through the coercive force of law. Since the coercive force of law is only possible through state monopoly of violence, world peace requires a universal state. Since, however, such a state is both impractical (given divergent state interests) and dangerous (world monopoly of violence would equal tyranny), anarchy is irreducible. The units within anarchy can change (regional organizations, etc.), but the condition of anarchy between them cannot. This argument is grounded on the simple assumption that world government *requires* the same coercive force as that of domestic law. Nothing in the Realist argument allows, therefore, for variation in the relation between law and force as one shifts from one level of legal and political organization to another. The Hobbesian monopoly of 'common power' is simply necessary for law and justice to function effectively in global terms. There is, however, neither theoretical model nor empirical evidence to suggest that this is necessarily the case. Realist leanings on historical precedent (John Herz's or Robert Kagan's 'fundamental historical lessons') do not provide sufficient argument. History works within certain material constraints; but the very modality of these constraints changes.

There is no reason to assume that the rule of law, in order to be effective, either should be, or needs to be, the same at the national, international and global levels. This is a crucial point regarding the enactment of duties and responsibilities. The human species is just beginning to enter something like 'world civilization'. The assumption on the part of Realism that power can only be trumped by the monopolistic force of law is ahistorical. The previous argument by Norbert Elias that increasing social differentiation brings with it increasing need for universal coordination may suggest another route. Namely, as this differentiation widens and deepens over the planet, universal coordination on specific issues of global reach does *not* need the full force of coercion akin to that of domestic law. This argument against anarchy is not institutionalist: it does not assume individual interests, in conditions of imperfect information, looking for institutional mediations to reduce transaction costs (compare Milner, 1993). Milner's assumptions are analytical and formal. My assumption is, rather, that the relation between law and force can change from one level of human organization to another because of the historical internalization of external constraint (individual and collective). This internalization intensifies in modern complex societies since increasing social differentiation is accompanied by growing universal coordination. Without this assumption, one cannot explain why conflicts in the world, however violent and murderous, remain an exception in a fairly stable world order.[4] Nor can one explain, without it, the increasing need for regional and global regulations of the capitalist system. The new threat of the use of nuclear arms in non-state hands proves, inversely, the point: nuclear terror presents a radical threat to human ordering because terrorism is, in essence, not rule-bound. From a cosmopolitan sociological perspective, therefore, the Realist aporia of the universal state constitutes an historical error of thought.

The second reason why the Realist line is problematic is because the terms of the domestic analogy are increasingly loose in contemporary use of them. At least, cosmopolitan response to Realism is effective *when* it uses the domestic analogy loosely: that is, when it shows awareness that the terms of the analogy – domestic law, on the one hand, international and cosmopolitan law on the other; domestic democracy on the one hand, cosmopolitan democracy, on the other – are *themselves* changing. The change suggests, in turn, the increasing need for differentiation in contemporary cosmopolitan argument. With regard to misuse of the domestic analogy and the 'legalistic-moralistic' fallacy, it requires, for example: (i) cosmopolitan engagement with state leadership; (ii) cosmopolitan exposition of the differences in legal modality according to level (national, regional, global); and (iii) exposition of differences in democratic polity according to context. I have begun to speak of the first, and return to it in the next section; I will turn to the last in the final section. I address here the second (differences in law) in the context of the domestic analogy.

The international human rights regime represents for cosmopolitans 'what is perhaps the most powerful expression of cosmopolitanism in the realm of global politics' (Hayden, 2005, p. 38). The major question, in response to Realism, has been whether these rules have moral and legal force on domestic state behaviour or not. I have argued above, in the context of Realist critique, that they do in terms of the legitimacy of power and given the changing nature of interest. A question still remains: do they *already* have a direct exogenous effect on state expectations and conduct, and, if so, what kind of law are we considering? I use this question to address a differentiated analysis of cosmopolitan law.

The dominant themes of post-1948 international rights documents are the equal entitlements human beings have to a sustainable and dignified life. The framework of this regime has motivated, fairly effectively, 50 years of civic critiques of state behaviour, and these critiques from domestic state constituents have had large influence on state conduct. The 1998 Rome Statute on the International Criminal Court (ICC) would, for example, have been much less extensive without the proactive role of the NGO community (compare Linklater, 1999; Hayden, 2005, pp. 110–11). One can, therefore, argue for the direct exogenous effect of international law on state behaviour in five ways:

1 Constituent pressure on governments (the liberal obverse of Goldsmith and Posner's 'rational choice' thesis on constituent behaviour).
2 International legal ruling trumps domestic legal ruling.
3 The rules of international declaration, treaty and legal custom inform the rules of domestic constitutions.
4 International legal ruling becomes a cited precedent in domestic legal case and judgement.
5 Making state leaders individually accountable for the government of their peoples shapes the terms of state power (we return here to legitimacy of political power).

It is for an expert of international law to show proper proof of the last four conditions of influence (see Cassese, 2005). My more modest claim is that, under historical terms of universal coordination and proactive global leadership, all five could be more satisfied than less satisfied. I concentrate, respectively, on (2) and (4) in order to loosen the terms of the domestic analogy between domestic, regional, international and global law.

In terms of explicitly legal institutions, the only example of (2) to this date is the European Court of Justice (ECJ).[5] The source of its legal decisions lies in the treaties of Union members, the European Convention on Human Rights and Fundamental Freedoms. It is concerned to uphold the primacy of EU law over divergent national laws and overlook its even application throughout member states. Its role is well understood to have been critical in creating common market policy across national borders, consistent decisions between the various institutions of the Union regarding national legislation, and for upholding high terms of entry for candidate states to the EU (see Pinder, 2001; McCormick, 2002; Peterson and Schackleton, 2002). EU law is not competent in criminal or family matters, but by making the EEC Rome treaty in 1963 a 'constitutional instrument', it imposed direct and common obligations on all member states (Shaw, 2000). Court rulings since have reinforced individual rights, free movement of European labour and reduced gender discrimination. Both conditions of accession to the EU (democracy, fulfilment of rights) and the ongoing activities of its main legal pillar, the ECJ, indicate the extent to which national governments of the member states have both changed their non-democratic behaviour to access the EU in the first place and subsequently transferred power to European institutions.

Goldsmith and Posner argued that the EU is not a generalizable model for supra-national governance (2005, pp. 221–5). The basic common values its members share as well as its contiguous geographical borders are singular. One can add that the precondition of the EU lies in the devastation of two world wars originating in Europe. Now, *Realists and cosmopolitanisms simply do not agree here*. For Cabrera, Habermas, Hayden and Held, the EU and the often underrated work of European law constitute post-national political inventions that will, in time, serve as a reference point for other, less integrated regional institutions. While the EU lacks the power to force its member states to implement European law and policy, its rulings are, for the main, obeyed. European legal duty has, therefore, its own consistency, independent from hard domestic law, on the one hand, and state interest, on the other.

For cosmopolitans, it is this consistency that sets a precedent for regional and global politics. In terms of my loosening of the domestic analogy, EU law names, therefore, a historically new relation between law, force and interest. This new relation will plausibly work at regional and global levels under conditions of increasing social differentiation and universal coordination. The Realist counter-argument that the European region is exceptional and particular is, from this perspective and understanding of law, only empirically explanatory within a short time-frame. Ongoing economic coordination in Africa, in Latin America and in Asia may well become the basis of regional legal and political associations that work with a structurally similar notion of 'weak' law, even if this law's content is not tied to substantive democratic principle. Again, there is no evidence or theoretical model to prove the contrary. I would suggest that cosmopolitan judgement departs best from this radical lack of counter-argument and is consistent and imaginative when it reinforces the similarity *and* difference between domestic and regional legal arrangements. From this perspective of the looseness of the domestic analogy, and *contra* Realist critique of EU exceptionalism, legal/institutional and normative modalities of cosmopolitanism are, I maintain, entitled to affirm the EU as a possible model for supra-national rule-based behaviour.

I stated in chapter 1 (sections 2.3 and 2.5) that Kant's essay 'Perpetual peace' expounds the aporia of the universal state in consistent liberal terms (Kant, 1795/1991, pp. 102–5, 128–9). Following the republican model of modern freedom, Kant emphasizes freedom under the rule of law and the necessity of the threat of force for this freedom to function legally. The necessary force of law provides the reason for his use of the domestic analogy. But force at the world level risks turning world republicanism into universal despotism. Kant therefore opts for the negative substitute of a 'federal alliance of Free States' (ibid., p. 129). This league is not a lawful state: it cannot therefore guarantee *human* rights *as* legal rights; nor can it transform these rights into *political* rights in strict analogy with the institutions of domestic political membership and legislation. On the one hand, the league wins back the freedom of national legislation; on the other, it loses the very issue of perpetual peace: the transfer of national sovereignty to a world power. 'Perpetual peace' enacts both a consistent liberal position of freedom/peace under the force of law and a consistent pragmatic position regarding relative freedoms between national law and global self-obligation. In other words, Kant's essay uses the domestic analogy *and* breaks it at one and the same time. Chapters 1 and 2 have expounded, in turn, Habermas's re-reading of the Kantian aporia in terms of the 'quasi'-juridification or 'quasi'-constitutionalization of international relations, with emphasis more on the legalization of human rights, less on nation-state behaviour. I wish to stress here, in the context of EU law and Kant's simultaneous threading and breaking of the domestic analogy, what 'quasi' entails.

It implies, precisely, the need to separate out relations between rights, law and force at the various levels of human jurisdiction in a globalized world. In part agreement with the theoretical moves of institutionalists and the English School, the cosmopolitan perspective looks to different understandings of legal obligation and motivation in a tiered system of legal governance. Strict critical reference to the domestic analogy, underpinning the Realist critique of cosmopolitanism, is consequently not appropriate in this context: the terms to be analogized are heterogeneous. The analogy only remains appropriate as a loose normative horizon of possibility and impossibility, one under which human societies invent the terms of international freedom under law (see chapter 1, section 2.3 and 2.6). This unmaking and making of the analogy is not that of Kant: Kant shifted between idealism and pragmatism *within* the aporia, but was unable to think out of it. If, however, one thinks about the relations between law and force, right and obligation, obligation and polity in differentiated terms, there is, strictly speaking, no aporia and no analogy to begin with! EU law and European legal obligation, underpinned by economic coordination, point us in this direction. 'We' consists here in an indeterminate humanity under material constraints. Realism is consequently incorrect to dismiss the immediate exogenous effect of law on state behaviour because, here, at a deeper conceptual level, it is wrong to fit contemporary cosmopolitan ideas into domestic analogical thought. Within the terms of the same argument, it is also incorrect to accuse this same thought of Eurocentrism.

I turn, finally in this section, to conditions (1) and (5): constituent pressure on governments and the shaping of state-power by making state leaders individually accountable for the government of their peoples. Here, cosmopolitan argument necessarily turns to the ICC (for example: Archibugi, 2008, pp. 168–71; Benhabib, 2006, pp. 73–4; Cabrera, 2004, pp. 73–4; Hayden, 2005, pp. 108–16; Held, 2004, pp. 123–5; Singer, 1972, pp. 117–24). The court came into force in July 2002 after prolonged NGO pressure led to 60 countries ratifying the 1998 statute. The court's remit is limited and clear. Where national governments are either unable or unwilling to prosecute their own citizens accused of genocide, war crimes or crimes against humanity, the ICC may intervene and demand remedy for the violation of the human rights concerned by prosecuting those in command (Rome Statute of the ICC, Part II 'Jurisdiction, admissibility and applicable law', articles 1–14). This remit implies three things:

1 Inscribed within the legal legacy of the post-Second World War Nuremberg and Tokyo trials, crimes committed against humanity do not only concern the victims. They concern humanity as a whole.
2 State leaders are no longer protected by the immunity of nation-state sovereignty (the fundamental move away from Article 2 of the UN Charter).
3 The principle of universal jurisdiction has become legally effective. That government individuals can be prosecuted anywhere in the world for criminal acts on their own territory implies the generality of a universal law.

The ICC is meeting major political problems. It has so far been unable to define 'a war of aggression'. It is not independent from the UN Security Council mandate and therefore does not function universally. Its timing of prosecutions has been politically wild, and, most importantly, it is unable to enforce its prosecutorial declarations. These qualifications do not, however, undermine the case for the ICC as such. This cosmopolitan case remains at present normative, not political. The ICC must become more independent and impartial in the years that follow, in order to gain a universal legal reputation. To cut its relations with the UNSC is a critical condition for this. Those who argue, therefore, that a regionalization of international justice would be more appropriate to prevent both conflicts and Western imperialism are mistaken (see, for example, Mamdani, 2009). Regional courts are to be encouraged, but they will themselves only work effectively in a larger network of judgement. The largeness of the network is more likely to improve impartiality and reduce particularism. And it is less likely, not more, to foster legal hegemony.

Even at this precocious stage of the ICC's life, one can make the argument, *contra* Realism, that the representatives of states will become legally bound at the world level: not because the rules of the ICC are not applied selectively (Goldsmith and Posner are right), but, rather, because states will gradually internalize the courts' norms (regarding specific crimes) as standard behaviour for themselves under conditions of universal coordination. This, at least, seems to me the best cosmopolitan claim.

With both these examples, I stress that the effect of international law on state behaviour is difficult to delimit conceptually because the relations between different levels and different modalities of legal obligation are in process. I have here moved the empirical Realist point to the conceptual point of 'category errors'. The cosmopolitan response to Realism has been made in normative, institutional and legal terms – on the condition that the normative is understood through historical process and that the legal is differentiated. The Realist focus on the absence of world government loses conceptual clarity in this move. That said, at a practical level, at this stage of history, states must lead: hence the importance of the Realist framework. It is this requirement of state-led global leadership that makes 'humanitarian intervention' and the 'moralization of politics' such hot issues. I now turn to the cosmopolitan response to Realist criticisms of this moralization and to a cosmopolitan understanding of prudence and a political ethics of the lesser violence.

4 Humanitarian Intervention: Towards a Cosmopolitan Realism

Patricia Owens's argument, outlined in chapter 2, was subtle and clear: violence is not simply empirical; it is structural to making the end of politics moral. Habermas and his followers rely consequently on the violence of humanitarian intervention to produce the global public that, *post factum*, legitimates such intervention. The failures of the second Iraq war show that the NATO intervention in Kosovo was not 'a benign model for humanitarian intervention' (Owens, 2007, p. 106). Williams's parallel argument for a prudential 'philosophy of limits' resists equally the liberal cosmopolitan wish ('rational universalism', in his terms) to subordinate international politics to high moral ends (Williams, 2005, p. 184). In doing so, he also makes a comparison between George W. Bush's neo-imperial policy of 'democratic globalism' and NATO's role of providing 'liberal order' in Kosovo (Williams, 2007, pp. 127, 146–7), a comparison that is more explicitly countenanced by the strong anti-Wilsonian position regarding US foreign policy by Tony Smith (Smith, 2009 and 2010). For Hawthorn and Zolo, the worst effect of humanitarian intervention from Bosnia onwards is the perception of, and consequent resistance to, liberal imperialism (Hawthorn, 2003; Zolo, 1997).

A Habermasian-type defence of the intervention in Kosovo, on the one hand, and criticism of the invasion of Iraq, on the other, needs, however, to be more carefully distinguished by these Realist arguments. Making this distinction precise promotes, I would claim, the cosmopolitan counter-argument for seeking *more* legal and political universality and generality among state-determined global arrangements. As I will argue again in response to IR postmodernism, conflation of liberalism and neo-conservatism, within wider traditions of the moralization of politics, loses the political importance of careful distinctions.[6]

The intervention in Kosovo, led by the Clinton administration, redounded to the particular power of NATO because of the Russian and Chinese vetoes. UN legal sanction was preferred, but made impossible given the particular constitution of the UNSC. Russian and Chinese obstruction was made in the name of the sovereign equality of member states of the UN, but its evident reason was power politics (see Michael Ignatieff's response to Robert Skidelsky in Skidelsky and Ignatieff, 1999). Obstruction was not therefore advanced in the name of *a greater legitimacy of power*. The point is important for a politics of the least bad or the lesser violence. Since Realist analysis is precisely concerned with such a political ethics, it fails to assume the point at theoretical cost.

The Kosovo intervention rode on the back of UN failure in Srebrenica in 1995, during which the Dutch UN peacekeeping force was instrumentalized to abet the murder of 8,000 Muslim males (see Robertson, 2002, pp. 81–2). NATO's concern to prevent the Yugoslavian President Milosevic from further ethnic cleansing in predominantly Albanian Kosovo worked with this previous failure. Weighing up the legitimacy of intervention, the risks of casualties and the potential for post-conflict development, NATO opposed its violence to what was considered the greater violence of Serbian aggression (see Freedman, 2000). This intervention can be considered to constitute a lesser violence in a given economy of violence.

The Kosovo situation obviously became complex. Both Albanians and Serbians were killed fairly relentlessly during the six-week period of NATO air-strikes. The strikes on Serbia produced the inevitable mistakes of war, but civilian death could have been further avoided. Common accusations, however, that the intervention actually *increased* the likelihood of Albanians being killed and/or displaced by Serbian forces (or that the NATO air-strikes were too reckless in nature) should be rejected (Human Rights

Watch, 2000); the intervention actually came *too late* to prevent Kosovo Albanian victims (again, see Freedman, 2000; Sciolino and Bronner, 1999). Considerable efforts were made prior to the military solution to find a diplomatic solution, ending in the failure of the Rambouillet agreements (Weller, 1999). US and European ground troops should have been introduced into Kosovo earlier, both to contain the Serbs from within Kosovo territory and to stop the Kosovo Liberation Army taking revenge on Serb Albanians. Some 500 Yugoslav civilians were killed during the air campaign, while 10,350 Kosovars were massacred, and up to 863,000 were expelled and 590,000 internally displaced (Ball et al., 2002). After the initial accusation by Amnesty International that the NATO bombing of a Serbian state radio station (in which 16 civilians died) constituted a war crime, NATO was understood not to have committed any such crime by *post factum* reports on the 1999 air offensive (Human Rights Watch, 2001). NATO also handed control of Kosovo over to the UN after the end of hostilities. The UN committed itself to a fair trial of the Serbian offenders and to reconstruction under the aegis of the UN. Serb policy in Kosovo does not bear moral equivalence with the Holocaust, as argued at the time by President Bill Clinton and NATO commanders (Clinton, 1999; W. Clark, 2001). Serbs' explicitly planned persecution of the Kosovo Albanians (1.5 million people displaced) outweighed, however, a lack of response on the part of the leading states of the 'international community'. This 'community' is predominantly Western and highly selective: Rwanda was ignored five years earlier, with 800,000 Tutsis and Tutsi and Hutu refugees massacred (Vidal, 1998). But the point here concerns *whether the intervention in Kosovo was justified,* not *whether it was a selective intervention.* The question is a normative one of international principle of power. The above balance of factors adds up to a justification of the intervention for the barrister Geoffrey Robertson. Although it was internationally illegal, because of Russian and Chinese obstruction on the UNSC, Robertson argues that 'on balance, Kosovo was a just and lawful war' (Robertson, 2002, p. 448). This cosmopolitan logic of intervention is one of lesser violence or the least bad (compare Ignatieff, 2005, and Ian Clark on borderline legitimacy judgements in I. Clark, 2005, pp. 199–205). Cosmopolitan political argument for intervention in Kosovo is 'prudent' in this sense. I therefore adopt the political logic of classical Realism in order to justify one intervention against another and defend a prudent cosmopolitan calculation on the point of military intervention in general.

The difference in the second Iraq war is immediate. The coalition forces could have been legally sanctioned if they had allowed the UN inspectors to continue their work on the ground to the satisfaction of sceptics (violence as a last resort). France put forward no absolute veto until explicitly challenged by clearly preconceived US/UK determination. Too many indications, at the time, pointed to a lack of convincing evidence: Dick Cheney's linkage of Saddam Hussein with al-Qaida; Tony Blair's and George W. Bush's 'evidence' of long-range Iraqi gun manufacture; Colin Powell's self-defeating presentation of mobile chemical plants at the UNSC (see Sands, 2005, pp. 174–204, esp. pp. 177, 184, 188). It was also tragically and comically unclear in the lead-up to the war what the objects of intervention were: removal of weapons of mass destruction; regime change; settlement of old scores; *post-factum*, stopping crimes against humanity (see Bellamy, 2005) – all forming an integral part of the 'global war against terror'. Reasons for military intervention shifted according to personality, whim and resistant fact. After the invasion, the US government foolishly divided the spoils of victory (oil, infrastructure and private security contracts) among its corporate friends (mission states must not stand to profit). No commitment was given prior to the war either to reconstruct Iraq or to persuade the UN to return after hostilities had ended. No care was taken to give the Ba'athist leaders a fair trial before an international tribunal. The hanging of Hussein was done in a macabre ritual of revenge which, caught on a mobile phone and spun around the world, recalled feudal exercise of justice and intensified the international perception of injustice. Whatever the ultimate historical outcome of the war in Iraq (even, democracy in the Middle East), the war cannot be justified, given the above-mentioned flaunting of international legal procedure. The second Iraq war remains, from a cosmopolitan perspective, therefore, a critical moment of regression in moves towards global leadership and international legitimacy. Ethical vision in world politics remains in structural difficulty as a result.

The invasions of Kosovo and Iraq were both illegal; but the invasion of Iraq from the outset had neither legitimacy nor a sense of lawfulness. This distinction between the two wars is, I am claiming, critical for political judgement in the international domain regarding global rules. The first was perceived as legitimate, if difficult. *Post factum* considerations (the independence of Kosovo) continue to play a part in how that legitimacy will be understood. The continuing conflict between Serbian and Kosovo Albanians was one consequence of NATO's choice to employ air-strikes alone and not air-strikes with ground forces (Kupchan, 2005). The second was a caricature of international law to begin with, which no considerations after the event can contribute to its becoming retrospectively legitimate. A clear distinction between the two wars is possible and necessary: possible because of the manner in which international law was flouted; necessary because such distinctions foreground and validate prospectively international legal and military procedures. The second Iraq war has severely damaged the perception of these procedures. Examples of legitimate state practice in conjunction with international institution would clarify their more proper use in the future. Chapter 7 takes this point up again in response to the postmodern IR critique of universalism.

In *Just and Unjust Wars* Michael Walzer argues: 'The cardinal mistake of the realists is to suppose that if one fights for "universal moral principles," one must always fight in the same way, as if universal principles did not have concrete and diverse applications' (1977, p. 117). Regarding processes of democratization, Daniele Archibugi says, in similar vein:

> Democracy is a regime that must be constructed bottom-up and not top-down and that may be imported but not exported. The true dispute is therefore not whether or not to pursue democratization but, on the contrary, what ways and means must be used to achieve this objective. (2008, p. 279)

Whatever their respective differences (weaker and stronger forms of cosmopolitanism), both Walzer and Archibugi argue for distinctions between *different* means to the *same* end. These distinctions have been made clear in the above account of legal, diplomatic and military means in the Kosovo and Iraq wars. Realism's accusation against 'cosmopolitan' intervention that it does not distinguish enough between means and ends is, in this context, somewhat ironic! Hawthorn's, Zolo's and Owens's respective forms of scepticism with regard to the limitless logic of humanitarian intervention, together with Owens's, Williams's and Smith's conflations of neo-conservatism and liberal universalism, do not pinpoint this distinction as *the* critical criterion of judgement regarding intervention. Habermas's argument for a distinction between Kosovo and Iraq does (2006, pp. 85–6, 89). The juridification of international relations remains an important normative end in this context of legitimate and illegitimate wars.

For Habermas, violence must be seen to be one of last resort; the case for intervention must be persuasively argued; material advantages must be seen *not* to accrue to the enforcers of international criminal law; reconstruction plans must be in the offing; international trial of enemy leaders must follow their capture (if taken alive), etc. (ibid., pp. 121ff, 169–73). Only if due process and judicial review at the global level of law is instituted, will the legitimacy of international legality be shared beyond those who broker power in the international domain (ibid., p. 189). In the name of the lesser violence in the global public domain, an appropriate cosmopolitan response to Realist critiques of neo-conservative and liberal interventionism is, therefore, twofold. First, more reflection upon and enactment of universalization procedures are required, not less. This reflection and enactment refine the distinction between ends and means, but, second, they demand, as Realism requires, matching legal ends and legal means.

Such a legal cosmopolitan argument on juridification constitutes a convincing response, I would suggest, to both the Realist 'moralization of politics' argument and its insistence on aligning ends and means. For, it harnesses Realist argument and uses it against the Realist critique. Politically, however, the cosmopolitan position remains problematic. The problem concerns the question of prudence *qua* international political judgement. In his excellent rehearsal of cosmopolitan arguments, Robert Fine comments that Habermas's norm of juridification of international relations wishes to overcome political judgement (Fine, 2007, p. 93). In terms of the spectrum of cosmopolitanism, it anticipates, that is, a purely legal modality of cosmopolitanism. Fine writes:

> There is something unsettling in [Habermas's] repeated argument that political judgement is necessary *only* because the constitutionalisation of international law is not yet complete.... The question is whether political judgement is a stop-gap measure necessary in the absence of clear, concise and authoritative criteria of justification, or rather an irreducible aspect of justifying, authorising and monitoring military interventions. (Ibid.)

For Fine, the Habermasian transfer of responsibility from the political system of state interests and hegemony to the legal sphere looks attractive in the face of moral justifications of the use of force. He accepts, therefore, the above distinction between ends and means that Owens's partial conflation of the two wars ignores. That said, the turn to international and cosmopolitan law cannot 'substitute for cosmopolitan political argument' (ibid., p. 95). As Fine emphasizes, '[a] *politics* of intervention would not disappear in a world of cosmopolitan law enforcement' (ibid). In other words, the legitimacy *of* legality in a world without world republican government cannot be proceduralized. Government leaders in the international system must *make* the argument for military intervention. Judicial application of universal criteria to particular cases misses this crucial realist moment of judgement between norm and experience. Application of universal rule is never automatic; it has to be deliberated over and fought for. At this historical point in time, as I have argued throughout this chapter in symmetrical response to Realism's 'state-centrism', the political prudence of democratic state behaviour is therefore critical (see and compare Habermas on 'hegemonic liberalism', 2006, pp. 183–5). The argument upholds political cosmopolitanism in my second sense of cosmopolitan judgement and argument in the political domain (chapter 1, section 2.6).

The following distinction between *political moralism* and *moral politics* results from these arguments. For political realists, political moralism constitutes the moralization of politics: both neo-conservatives and liberals are political moralists. Realism overrides, here, the Kantian distinction between 'moral politics' (the subordination of politics to morality through law) and 'political moralism' (the fashioning of morality to political expediency and interest) (Kant, 1795/1991, pp. 118, 123–4). Habermas argues persuasively that juridification of international relations breaks, precisely, the arbitrary moralization of politics. His Kantian argument for legal mediation between morality and politics is, however, too rigid. Realists are accordingly right to be vigilant regarding the evacuation of political specificity in legal cosmopolitanism. The manner in which they criticize Habermas's position is, however, misplaced. The argument for impartial procedure is the correct normative horizon since it will give human rights increasingly 'legal' status. The argument for basic cosmopolitan freedoms under weak global law can only be refuted if a better understanding of both interstate and cosmopolitan freedoms is proposed. Tolerance of other values is not a good enough argument. Williams's reasoning, as we saw in the last chapter, that prudence requires 'recognition of the *particularity* of *all* values' (2005, p. 188, my emphasis) is not conceptually strong enough; it also goes against Morgenthau's own thinking of universal moral constraint on political action (Morgenthau, 1971, pp. 231–2). Universal coordination requires agreed-upon principles effective behind institution-building. These principles can be realistically appraised as minimal; but such principles require some set of universal values. The general principles of the dignity of life – food, shelter, freedom from bodily harm, freedom of expression, social recognition – can be supported by all nation-states that work with international institutions. At the international level these principles must be purposefully embodied by the relevant agents of power: leaders and representatives of government.

Such embodiment is a *risk* and a *decision* and not simply a matter of procedure. It is the risk and decision of political judgement that the classical version of Realism correctly embraces. This risk and decision could go something like the following from a cosmopolitan perspective: 'Our country believes that military intervention for the protection of human lives is appropriate in x case. This is the ideology we are accordingly defending, and these are our reasons why it applies here and now to x. We are prepared to defend these reasons under close scrutiny, and we wish in so doing to persuade others (whose interests will not necessarily be ours) of our point of view. If we cannot do so, but our point of view nevertheless carries weight due to skewed conditions of executive decision-making in the UNSC, we have failed the cosmopolitan political argument, and we are not offering global leadership. Resistance to the legitimacy of the decision in the name of anti-imperialism will necessarily emerge, whether the decision is right or wrong. If we can do so to the extent that a perceived majority is in agreement, or a new majority has emerged from out of the struggle of debate and interest, we are beginning to make cosmopolitan political argument, and we will begin to be perceived as legitimate global leaders. Our further actions will confirm or belie our words.'

At state and interstate level, this is a moral politics that both cosmopolitanism and classical versions of Realism can countenance. It constitutes a clear defence of cosmopolitan judgement and something like a 'cosmopolitan realism'.[7]

5 From the Principle of Sovereignty to the Principle of Subsidiarity

Let me return, finally, to the first definition of political cosmopolitanism: the project of cosmopolitan democracy, and see how, slightly reconfigured, one can make an argument for it in response to Realism and on the basis of a differentiated universalism. No section of my exposition of the Realist critique of cosmopolitanism attended directly to the issue of democracy. That said, Realism's use of 'category errors' underpins its simple dismissal of the cosmopolitan democratic project, and Goldsmith and Posner's more local arguments against it were based on the weakness of global motivation, the trade-off between weak democratic institutions and strong global governance, and the complexity of nation-state interests (see chapter 2, pp. 60–3). My argument differs, in emphasis, from the general democratic colours of Archibugi and Held's positions, but, as said, I consider the following argument necessary to meet the Realist critique.

Held and Archibugi consider the fate of democracy in a globalized world in the form of a chiasmus (see chapter 1, section 2.6). On the one hand, democratic nation-states require global coordination in order to maintain their democratic credentials at home; the domestic democratic deficit will otherwise grow, and the democratic principles of self-determination and freedom will likely give way to new forms of populism and nationalism or to oligarchy. On the other hand, global coordination itself requires democratization, and such calls for democratization necessarily borrow from domestic models of democracy to conceive of reform. This chiasmus both makes and loosens the analogy between global and national democratic polities. It compels us to consider cosmopolitan democracy less, I argued in chapter 1, as an analogous extension of democracy to the global realm, but more as a *reinvention* of it under conditions of globalization. I now emphasize this point of reinvention in response to the Realist critique that political cosmopolitanism commits a 'category error'. Held has increasingly insisted that the argument for cosmopolitan polity seeks 'the creation of an effective and accountable administrative, legislative and executive capacity at regional and global levels to *complement* those at the local and national levels' (2003, p. 182). He is therefore arguing beyond an obsolete opposition between world government and nation-state. Public decisions must provide and deliver public goods at the appropriate level of effective governance and be placed within a wider context that should embrace, as far as possible, democratic principle (ibid., p. 168). As I stressed in chapter 1, such transformation requires, in analogy with domestic democracy, fundamental reform of the UN system so that it may become something like a just civil constitution: a two-tiered assembly of states and of peoples, a curtailed executive, an impartial judiciary, etc. The price of theoretical rigour is, precisely, Realism. To respond to Realist critique, this normative horizon requires, rather, emphasizing that theorizing and practising the levels between municipal, national, regional and global forms of governance should be done in terms of the principle of *subsidiarity*. I argue here that the present solution to the above chiasmus is first and foremost this principle; the latter also works, as a normative horizon, with the historical reality of 'weak' law.

The principle of subsidiarity means that decisions are taken at the lowest level at which they are both effective and legitimate regarding the people that these decisions affect (Cabrera, 2004, pp. 95–8; Follesdal, 2000, p. 86; Held, 2005a, p. 14). Concepts of multilevel governance are now commonplace in international relations theory. The political cosmopolitan position is particular in that, to one side of effectiveness, it insists on democratic legitimacy, not simply accountability (compare Kahler and Lake, 2003; Keohane and Nye, 2003).

One must be careful here. Kant's, Miller's, Nagel's and Zolo's different emphases on the legitimate and functional constraints of the modern nation-state are important (see chapter 1, pp. 25–7; chapter 2. pp. 64–5). Effective response to the 2008 financial crisis would not have been possible without the principle of national fiscal sovereignty (the central banks as lenders of last resort). The political theorist Jean Cohen has argued persuasively that the principle of the sovereign equality of states is not Westphalian (Cohen 2004, 2005, 2008). Article 2/1 of the 1947 UN Charter instituted the latter for the first time in history, and guaranteed, in so doing, decolonization in the second half of the twentieth century. Cosmopolitan commitment to the dignity of moral personhood risks, she argues, overriding the political gains of this equality. In this sense, she is right to consider it a bulwark principle against neo-imperial manoeuvres on the part of Great Powers. That said, the fiscal response on the part of sovereign macroeconomic policy would have been impossible *without* the simultaneous global coordination of central banks and governments: through the G20, informal procedure, the Basel-based Bank for International Settlements (BIS) and the IMF. Political judgement regarding the importance of intervention in states to protect the dignity of life is, I have also argued, necessary as well. The principle of subsidiarity goes some way towards reinventing supra-national *and* national democratic polity without either compromising unduly national autonomy or falling into the trap of a universal state. At the very least, it constitutes a principled response to the twenty-first-century condition of interdependence, which is not unrealistic, but which will have to be fought for ideologically.

The principle was first called upon at a supra-national level by the European Union, although it does not work effectively within the EU decision-making process (see Constantin, 2008). There is a priori no reason why, as a principle, it cannot gradually apply to multitiered forms of world governance. This application implies several things that re-configure the concept of cosmopolitan democracy.

First, the democratic idea of self-determination must be rethought *within* the differentiated terms of the principle of subsidiarity. Self-determination of the world's peoples *as* a world people is a non-starter (unless humanity comes to differentiate itself from external enemies). The democratic principle of autonomy must be reinvented as both the crucial ground of the principle of subsidiarity (those people who are affected by decisions must in some institutional way belong to the decision-making process) and as a derivative of it (subsidiarity trumps collective deliberation where the latter is impossible or too inefficient in the circumstances). Use of the domestic analogy, the brunt of the Realist critique of political cosmopolitanism, is here replaced by political invention of legitimate, tiered governance.

Second, the reinvention of the principle of autonomy leads to thinking of multitiered governance in terms of 'constitutional mixes'. There is nothing new in this mixed 'extension' of the concept of democracy. This is the fifth major historical moment of democratic invention. Direct, representative, communist and social variants of democracy precede it. The second moment – from 'direct' to 'representative' democracy – accompanied the formation of the nation-state. It is worthwhile focusing on American representative democracy, given its size constraints. The fathers of the American Republic argued that representation meant both representation of sub-federal interest and presentation of federal interest. Democracy was accordingly rethought at two levels: republican self-determination *and* republican election and selectivity. As the political theorist Bernard Manin carefully argues (1996), the reinvention of democracy in the eighteenth century was *never* democratic in the first place. Representative democracy is, in Aristotelian terms, a 'mixed constitution' that has both democratic *and* aristocratic elements (ibid., pp. 204–5). Regular transparent elections and an independent judiciary guarantee popular and constitutional constraint on legislative and executive power. Representatives to both houses of Congress are, however, necessarily different from the people: it is, in principle, their 'superior' political talents that take them to Congress; not either money or populism. Once there, their interests are also independent from their voters, and that independence is structurally crucial to block lobbying. On both accounts, Manin argues, what is democratic is the consent given to, or withdrawn from, a substantive and functional superiority (the elective system). What is not democratic is the 'superiority' itself. A good democracy functions, precisely, with leaders who are effective because they are able to stand at a distance from particular interests; it cannot only perform democratically through a vigilant, proactive people. The implications of this argument are clear and rhyme with the theses of the chapter as a whole *qua* a cosmopolitan response to Realism.

The reinvention of democracy today will break in part with representative democracy, as representative democracy did in part with direct democracy. The failure of the communist model of modern direct democracy places the realities of self-determination and collective deliberation only at the *local* level in complex societies of functional differentiation and universal coordination. Representative democracy is informed by aristocratic elements because of the structural disjuncture between governors and governed. Given – as Goldsmith and Posner unduly emphasized *contra* democratic global governance – the widening gap between governors and governed at regional and global levels, cosmopolitan democratic inventions must embody these 'aristocratic' elements. The necessary complexity of global electoral systems, the governance gap between principals and agents, and the crucial presence of intergovernmental officers require constitutional mixes. It would be counter-effective to the cosmopolitan democratic argument to argue otherwise. From this perspective, advocates of cosmopolitan democracy could be considered, rightly, to be arguing that the given 'aristocratic' elements of global governance need new terms of consent based on the principle of subsidiarity.

The argument that democracies are becoming 'decentralized' is made effectively by the French political historian Pierre Rosanvallon (see, particularly, Rosanvallon, 2006 and 2008). The moment of popular sovereignty is increasingly reduced to the electoral moment, while governmental and non-governmental commissions are asked to provide the terms of public reason on issues like immigration and integration, energy policy, climate change, and food and health policy. This decentralization harbours dangers of bureaucracy and elitism; but, for Rosanvallon, it is in principle to be affirmed. It provides the occasion both for more local democracy (particularly urban democracy) and for impartial reflection on difficult issues pertaining to complex societies that require domestic, regional and global analysis. Public servants, rational experts and consultants, bureaucrats, non-state actors – all are important members of this decentralized public reason. Decentralization accompanies universal coordination; it does not go against it. The more differentiated societies become, the more universal coordination is required, but the more likely this coordination will take place in decentralized forms (compare, again, Slaughter, 2004). This is a structural given of international and global society, and is distinct from the centralization of nation-states. There is a growing convergence, I would therefore argue, between new democratic forms at the domestic level and institutional growth at the global level. In this second sense, the political cosmopolitan argument for cosmopolitan democracy is empirically meaningful.

It is not a question of replicating a centralized democratic model at the global level; rather, globalization is changing *all* levels of governance: at the democratic governmental level and at the regional and global governance levels. Within this change, there is both convergence and divergence, and the large challenge of cosmopolitan theory and practice is to conceive of a tiered democratic system within the principle of subsidiarity. I suggest that, broken down in this manner, the cosmopolitan democratic argument looks much more persuasive than the Realist critique of the domestic analogy and of global motivation would lead us to think.

6 Conclusion

This chapter responds to the Realist critique of cosmopolitanism in five rounds of argument. First, it places the normative in relation to history and under conditions of interdependence; as a result the Realist distinction between normative prescription (international law) and empirical motivation (state interests) is considered simplistic. Second, it focuses on the intertwining of power and justice with regard to legitimate international behaviour in an interdependent world, and it looks to a more expansive notion of national interest, under conditions of interdependence, with regard to global collective action problems that ensue from these conditions. On both accounts, state-led global leadership is considered to require minimal cosmopolitan responsibilities. It then looks, third, more widely at Realist use of category errors to undermine universalism in the international political field. In section 3 my focus is on international law; in Section 5 on cosmopolitan democracy. Section 3 reflects upon a differentiated account of international law that undermines, in response, the liberal analogy between domestic and international law and seeks to identify the particularity of post-national law under conditions of regional and international differentiation. It makes an argument for the paradigmatic value of the EU in these terms. Fourth, the chapter then addresses the Realist critique of interventionism; it seeks distinctions between different interventions on the basis of principle and argument; and it advocates, in complementary manner, both legal cosmopolitan mediation between morality and international politics and cosmopolitan political justification and leadership. Section 4 consequently defends a cosmopolitan politics of the lesser violence that meets cosmopolitan requirements of international responsibility and Realist requirements of prudence. Fifth, having made this argument for a more minimal political cosmopolitanism, the chapter then returns to its maximal definition, the project of cosmopolitan democracy, and rehearses its interest to IR through exposition of the principle of subsidiarity and its differentiated entailments.

All five rounds of argument bring to bear upon IR Realist theory the following claims:

1 Contemporary cosmopolitan ideas should be understood within a broad tradition of liberalism, which address the practical reality of interdependence, and not pinned to an abstract, normative 'utopianism'.
2 These normative ideas should be articulated historically and, at one and the same time both legally and politically, within differentiated understandings of interest and universalism. They must, therefore, also be differentiated in content and reach according to the agent concerned.
3 Given both interdependence and the state system, democratic states should lead by example, by good political argument, and by assuming minimal cosmopolitan commitments in order to address global collective action problems.

These arguments imply, at this moment in history, that non-democratic states should be increasingly locked in to global commitments, obligations and rules. The future struggles between non-ideological power and ideological value are obviously critical in this respect. Cosmopolitan argument assumes, here, an optimism of political will in relation to the practical reality of interdependence.

The difficulties that this cosmopolitan argument meets suggest four research agendas that are closely related to the international political field and its realist specificities: (i) a systematic reconsideration of the role of the state in cosmopolitan politics; (ii) a careful elaboration of a cosmopolitan political ethics; (iii) a differential analysis of law; and (iv) a consistent theory of differentiated democracy following the principle and institutional possibilities of subsidiarity. With these agendas, I claim, cosmopolitanism may be an effective argument within IR theory.

Institutional and political cosmopolitanisms constitute normative, but concrete, responses to processes of globalization. These processes are correctly understood as an economic phenomenon, whatever else they also are: technological, communicational, social and cultural. This chapter has pushed the argument for a sophisticated liberal cosmopolitanism in the context of Realist insight. It has made little attempt, however, to articulate different conceptions of the liberal within it. Marxism in IR is both an economically driven theorization of world politics and a good critic of liberal formalism. A cosmopolitan response to it requires an account, and defence, of what a progressive liberal approach to politics means at the global level. The next two chapters look at the Marxist critique of cosmopolitanism and a cosmopolitan response in this light.

4

The Marxist Critique of Cosmopolitanism

The previous response to the Realist critique of cosmopolitanism made a great deal of the constraining effects of growing dependence between states. Going back to the ground-breaking work of Keohane and Nye, *Power and Interdependence* (1977), interdependence can be considered a predominantly economic phenomenon. Under the more recent term of 'globalization' (Defarges, 1997; Steger, 2003), its most trenchant critic is to be found in the school of Marxism and its avatars (Neo-Marxism or post-Marxism).[1] As a critical body of thought regarding liberalism, Marxism survived the end of communism, although the orthodox postulates of revolution, of a revolutionary agent of change, the international proletariat, and belief in the efficiency of a planned economy have not. Marxism's residing interest – whether it is in political sociology, political theory or IR – lies in the nature of its critique of economic and political liberalism. In the specific field of IR, it offers tools of analysis through which: (i) power and interest are considered in economic terms; (ii) political economy is diagnosed in explicitly political terms, but with moral commitments; and (iii) a critique is made of liberal universalism, in general, and of neo-liberalism, in particular (see Frieden et al., 2009). Despite the theoretical and practical failures of communism, Marxism's value lies in its analysis of the inextricable relation between economics and politics in the domestic and international domains.

Since cosmopolitanism embodies basic liberal principles, a Marxist critique of cosmopolitanism necessarily deepens its constitutive criticisms of liberalism. In the recent contexts of globalization and the doctrine of neo-liberalism, this critique concerns directly the shape and role of the global economy in world politics and the relation between economics and politics in a global capitalist system. If one follows the work of David Held, cosmopolitanism constitutes the right response to globalization (Held, 2004). Marxists argue, conversely, that cosmopolitanism is far from providing an adequate response because of the nature of *economic power*. The debate between Marxist-inspired critique, on the one hand, and cosmopolitanism, on the other, may have just begun with the contemporary shift of economic power to Asia. In this chapter and the next, I consider this debate from a specific, narrow angle. I wish to see in what way cosmopolitanism responds to a radical critique of liberal universalism in the economic field and of the internationalization of liberal economics, and how, in response to this critique, it frames institutional arrangements to further the widest possibility of self-fulfilling lives. What concerns me, then, over the next two chapters, is how *economic globalization* should be *governed*.

Before giving a breakdown of this chapter, I should say what I am not doing so that the terms of debate are clear.[2] The debate which I set up here between Marxism and cosmopolitanism does not concern an explicit exposition of 'global justice'. Commitments to global justice concerns are, loosely, assumed; it is the institutional implications of such commitments that interest me more. As I expounded in chapter 1, section 2.2, moral cosmopolitans are roughly divided into two groups: those, like Charles Beitz, Thomas Pogge, David Held and Simon Caney, who emphasize moral personhood and commitments to moral personhood; those, like David Miller, Thomas Nagel and John Rawls, who emphasize the difference between the moral equivalence of persons and our commitments to people beyond national borders (see pp. 23–8 and 34–6). The difference is important when considering the extension of social justice to the global level: strong cosmopolitans advocate this extension and look to ways to address it; weak cosmopolitans refuse such extension given the particularity of the political conditions under which social justice functions. Following Pogge (2008), I argued that concerns with global justice have an important economic dimension since they address the systemic nature of world poverty and inequality: institutional cosmopolitanism follows from moral cosmopolitanism as a result. I do not believe, however, as Pogge argues, that there is a 'single criterion of justice for the world as a whole' (ibid., p.145). My own argument is threefold. First, increasing interdependence creates widening sensibility to harm and widening responsibility to the causes of such harm. Second, given the nature of the interests the agent represents, these responsibilities differ according to the agent: a wealthy state's commitments to the alleviation of world poverty are clear, although its first commitment is to a threshold of minimum wealth at home; a transnational civil NGO like Oxfam, on the other hand, looks at poverty in countries in an equal manner. Third, as interdependence tightens (a long-term historical assumption), a state's commitments become more inclusive on specific global issues, since its own interests are defined through others' interests. Now, in a debate between Marxism and cosmopolitanism, discussion of principles of global economic/distributive justice is certainly important: this is, however, not my focus for two reasons.

First, following the three points above, I assume a loose framework within which to discuss global justice: I understand by it a duty to provide all human beings, as far as possible, with the opportunity to lead a self-fulfilling life. *Qua* institutional, such provision should be concerned to provide opportunities of material resource so that human beings are not *materially* prevented from determining what these lives are for themselves. I agree, therefore, with Pogge that moral cosmopolitanism has institutional entailments (see also Cabrera, 2004, 2005); but I also agree with Miller and Rawls that political and civil arrangements cannot be imposed on other countries either theoretically or empirically. That said, returning to my second definition of 'political cosmopolitanism', I think that one can *argue for* such arrangements and that one can *argue for* a loosely defined progressive liberal cosmopolitan position *in order to* change the overall philosophical and economic framework of global public policy (where this policy has had, and continues to have, nefarious empirical effects). I therefore work with David Held's understanding of 'global social democracy' in the next chapter as a general lens through which to think and practise the reform of global capitalism, even though I consider the term theoretically too expansive and imposing. I am interested, in other words, in the institutional implementation of basic duties that form a precondition of the possibility of self-fulfilling lives, not in further exposition of these duties as such.

My second reason returns me to this chapter's concern: the Marxist critique of liberalism and, therefrom, contemporary cosmopolitan ideas. I do not address explicitly principles of global justice within the exposition of Marxist critique since the attainment of justice is not an overriding concern in Marxist theory (rightly or wrongly). Following Allen Wood's interpretation of Marx (Wood, 1972, 1979, 1986), I consider that distributive justice (who deserves what) is, for Marx, a function of economic production and the relations of production (under what relations of property is what produced and consumed); and that the major philosophical and practical concerns that Marx has regarding capitalism and its overthrow are, on the one hand, class-conflict and, on the other, freedom, community and self-fulfilment (see, also, Mészăros, 1975). As we can see from the Marxists' arguments expounded in this chapter, questions of justice cannot be divorced from social and economic preconditions. Deliberation, therefore, upon abstract principles of justice is not a Marxist priority since the terms of justice are determined by the economic modes of production and what they entail socially: economic power and its reorganization constitute the object of Marxist theory (Harvey, 1982; Poulantzas, 1978; Wood, 1979). That said, any concern with the relation between capital and labour at a domestic or international level obviously assumes basic moral commitments: towards a general sense of equity and towards a general sense of equality (Lukes, 1987). I am therefore concerned in this chapter with (again, but for this second reason) a *loose* sense of these commitments in the context of the Marxist critique of cosmopolitanism. My focus is trained on the overall functioning of the capitalist system and institutional responses to it.

What interests me, then, in the debate between Marxism and cosmopolitanism is the position one assumes to globalization and how one considers progressive change within it. This change concerns the *institutional* implications of a basic normative vision that is committed to reducing world poverty and radical inequality. My theoretical analysis is pitched, accordingly, at basic tenets of Marxist analysis with regard to liberalism and capitalism, their consequences for contemporary cosmopolitanism, and general questions of macroeconomic policy in a globalized world.

The chapter contains three sections. Section 1 rehearses the most important tenets of Marxism in the context of classical liberal thought and globalization. Section 2 looks at the contemporary global ideology of neo-liberalism from a Marxist perspective in IR theory and considers the 2007–9 global financial crisis and economic recession in its light. Section 3 then turns to specific Marxist criticisms of cosmopolitanism, which redound to the cosmopolitan substitution of politics by ethics. The reason for the organization and pace of this chapter is straightforward: only with an understanding of the Marxist approach to international relations can its critique of cosmopolitanism *qua* cosmopolitan liberalism be appropriately appraised. Chapter 5 will then make an argument for a progressive liberal cosmopolitanism in response.

1 The Major Tenets of Marxism

I focus on five major constants of Marxist thought, which I foreground in the contexts of both classical liberalism and globalization.

(1) The discourse of *globalization* is nothing but *the ideology of capitalism gone global*, once the communist alternative of a planned economy

proved impractical. For Marxist discourse, globalization constitutes a fundamentally economic process that is contained within capitalist social relations. These relations are founded on the dynamic of capital accumulation, are to the disadvantage of wage-labour, but are veiled under a universalist discourse of 'global interdependence' between nations, peoples and citizens. It is worth recalling on this point Marx and Engels' initial encomium to capitalism in the *Communist Manifesto*:

> The need of a constantly expanding market for its products chases the bourgeoisie over the entire surface of the globe. It must nestle everywhere, settle everywhere, establish connections everywhere. The bourgeoisie has through its exploitation of the world market given a cosmopolitan character to production and consumption in every country. . . . In place of the old local and national seclusion and self-sufficiency, we have intercourse in every direction, universal inter-dependence of nations. And as in material, so also in intellectual production. The intellectual creations of individual nations become common property. National one-sidedness and narrow-mindedness become more and more impossible, and from the numerous national and local literatures, there arises a world literature. The bourgeoisie, by the rapid improvement of all instruments of production, by the immensely facilitated means of communication, draws all, even the most barbarian, nations into civilization. (Marx and Engels, 1848/2005, pp. 71–2)

This passage marks the first theory of globalization (compare Desai, 2002, pp. 4–5). Industrial innovation and the institution of the market economy propel the nineteenth-century European middle class onto the stage 'of universal inter-dependence of nations' and fosters the gradual capitalization of the life-world. For Marx and Engels, the ensuing world market creates 'economic cosmopolitanism' and, concomitantly, the civilization of 'cultural cosmopolitanism'. Contemporary processes of globalization are thus the extension of a dynamic set in place by the emerging Western middle class. This civilizing dynamic is neither just nor unjust: it produces an extraordinary increase in wealth and productive capacity, but at great human cost.

(2) This dynamic is promoted by the *partial* tenets of *classical liberal thought: the theory of free trade and comparative advantage.* These tenets invite critique. Following the work of Adam Smith and David Ricardo, the theory has three components: (i) trade between nations leads to economic growth and national prosperity; (ii) trade encourages nations to find their own production advantage, in relative comparison with those of other nations, and to specialize in that production-capability; and (iii) country-specific specialization enhances overall world growth. As is well known, the theory has large implications (see Hiscox, 2005). *Economically*, it

makes trade a causal factor of national and international growth. Denying that wealth is due either to territory (spoils of war) or to given endowments (natural resources), classical liberal thought refuses autarchy and protectionism and makes the commercial dependence between nations a condition of rising living standards. *Politically*, it affirms the separation of economic civil society from government interference and considers the institution of a transnational market economy to be the major bearer of peace between trading partners. If the latter trade according to their comparative advantage, they will not wish to acquire territory. Classical liberal thought forms the theoretical underpinnings of the beginnings of globalization (Berger, 2003; B. Cohen; 2008, Ravenhill, 2005). It separates the economy from politics and foresees an international economy that functions most efficiently through a self-regulating set of markets, predicated on geographically relative advantages, and curtailed domestic government (Salvatore, 1999).

For Marxism, this theory comprises an 'ideology': that is, a set of ideas, seeking broad if not universal consent, rooted in material interest. There are two reasons for this. First, economic cosmopolitanism hides particular class interests and/or power relations. As an economic system, capitalism depends upon capital accumulation: the realization of surplus value. This accumulation cannot be a 'win–win' situation, as the liberal theory of comparative advantage assumes. Domestically, the 'losers' are the working-class, whose labour power is exploited in order to create surplus value. Internationally, the 'losers' are both those classes and those regions of the world which become disadvantaged by systemically unequal terms of trade and exploitative flows of capital between developed and developing nations (Baran, 1976; Frank, 1971). From a Marxist perspective, the capitalist system consequently presents a structurally agonistic 'zero-sum' game informed by necessarily adverse class and regional interests. Second, from a Marxist reformist position, economic cosmopolitanism downgrades the purpose and outcomes of government. Classical liberal thought was radical at the historical moment of hierarchical societies. With the advent of industrialization, the increasing complexity of modern society and political franchise, liberal advocacy for the curtailment of government failed to address, however, the social consequences of market failure. It thereby underestimated the need for strong government to provide a base-line opportunity for all. Without the massive intervention of government, a freer society is impossible. Inversely put, curtailed government necessarily produces huge disparities of wealth: poverty and inequality, both domestically and internationally (Harvey, 2007).

As a result of these two different points, the argument for the separation of the economic from the political realm, in the name of efficiency, legitimates the national and international rule of capital (the business and financier classes). This separation is endorsed by the universality of formal rights. In liberal capitalist societies, Marx argued in 'On the Jewish Question' (1843), each individual is in principle formally free; but, for the majority, civil and political rights are socially and economically ineffective. The liberal order thus covers over the source of its own power by claiming that the economic sphere is *not* political (Bernstein, 1991; Rose, 1981). Or rather, under the name of the self-regulating market and the rights of freedom, security and property, liberal class-power expresses itself *as* the drive to separate economics from politics. It is not simply that economic forces are forms of power; the very institution of the market is an act of political power. This drive to create efficiency, unfettered by government, leads to the depoliticization of economic society. For revolutionary Marxism, the (re-)politicization of social relations constitutes the only response to classical liberalism: revolutionary overthrow of capitalist relations through the political agency of a class with universal interest (Tucker, 1969). The major failure of communism ensues, however, from the saturation of civil society by communist party interest (see Kornai, 1992). Much Marxist theory has become, as a result, politically reformist – the state no longer reflects the ideology of the middle class – and economically 'Keynesian': the state serves as the appropriate vehicle to institute a compact between capital and labour (Roemer, 1994). Unlike Keynesianism, however, Marxist-inspired critique remains steadfastly critical of capitalism. The reason for this radical scepticism lies in the third major tenet of Marxism.

(3) If capitalism creates growth and opportunity for some, *it is at the same time crisis-prone*. Whatever compromise is possible between the divergent interests of capital and labour, the inevitability of capitalist crisis proves that the process of capital accumulation is irreducibly divisive and in the long-term unsustainable (Harvey, 1982). In his critique of political economy, *Capital*, Marx sets out two logics of capital accumulation and immanent crisis to explain the structural entropy of capital: those of industrial capital and of financial capital. The following summarizes argument from: (i) *Capital*, 1, 'The general law of capitalist accumulation' (Marx, 1867/1990, pp. 762–801); and (ii) *Capital*, 3, 'The law of the tendential fall in the rate of profit' (Marx 1894/1991, pp. 317–78). It is worth considering them in detail here given their institutional implications. For, although the labour theory of value (value is exclusively produced by the factor of labour) is now considered obsolete by economists, and although cosmopolitan literature has shown little interest in Marxist economic theory, the Marxist critique of international political economy still emphasizes these basic logics because of the overall analysis of capital that they

permit. A debate between Marxism and cosmopolitanism requires, accordingly, their understanding.

For Marx, capital is the exchange-value of money which becomes an end in itself (profit), rather than remaining a means to satisfy a need (money's use-value). Industrial capital is nothing but value that valorizes itself through the production process. This accumulation of capital is achieved through the value that labour adds to the means of production, the result of which is sold at a higher value than both the value of the capital originally invested and the value added by labour power ($K-P-K^1$). Following the labour theory of value, the source of profit lies therefore in the ratio of difference between the labour time actually paid and the surplus value realized at the moment of sale. The profit itself resides in the ratio of difference between this surplus value and the overall costs of production. The profit is then reinvested in the production cycle and/or consumed by the owner of the means of production, the capitalist.

The second circuit of valorization is that of loan-capital or financial capital: capital that accumulates through interest alone ($K-K^1$). For Marx, financial capital represents the purest form of capital because its only visible end is to valorize itself. Financial capital can only accumulate, however, if it is predicated on the circuit of industrial capital. While value is only produced through the production process, finance capital is nevertheless itself productive because, as loan capital, it is present both at the beginning and the end of the production process. The financial system constitutes, in other words, the backbone of the real economy, since, without efficient allocation of credit, the capitalist production process would be impossible in the first place. The risk that financial institutions take when allocating money to particular economic agents provides the background condition of growth. That said, for Marx, financial capital remains structurally secondary to, and parasitic upon, the production process. The recurrent temptation of financial capital is to withdraw money from this process and assume that it can valorize itself by itself (that 'one can make money with money alone'). As the historical trajectory of speculative bubbles underlines, this temptation ends up damaging the system of capital accumulation as a whole.

There are, for Marx, two major contradictions in these interrelated circuits of capital valorization.

The first is the tension between the source of value in the production process (labour power) and its increasing diminishment (through increased productivity) to create surplus value. With the growing replacement of manpower by technology to increase value in the short term (under conditions of market competition), the capitalist reduces his profits long term, since labour remains the sole source of added value. Technology transfers value to products, for Marx; it does not produce it (see 'Machinery and large scale industry', in Marx, 1867/1990, pp. 508–17). With increasingly fewer workers to produce added value, the rate of profit will therefore tend to decline. This first contradiction is mitigated within capitalism by a series of 'counteracting factors' for Marx (ibid., pp. 339–49): extension of the working day, cheapening of wages through a surplus idle population ('the industrial reserve army'), extension into foreign markets, constant techno-logical innovation, centralization of capital (takeovers and mergers) or war (destruction of value and stock). 'Economic cosmopolitanism' (global capitalism), initially applauded by the *Communist Manifesto*, constitutes, in essence, a *derivative* effect of this first contradiction. The globalization of capitalist relations saves the system temporarily from immanent col-lapse. In other words, as a socioeconomic system driven by the structural contradiction of capital accumulation, capitalism is both prone *to* crisis and, at the same time, resolves its contradictions and tensions *through* crisis. The fall in the rate of profit is a 'tendency' only (not a strict law in the social scientific sense), since capitalism is able to transform its internal barriers to further valorization into, precisely, occasions for renewal. As a non-economist, I consider this observation to be the major contribution of Marxism to the critique of liberal political economy.

The second contradiction is the relation between financial capital and industrial capital. Financial capital tends over time to pull back and seek autonomy from the production process, seeking to make money with money alone. The valorization of the production process is slow and too dependent on the fluctuations of the labour market (the price of labour). Capital valorization is consequently sought within capital alone: on the stock exchange, through speculation on exchange rates and weak national currencies, and through the buying and selling of real estate. As the depen-dence between nations increases economically during the nineteenth and twentieth centuries, the occasion for speculative capital grows apace. The second contradiction lies in this growing autonomy of financial capital away from industrial capital. Required for the latter to work in the first place, still-born without the profits of industrial production, finance capital nevertheless seeks independence from its twin brother. This contradiction has, however, no 'counteracting factors' that defer its systemic effects. It is only resolved by crisis (the destruction of stocks of value): liquidity and insolvency crises for banks, stock-exchange crashes and the burst of specu-lative bubbles. The last few years have reminded us of these capitalist practices: hence the recent revival of interest in Marx (Mészáros and Foster, 2010).

Both contradictions of industrial and finance capital inform the cycles of capitalism. In sum, from a Marxist/post-Marxist position, general crisis is structural to capitalism but is mitigated by counteracting factors and/or by effective management of the crisis itself. Barriers to capital accumulation can be overcome; the internal scissions between constant and variable capital and between industrial and financial capital cannot. Globalization is, in this sense, the 'negentropic' effect of an entropic system that is structurally fated by these scissions.

(4) The fourth tenet of Marxism can be laid out briefly given the above expositions of classical liberal thought and capital accumulation. As an economic system of power, structurally subject to crisis, *capitalism must constantly legitimate its order and disorders. This legitimacy will depend on the major purveyors of capitalist relations.* Robert Cox and Stephen Gill have theorized these points in IR through the work of Antonio Gramsci and the concept of 'hegemony' (Cox, 1987; Gill, 2003). If the dominance of world order is predominantly economic in the modern era (Lenin, 1917), this dominance is best achieved through a hegemonic ideology that gains, following Gramsci, the consent of the principal economic and political players (Gramsci, 1971, pp. 343–77). US power underpinned the capitalist order of the second half of the twentieth century. After the end of the Cold War and the short-term disappearance of a liberal 'enemy', this hegemony was again secured through the language and values of 'globalization'. Globalization, together with the economic and cultural cosmopolitanism it promotes, serves therefore not simply to legitimate global capitalism (compare point 1), but to assure the hegemonic power, the US, which underwrites it: the process of globalization is, in other words, a neo-imperialist economic phenomenon that is hidden by the concept of the 'globalized world' (Gill, 1990; Gowan, 1999; compare Wallerstein, 2003). The next section will look at the Marxist critique of recent neo-liberalism in the context of American hegemonic power.

(5) Fifth, and finally, Marxism is highly vigilant concerning *the politics of exclusion that ensue from the liberal separation of the economy from politics*. This tenet may seem redundant given tenets (1)–(3). It will be important for later discussion, however, in the context of 'embedded liberalism'. Karl Polanyi's *The Great Transformation* (1944) opens up this aspect of reformist Marxism best. In the nineteenth century, liberal economic thought maintained the gold standard to effect stable flows of goods between trading nations. With economies fixed to a certain amount of gold, national currencies and domestic economies operate, economic liberals argue, in a 'self-regulating market'. One nation's trade deficit leads to a reduction in domestic money supply, resulting in turn in a downturn in economic activity and a reduction in demand for imports. The inverse effect takes place for the trading partner with a trade surplus: more exports lead to an increase in domestic money supply (more gold or its currency

equivalent) and an eventual rise in imports. Imbalance between the two trading partners is thereby corrected through the international coordination of markets under the 'universal' mechanism of 'species flow' (Hume, 1777). The gold standard allows the market to achieve 'general equilibrium' *without* government intervention (see Eichengreen, 2008; Helleiner, 2005). Looking back from the Second World War to the 1920s and 1930s, *The Great Transformation* argues that this liberal creed of the gold standard is partly responsible for the emergence of Nazism and fascism. As a result of a fixed exchange rate policy, domestic macroeconomic policy became, it is argued, dysfunctional. In order to maintain their currency peg to gold, trading partners were forced to reduce the supply of money in circulation and to raise interest rates. The resultant downturn in economic activity led to massive domestic unemployment and social unrest. Under the doctrine of a self-regulating international market the 'losers' of international trade (in the West of the early twentieth-century: the working-class) turn to protectionism and nationalism.

For Karl Polanyi, it is only because Britain, the US and France left the gold standard by 1931 and depreciated their national currencies to raise exports that they averted, unlike Germany, Italy and Japan, the risk of extreme nationalism. In other words, for Polanyi and his legacy, *fascism constitutes the twentieth-century political solution to the failures of the market economy*. To one side of the viciousness of the Versailles treaty, the internationalization of liberalism leads from a Marxist economic perspective to the modern politics of unfreedom. The liberal separation between the economic and the political in the name of national and world growth paradoxically ends up in an anti-liberal politics of racial identity. As Eichengreen notes, Polanyi's thesis is too clean (Eichengreen, 2008, pp. 77–8, 107–8). Governments had to make political reforms given the widening franchise at the beginning of the twentieth century. The gold standard was doomed as soon as the working class achieved electoral representation. Polanyi's thesis has nevertheless remained telling for critiques of economic liberalism, both between the two world wars and after the end of the Cold War. For it emphasizes the possible social and political consequences of liberal economic autonomy. The replacement of political choice by the fundamentalism of the 'self-regulating market' leads not only to the depoliticization of society; this depoliticization may result, in turn, in a politics of the worst violence. In the name of efficiency and growth, the liberal separation of the economy from society can produce the worst: fascist appropriation of social alienation. One could argue that the sources of contemporary international terrorism lie, in part, in this recurrent liberal paradox.

These five major tenets of Marxism in the context of classical liberal thought and globalization can be summarized as follows:

1 Globalization is an economic process that accelerates from the nineteenth century onwards and translates the power of capital in contradistinction to that of labour.

2 This power emphasizes growth through trade and the efficient self-regulation of markets both at the domestic and international level. Liberal power is consequently grounded on the separation of the economy from polity.

3 This separation is, however, radically unsustainable given the tendential fall in the rate of profit and the recurrent crises that follow the freeing of finance capital from the market constraints of industrial capital: capitalism is crisis-prone.

4 The separation needs to be constantly legitimated by a hegemonic ideology, which, in the modern era of nation-states, is underpinned by specific states (Great Britain; later the United States) that shape the relations between them within the capitalist system in a neo-imperialist manner.

5 This separation leaves the losers of capital accumulation poor and disinherited. Left to the logic of the market at both domestic and international level, social relations worsen, people find themselves deprived of political choice and, in periods of capitalist crisis, a politics of the worst violence can result. The classical liberalism of the early modern age ends up, in the 1930s, producing fascism.

2 From Embedded Liberalism to Neo-liberalism

From the 1980s onwards critical international political economy in IR works to a lesser or greater degree with these five tenets of Marxism. IR scholars – for example, Susan Strange (not a Marxist, but inspired by Marxism), Robert Cox, Ronen Palan, Stephen Gill and Peter Gowan – all focus from the 1980s and/or 1990s onwards on the contemporary formation of globalization as a particular evolution of capitalist relations, shaped, in large part, by the power of the United States (Cox, 1981 and 1987; Gill, 1990 and 2003; Gowan, 1999; Palan, 2003; Strange, 1996 and 1998). This body of work takes shape in the context of two historical events that move the ongoing problematic of globalization beyond the parameters of classical liberal thought and its critique: (i) the founding of the International Monetary Fund (IMF) in 1947; and (ii) the demise of the Bretton Woods system in general in 1971 when Nixon took the US off the gold standard. It is accepted by all the above thinkers that the Bretton Woods agreements at the end of the Second World War inaugurated an age of multilateralism and domestic stability, at least for the West. A pegged exchange-rate system, together with national capital controls, permitted a stable re-expansion of international trade after the war, all the while allowing domestic government freedom of movement in monetary policy, that is, control over inflation and interest rates (see, in particular, Palan, 2003, pp. 127ff; compare Eichengreen, 1998, pp. 93–131). This compromise between international and domestic economic policy allowed the value and end of full employment to be sustained: a crucial outcome in the context of ideological rivalry with communism. The compromise between capital and wage-labour is one between international capitalism and territorially determined democracy: following Karl Polanyi, the IR theorist John Ruggie calls it 'embedded liberalism' (Ruggie, 1982, p. 393).

Within terms of the Marxist tenets above, 'embedded liberalism' attempts to mend the classical liberal separation between economics and politics by re-privileging social relations over economic relations with strong government intervention in market society: the domestic policies of redistributive tax system, universal health coverage and equal access to education. Embedded liberalism names, consequently, the post-1945 compromise between labour and capital in the industrialized countries. This compromise allows, on the one hand, industrial capital access to international markets, and, on the other, labour social benefits. This 'social embedding' of liberalism comes to an end during the 1970s with the simultaneous emergence of a floating exchange-rate system, the 1973 and 1978 hikes in oil prices and increasing international movement of capital, beginning with the Euromarkets (see Helleiner, 2005; Palan, 2003; Strange, 1998).[3] From this period onwards, the international economic order is considered by both Marxist and Marxist-inspired writings as increasingly subordinate to the will of *Pax Americana* (the US and its close allies) and the interests of financial capital (see Cox, 1987, pp. 211–67; Gill, 2003, pp. 1–9; Gowan, 1999, pp. 8–19; compare Strange, 1996, pp. 190–8). From the inception of Margaret Thatcher's and Ronald Reagan's governments in the early 1980s a normative shift from the above 'embedded liberalism' of the post-war era to 'neo-liberalism' takes place.

There is a great deal of critical literature on neo-liberalism (for a concise review, see Harvey 2007). For my purposes I consider it here from a Marxist perspective alone: neo-liberalism constitutes, in essence, an ideological struggle against the embedded liberalism of the post-war era. Historically situated at the end of the 1970s, it names the political doctrine of a broad sector of economic and political interests that wish to curtail inflation, large government deficits and sectoral interests (wages). In doing so – from the deeper Marxist viewpoint of the capitalist system as a whole – *neo-liberalism seeks to redress a general decline in the rate of profit*, one that followed the Keynesian compromise between capital and labour after the Second World War (see especially Brenner, 2002 and 2006). Neo-liberalism rejoins classical liberal thought when it affirms free trade and the removal of trade barriers, regional specialization and general market efficiency. The first neo-liberal democratic states, Great Britain and the United States, argue against an 'outcomes-oriented' concept of government and adopt a market-oriented approach to monetary and fiscal policy (see Cerny, 2008, pp. 24–5). Following Adam Smith and Frederick Hayek, in particular, neo-liberals believe that the market, with its emphasis on individual risk and competition, offers the best way to organize the economy, if not society as a whole. Government spending is not retrenched (despite neo-liberal rhetoric of the time); but the government changes in *function* (Hirst and Thompson, 1998). Rather than intervening in society to correct market failure and provide extensive public goods, it lays out a 'regulatory' framework of 'governance' within which efficient markets can be generated, obvious market failures addressed (rule of law, defence, basic infrastructure), and the internationalization of both finance and industrial capital can be extended (primarily through the dropping of domestic capital controls).

There are, as a result, three important differences between 'neo-liberalism' and 'classical liberalism' given the intervening period of 'embedded liberalism':

1 Neo-liberalism offers a regulatory framework of governance (Cerny, 2008), whereas classical liberal thought tends to affirm the virtues of the self-regulating market and minimal government. This change of emphasis would seem to be underestimated by neo-liberals themselves in their ideological struggle against corrupt government.
2 Neo-liberalism is explicitly resituating nation-states in the context of an expanding world economy. While this goal can be inferred from classical liberalism (as the Marxist tenets above assume), neo-liberalism *overtly* appropriates globalization to forge a set of interrelated market societies.
3 This form of globalization depends less on the internationalization of production and productive investment than on financial growth. Under neo-liberalism domestic and international growth is 'finance-driven' (Brenner, 2006; Crouch, 2009; Gamble, 2009; Gowan, 1999 and 2009; Strange, 1986, 1996, and 1998).

The last point has become a common-place of media coverage of the current global economic crisis. A Marxist analysis of neo-liberal globalization drives home the *self-contradictory* nature of this model of growth.

The neo-liberal 'financialization' of the economy works at two levels: domestic and international. At the domestic level, the ideological shift from embedded liberalism to neo-liberalism lies in making the individual responsible for his or her life. From the 1980s onwards in the US and the UK, capital markets were developed to increase access to money, life-pensions were diverted to the private sector and 'securitized' (turned into investment assets), shareholders gained primacy over managers in firms, property was 'democratized' (homeownership increased to 80 per cent of the population in the US and UK between 1980 and 2000) and public debt was replaced by private debt. Robert Brenner and Colin Crouch have wryly called this aspect of neo-liberalism 'privatised Keynesianism' and 'stock-market Keynesianism (Crouch, 2009, p. 387; Brenner 2006, p. 293). The point is critical.

Between 1980 and 2007, Western wage-earners were no longer able to save, since wages, outside the financial and top management sectors, were either depressed or stable (Brenner, 2006). *Private debt became a substitute for public debt*. Wage stagnation was compensated for by a credit-led boom (or debt-led growth). The massive allocation of credit to individuals by financial capital led, despite depression of wages, to increasing consumption and the housing boom, and to ever deeper private debt on the basis of individuals' rising assets (Brenner, 2002; Crouch, 2009; Gamble, 2009). Given the growing autonomy of the financial system from the real economy at this time, but also its crucial role in driving growth, financial systems became increasingly sophisticated. They also became reckless, especially in the Anglo-American model of neo-liberalism. As is now common knowledge, inter-bank lending and individual loans to consumers were made with depleting bank reserves and with ever-diminishing protection against individual defaults. At the same time the whole finance-driven growth model was only made possible because of the export savings of China and the rentier states (most importantly, the sovereign funds of Russia, Saudi Arabia, Qatar and Kuwait). Through the purchase of Western government bonds, they lent to wage-stagnant, over-indebted Western consumers. The French economist, Patrick Artus, has calculated, prior to 2008, a staggering total private debt of $4.5 trillion among the leading Western democracies (Artus and Virard, 2008, p. 33). Despite volatility, the global imbalance between vast non-Western savings and Western debts was, from the Marxist perspective, held in order to grease the wheel of finance-based capital accumulation and maintain the status quo: the economic power of Western financial centres and their nations – specifically Wall Street and the City of London. Under an undervalued RMB, Chinese exports, for example, were bought by US consumers, whose increasing debts were paid for by Chinese reserve loans, themselves the savings from Chinese exports to the US.

A Marxist understanding of the post-1970s shift from labour back to capital proves very helpful for understanding the deeper causes and interests driving these unintended loops and makes clear critical sense of both post-1970s globalization processes and the economic cosmopolitan ideology of globalization. The neo-liberal, finance-driven response to the post-1970s crisis of embedded liberalism turns out to be domestically and internationally unsustainable. Growth cannot be purchased indefinitely on future growth, mortgaged in the meanwhile on external loans from emerging world powers. Under neo-liberalism the first structural contradiction of capitalist accumulation (tendential decline in the rate of profit) is deferred through the dual effect of wage freezes and consumer credit; the second structural contradiction (autonomization of finance from industrial capital) breaks out through the US sub-prime mortgage crisis (for a non-Marxist analysis of the details, see Gamble, 2009; compare Krugman, 2008, pp. 165–91).

At the international level, the neo-liberal 'financialization' of the economy took place in a more roundabout manner. Neo-liberal doctrine became international public policy during the 1980s and gained complete governance-power at the end of the Cold War. The IMF, the World Bank and the GATT/WTO endorsed the neo-liberal programme project during this period and, already enfeebled as an international regime of policy coordination after 1971, placed themselves squarely under American hegemonic rule. The international neo-liberal project came to be called 'The Washington Consensus' following, somewhat ironically, John Williamson's important article on convergence of economic policies at the beginning of the 1990s (Williamson, 1993). As Williamson argues, several policies had found international consensus among economic policy-makers by the end of the 1980s. These were fiscal discipline, public expenditure priorities, financial liberalization, trade liberalization, privatization, deregulation and property rights (ibid., pp. 1332–4). What made this consensus 'neo-liberal' was the *predominant stress put on market efficiency and regulatory government together with disregard for concerns with equity.*

Overseas development aid and project-based development were, as a result, called into question, 'export-led growth' was pushed to the forefront of the development agenda and priority of loans and grants were given to the institution of market economies and light, 'regulatory' governments. During the 1980s and 1990s the IMF and the World Bank tied their loans and aid for the emergent democracies in Latin America and developing countries in Southeast Asia and Africa to market-oriented monetary and fiscal policies (see Mold, 2007). The strong arm of Western neo-liberal power emerged in the 'structural adjustment programmes': loans based on the 'conditionalities' of privatization, deregulation, tax reform, competitive exchange rates between national currencies and trade and fiscal liberalization. As Williamson (1993) argues, many of these ideas are not wrong policies per se and found consensus on both the right and the left of the political spectrum (a point to which I return in the next chapter). However, for Marxist-inspired analysis, the Western domination of international finance and trade markets skewed, from the first, *any possibility of reciprocity between the developed and developing countries on the basis of neo-liberal doctrine.*

Indeed, this analysis would go further. For Gowan, for example, the global campaign of neo-liberalism, with its policy stipulations as stated above, has in fact provided the 'ideological bluff' for a finance-driven growth model (2009, p. 30). The tenets of neo-liberalism are, in other words, nothing but an ideological cover for a finance model of growth, predicated on stagnant wages and irrational production patterns. The observation may sound conspiratorial. But basic statistical analysis – on increasing inequality within the neo-liberal states, on increasing inequality between developed and developed countries, on the neo-liberal transfer of growth stimulation from industrial capital to finance capital from the 1980s – bears out a major structural problem in the neo-liberal growth model, one that certainly ends up to the general advantage of continuing US hegemony and to the particular advantage of Anglo-American financiers (for some statistics, see below, pp. 135–6). Whether neo-liberalism harbours particular power ends or not, and a particular economic international agenda after embedded liberalism or not, consensus around the doctrine reinforces US economic and political hegemony at a moment of increasingly felt contradiction in the capitalist model of accumulation. With the failure of this model, continuing attempts to maintain US economic and political hegemony through neo-liberal policy necessarily come to an end.

In sum, from a Marxist perspective, the internationalization of the neo-liberal agenda has allowed American power to reorganize itself economically, the West as a whole to maintain the status quo, and for both to dictate highly hierarchized terms of entry into the world economy. Globalization and neo-liberalism thereby dovetail into the explicit subordination of the developing world (compare Strange, 1996). The benefits have mainly accrued to Western financial elites and to the maintenance of the status quo. The social costs have been borne by a stagnant working class and by the developing world, and they have led, in the context of international security, to increasing resistance to American and Western 'neo-imperialism'. However, with the 2007–9 financial and economic crises, the domestic and international levels of neo-liberalism imploded into each other, creating a systemic change at the international level that is increasingly reflected at the domestic level. For the present, the costs produced by speculative financial capital are borne by the poorer countries, the Western taxpayer and, increasingly, social programmes; the gains have remained private (the bail-out of 'banks too big to fail') (Johnson, 2010). After the 'ideological bluff' of finance-driven growth, however, the shift of economic power from the West to Southeast Asia has become visible in the geopolitical dissolution of the G7 and its replacement by both the G20 and the G2 (US and China) (see Deeg and O'Sullivan, 2009). It is – that said – still unclear what will emerge ideologically and geopolitically after the post-Second World War periods of 'embedded liberalism' and 'neo-liberalism'. Two concluding points are nevertheless evident from the preceding analysis. They lead me from this long, but necessary, analysis of contemporary Marxism in world politics to the Marxist critique of contemporary cosmopolitanism:

1 The deep process of liberal globalization will likely continue, but in the lesser form of regional areas of economic power, although environmental crisis may well re-spark economic nationalism.
2 Even if liberal globalization continues in some form or other, contemporary cosmopolitanism falls far short of providing an adequate intellectual response to it: it does not constitute, therefore, an ideology or normative vision that fits the world's economic future.

3 The Marxist Critique of Cosmopolitanism

With the foregoing as intellectual and historical background, I can be precise and to the point. Given the major tenets of Marxism in the context of liberalism and globalization processes, Marxist theory in IR focuses on the ideological separation of politics from economics, on the overall dynamic of the international economic system as a whole, on the terms of economic power and on the overall forms of exploitation and exclusion that result from them. From out of these foci, Marxism critiques the normative, institutional and political variants of cosmopolitanism (ostensibly, the project of cosmopolitan democracy). The issue between these two bodies of thought concerns, therefore, *the correct understanding of globalization* and, consequently, *the right normative and political strategies to adopt regarding the dynamic of global capitalism*. This issue came recently to the fore in a debate, hosted by the British neo-Marxist journal *The New Left Review*, between the political cosmopolitan Daniele Archibugi and neo-Marxists, published in amended form in *Debating Cosmopolitics* (Archibugi, 2003). This section uses the economic arguments in this work and supplements it with three other writings from one of the original contributors, the journal's editor Peter Gowan (1999, 2003a, 2003b and 2009). I also make more general comment based on the work of the two previous sections. I first develop the overall argument.

David Held and Daniele Archibugi's original project of cosmopolitan democracy in the early 1990s was, in part, justified by the wish to counter the post-Cold War triumphalism of liberal democracy and to give, in contrast to it, a normatively attuned political response to the realities of interdependence. Their argument that democracy only remained possible nationally, if extended post-nationally, led to the extension of the principles and institutions of domestic democracy to the global level. Chapter 3 reconfigured this argument, in response to Realism, as a call for the reinvention of democracy under conditions of globalization. The Marxist critique of liberal globalization necessarily implies a critique of this project as well in Realist terms of economic power, and I will use this criticism as a way in. The fundamental Marxist point is this: however *critical* cosmopolitanism is of the present world order, its position remains complicit with the 'economic cosmopolitanism' of classical liberal thought and with its neo-liberal legacy (global capitalism). Not attentive to economic power, cosmopolitan normative vision flirts unwittingly with it. Furthermore, since the economic cosmopolitanism of globalization ideology disguises capitalist hierarchies of domestic and international power, cosmopolitanism (*qua* a response to globalization) at best ignores the neo-imperialism of the US and its closest allies or, at worst, ends up legitimating it. Thus, the 'economic cosmopolitanism' of global capitalism and the critical cosmopolitan disposition analysed in this book end up, for Marxism, the same – despite cosmopolitan concerns with global justice and democratic legitimacy of power. The Realist critiques of cosmopolitan interventionism and the Marxist critiques of the cosmopolitan appropriation of globalization dovetail at this point. Both critiques are essentially concerned with cosmopolitan 'errors of thought' that ensue from the refusal of international reality. For Marxism, however, the cosmopolitan *moralization* of politics is most appropriately considered as the *replacement* of politics by ethical prescription (rather than the imprudent subordination of politics to morality). It is only when forms of social solidarity have been achieved in global terms and have held global economic suasion that a cosmopolitan response to globalization will become appropriate. Until that historical moment, given social and functional constraints, cosmopolitanism is fated to being a *moralizing* discourse that reverts, unintentionally, to the (neo-) liberal practices of 'global governance' and 'regulation', de-politicization and global elitism. Universalism is, consequently, not wrong per se. It is the wrong discourse for this moment in history, given practical economic reality: namely, the skewed economic playing-field and the role of US

hegemonic power. Moral and political ambition in world politics is, consequently, better served by attending to *particular* strategies of resistance
that work with the principle of nation-state sovereignty. It is not a question,
therefore, of extending democracy beyond the nation-state under conditions of interdependence, but of instituting and reinforcing democratic
conditions within the state in resistance to global capitalism.

Let me now untangle the details of this sharp critique with regard to
cosmopolitan universalism in general. Section 3.1 considers the cosmopolitan complicity with global capitalism; section 3.2 expounds the structural reason for radical inequality from a Marxist perspective; section 3.3
considers the cosmopolitan moralization of politics; and section 3.4 points
to the particularist strategy of the nation-state *contra* universalism. The
conclusion summarizes the arguments of the chapter as a whole.

3.1 Cosmopolitan lack of economic analysis and complicity with global liberal governance

On the first point, regarding the cosmopolitan lack of strong economic
analysis, Timothy Brennan's response to Daniele Archibugi is categorical
(Brennan, 2003, pp. 40–50). The latter's political cosmopolitanism – the
claim of 'cosmopolitical democracy' (ibid., p. 7) – denies neo-liberal realities and serves the interests of the US hegemon by subordinating all states
under 'international democratic polity' (ibid., p. 48). Worse, it does not
take effective distance from the historical relation between economic and
political liberalism and colonialism (one recalls Owens's critique of
Habermas as outlined above in chapter 2). As a result, the liberal universalism of cosmopolitan democratic discourse is complicit with 'the comfort-
able culture of middle-class travelers' and the 'neoliberal orthodoxy' of
transnational economic practices (ibid., p. 42; compare Craig Calhoun's
excellent 'The class-consciousness of frequent travelers', 2003, pp.
87–117). Indeed, for Brennan, it can only be this community, given its
global network and its power base in the US hegemon, that constitutes 'the
core of any future community that could plausibly be called cosmopolitical' (Brennan, 2003, p. 43). For lack of economic mediation, then, the
project of cosmopolitan (or cosmopolitical) democracy does nothing but
reflect '*Pax Americana* dressed up as international law' (ibid., p. 45). David
Chandler (2003) makes a similar point regarding the complicity between
cosmopolitanism and neo-imperial rule. Neither Brennan nor Chandler
enters into economic detail. Peter Gowan's response does.

Prior to replying to cosmopolitanism in *Debating Cosmopolitics*, Gowan
had argued in *The Global Gamble: Washington's Faustian Bid for World*

Dominance (1999) that financial neo-liberalism was underpinned and, specifically, instrumentalized by US foreign policy. My last section made large reference to this argument. The US used neo-liberal economic policy to shape its relations with other states during the 1980s and 1990s. In doing so, it legitimated global capitalism in terms of the 'American way of life'. In *The Global Gamble* Gowan distinguishes cosmopolitan aspiration from globalizing Anglo-American neo-liberalism. He writes:

> There are many in the Atlantic world and elsewhere who would hope, for the best of reasons, that the political fragmentation of the world into a Balkanised patchwork of states could be overcome by steps towards genuine world government. This would indeed be a desirable goal. But it would be a grave error to assume that the current IMF/WB structures are a genuine step in that direction. The reality is that these structures are less genuinely supranational in their functioning than they were under the Bretton Woods regime, are far less so than was envisaged by Keynes and Dexter White when they negotiated the Bretton Woods regime during the war. What is overlooked by the proponents of developing these institutions further along their current lines is the fact that the principle obstacle to the construction of genuine organs of global governance lies in the post powerful states themselves. It is they who have most to lose from such a development because at present they control these multilateral organizations for the purpose of furthering their own power and interest. . . . [T]he entire IMF/WB system is designed to shift the costs of the power-plays of the Atlantic world on to the bulk of humanity, which lives in the South. (Gowan, 1999, pp. 28–9)

A political cosmopolitan vision offers, then, a 'desirable goal'; global governance is not here reduced to neo-liberal terms of regulation. But the practical reality of US (and its allies') power and interest has diverted international institutions from the supranational path that Keynes and White set out for them at the end of the Second World War. This diversion – we have seen for Marxist analysis in general – accelerates from 1971 with the increasing neo-liberalization of international liberal policy and institution. Gowan accords, therefore, intellectual integrity to normative cosmopolitan argument, but argues that the norm of international economic cooperation was immediately undermined by the politics and economics of state interest. The main argument of his book concludes with a similar normative/empirical distinction, one that ends on a note of Marxist impatience regarding the 'The Third Way' thinking of the 1990s social democrats. I quote again at length:

> If there is no effective European social democratic challenge to the globalisation drift, the next phase of international politics will be a turbulent and

ugly one. The lesson of the East Asian crisis that will be drawn in many parts of the world is that the Atlantic powers are prepared to use economic statecraft to block capitalist catch-up development. . . . The 1990s were a unique moment when real global institutional reform for sustainable development, based upon global political co-operation and international institution-building, could have been achieved under Atlantic leadership. But that opportunity has been utterly squandered as so often in earlier moments of victory. . . . Nothing demonstrates the vapidity of the 'new thinking' more graphically than the current catchphrase of the 'The Third Way': this is simply a slipway to enable European intellectuals, whether liberal or social democratic, to abandon their social liberal or social democratic values, for the sake of overcoming their cognitive dissonance with an Americanised Europe. Insofar as they abandon the struggle for egalitarian and cosmopolitan solutions to international problems, these banners will be taken up by more radical currents. They will draw the conclusion that Marx was right about capitalism being ultimately incapable of providing a viable framework for sustainable human society on this planet. (Ibid., p. 138)

Gowan's position clearly captures the *raison d'être* of 'anti-globalization' movements that started to have effect from late 1998 after the blocking of the WTO annual meeting at Seattle. A post-Cold War chance for global coordination and more equitable economic development was, for him, squandered again by the neo-liberal separation of the international economy from world politics, a separation working for the interest of the hegemon and the geopolitical status quo. From this perspective, the 1990s social democratic thought that bought into part of the neo-liberal agenda – a more market-oriented approach to monetary policy, private/public partnerships, more regulatory governance, etc. – did nothing to further the cosmopolitan norm of global coordination: fundamentally neo-liberal, it remains complicit with the US treasury appropriation of the IMF/WB and depoliticizes Northern and Southern societies. Gowan would have no time, for example, for either John Williamson's analysis of international convergence on specific policies, endorsed by both left and right, or John Ruggie's move to make more responsible large market actors with the concept of 'corporate social responsibility' (Ruggie, 2003).

In his response to Archibugi, Gowan (2003a) continues this line of argument. The political cosmopolitan point – the norm of global governance appropriate for equitable and sustainable development – quickly loses out to the liberal and neo-liberal practices of economic cosmopolitanism undertaken by the US and the EU. Gowan's major argument is, therefore, the fact that the cosmopolitan disposition constitutes a conflation of norms, which legitimates Western policies, *with* the policies themselves. Consequently, political cosmopolitanism needs to take much greater distance from contemporary neo-liberal practices (therefore, to be far less American-prone) in order to have any effective international ideological weight. These practices make up, for Gowan, the 'new liberal cosmopolitanism' (ibid., p. 50) of existing capital relations.

The new liberal cosmopolitanism sets in stone the internationalization of neo-liberalism analysed in the last section. It is characterized by the simultaneous call to liberal democracy and open free markets, capped by the light hand of regulatory global governance. However, 'free trade' constitutes a norm belied by the radically unfair terms of trade between North and South. Through a variety of protectionist mechanisms, mostly subsidies, the first world protects sectors that are increasingly important to countries outside it: agriculture, textiles and basic research and development (ibid., pp. 57–8). This accusation is now well substantiated and is endorsed by intellectually consistent free-traders like Martin Wolf who have targeted Western hypocrisy regarding trade liberalization (Wolf, 2004, pp. 212–18). Agricultural subsidies (to the sum of $100 billion in the West) and textile tariffs skew terms of trade in favour of the richer countries. Dissymmetrical investment in R&D prevents technological catch-up in developing countries (see also Chang, 2007, pp. 65–83). The neo-liberal world order safeguards flows of trade and finance explicitly in the developed countries' own interests: the contemporary reinvention of liberal 'economic cosmopolitanism' promotes particular interests. The massive development and dissemination of intellectual property rights that have taken place since the 1980s have allowed foreign operators to 'gain ownership of domestic assets . . . and integrate them into their profit streams' (Gowan, 2003a, p. 59), redirecting capital gains back to the North. The economic crises that predominantly ran in the South from Mexico in 1994 to Argentina in 2003 were largely caused by capital volatility. This capital volatility was the effect in turn of the end of domestic capital controls, of the liberalization of financial markets, of global trade imbalances fuelling fluctuations in exchange rates and, therefore, the increasing possibilities of short-term speculation. For Gowan, the profit streams from these practices – unfair trade regimes, foreign-owned assets and liberalized capital markets – all flowed back to the US and its allies. The 'liberal cosmopolitan regime' of neo-liberal global governance assumed by the IMF/WB and WTO has been US unilateral strategy, with the EU as 'its regional subordinate' (ibid., p. 57).

Accordingly, there is 'overwhelming evidence of a huge and growing polarization of wealth between the immiserated bulk of humanity and extremely wealthy social groups within the core [Western] countries. . . . One of the main bases for perceptions of common cause between the US and its allies is precisely their joint interest in perpetuating the drive for control of new profit streams from non-core economies' (ibid., p. 60).

From a Gowan-like perspective, we can therefore argue the following. Legal, institutional and political modalities of cosmopolitanism (Beitz, Pogge, Caney, Archibugi, Held, etc.) may wish to address this growing disparity with their focus on global justice and/or on the reform of international institutions. However, by failing first to focus on American power and on specific patterns of socioeconomic relations, these modalities of cosmopolitanism divest themselves of the theoretical and practical means to do so. The cosmopolitan target is accordingly misplaced.

3.2 Deep reasons for global inequality: beyond cosmopolitan surface

It is now accepted across the ideological spectrum that the neo-liberal order of capitalism has produced increasing inequality at the same time as growth and wealth, but that extreme poverty has been reduced (see Wolf, 2004; Held and Kaya, 2007). The Marxist point is, rather, that these inequalities have massively favoured the US and its allies over the South and, within the US and its allies, massively favoured the wealthier sectors of the working-population over the poorer sectors. It also argues that the finance sector has accrued most of the profits given the way capitalism reorganized itself, from the early 1970s onwards, through finance-led growth. As a result of these three directions of capital – to the Northwest, to the rich, to finance – the economic and geopolitical status quo, post-Second World War *Pax Americana*, was salvaged, if not reinforced. This salvage job was relatively successful despite the fall-off in the decline of the rate of profit, despite the systematic lack of investment in industry and despite the increasing share in world trade by the developing countries (from one-fifth to one-third of world exports from 1997 to 2005: Artus and Virard, 2008, p. 21). I return to all these points in the next chapter.

The above Marxist argument against political cosmopolitanism is based on the 'crisis-prone' understanding of capitalism analysed above in section 1: tendential decline in the rate of profit and autonomization of finance capital from industrial capital. For Marxists, American hegemony was, of course, always going to slip because of the competitive dynamic of the capitalist system it underpinned (Wallerstein, 2003; Harvey, 2007). It is, however, a question of *what* strategies could hold a Northwest-favoured arrangement of capitalism in place for so long. Without an account of these strategies and their power politics – for Gowan, precisely, 'the new liberal cosmopolitanism' – a counter-cosmopolitan argument remains purely normative and abstract. It fails to show how, or why, the cosmopolitan norms of the original international institutions were so quickly undermined and how, and why, a more cosmopolitan post-Cold War order never materialized. Having answers to both questions suggests a particularist economic strategy for the mid-term future. A few statistics concerning intra- and international inequality should now be given to back this argument up.

As an example of the first, I take the intra-country inequality of the US. Prior to the 2008 crash, the top 1 per cent of the population received 16 per cent of income with the top 10 per cent receiving 46 per cent of income (Gamble, 2009, p. 160). The average income of the bottom 90 per cent in 2005 was $29,000; the average income of the top second highest quintile (90–95 per cent) was $110,400; the average income of the top 1 per cent was just over $8 million (US Average Incomes, 2005, cited in Cammack, 2008, p. 296). In the US in 2008 there were 469 billionaires and 51 million people living in poverty (D. Smith, 2008, p. 38). Robert Brenner has calculated that from 1979 to 2000, US wages decreased, with regional variation, between 8 and 12 per cent (2006, p. 248). During this same period the stock market tripled in size (ibid., p. 254). From 1994 to 2000 housing assets in the US tripled from $4 trillion to $12 trillion, while, during the same period, savings dropped from 2.3 per cent of GDP to −1.8 per cent of GDP (ibid., p. 297). In the 1950s savings in the US had been, on average, 11.2 per cent of GDP (ibid., p. 332). Finally, US debt rose from 163 per cent of GDP in 1980 to an extraordinary 346 per cent in 2007 (Wolf, 2008). Two sectors of the US economy have been responsible for this rise: household debt increased from 50 per cent of GDP in 1980 to 100 per cent in 2007; financial debt rose from 21 per cent of GDP in 1980 to 116 per cent in 2007 (ibid.).

The above statistics clearly indicate, when taken together, a huge redistribution of income since the 1980s in favour of capital, with private debt replacing public debt in order to maintain consumption and demand-led growth. From a Marxist perspective, the recent model of finance-led growth organizes, therefore, a shift of capital to the wealthy, encourages increasing social inequality, but masks this inequality under debt-led consumption patterns. Brenner has also calculated that from 1994 to 2000, 75 per cent of increase in US profits came from the financial sector, with no increase on average for profits in the non-financial sector from the early 1990s (2006, pp. 298–9). Despite the economic paradigm of the new technologies, average investment of industrial capital in the US has been stagnant throughout the neo-liberal era (see Brenner, 2002, pp. 218–64; 2006, pp. 250–63). Brenner's point is clear and profound: growth has been finance-driven in relation to the *consumer*. The post-oil crises model of finance-led growth in the US has been rooted on ephemeral consumerism and the structural absence of domestic industrial policy (for the UK, see Crouch, 2009). I turn now to international inequality and global financial flows.

As mentioned above, there is general agreement that extreme poverty, calculated by the UN and the IMF/WB at one dollar per day purchasing power parity (PPP) has decreased. This decrease has been ignored by alternative globalization movements (see Wolf, 2004, pp. 138–72; Held and Kaya, 2007, pp. 8–9). It has now fallen as much as 18 per cent since the 1990s, from 40 per cent of the world's population to 22 per cent (Dollar, 2007, p. 84; Harrison, 2007, pp. 1–2), although the economic crisis of 2007 onwards is likely to affect the rate of fall. I return to this figure and its implications in the next chapter. Inequality has, however, soared. Since the 1990s, the number of people living for less than two dollars a day (PPP) has risen from *one-third* of the world's population to *just under a half* (Dollar, 2007, p. 74). The income of the richest 1 per cent of the world's population is equal to the income of the poorest 57 per cent (D. Smith, 2008, p. 38). One major reason for this is straightforward. With the exception of ten emerging countries (China, India and Brazil being the most important), capital flows remain almost exclusively between *developed* countries (Plihon 2001, pp. 35–6; Thompson 2007, pp. 184–5). Thompson argues that the stock of FDI diminished proportionately by over half from 1914 to 1990 and that the richest 20 per cent of the world population was receiving 80 per cent of FDI in 1990, with the poorest 20 per cent receiving only 0.7 per cent (ibid.). These calculations need to be updated to include up to the first five years of the twenty-first century, but they clearly suggest, empirically and theoretically, what the pattern of global distribution and investment was to be for the following ten years. For Thompson, they indicate that the international economic system has continued to develop throughout the neo-liberal era along regional lines: the NAFTA bloc, the East Asian bloc and the EU. Robert Wade suggests similarly that 50–60 per cent of world economic growth over the 1990s accrued to people in the top half of the rich countries' income distribution – that is, only 8 per cent of the world's population (Wade, 2007, p. 111). Since almost all the other half went to China's rising middle class alone, global income inequality has risen inevitably very fast (ibid., p. 114). The structure of global capitalism has, in other words, worked to increase radical inequality.

From the Marxist perspective, this rise of radical inequality has, therefore, a structural reason: it redounds to the power relations of leading states' interests (the US and its allies) in a crisis-prone, but expanding, global capitalist system. The finance-led growth and debt regime has allowed for this continuing Northwestern domination of the South, since the US has not needed, since the 1980s, to redress stagnant wages at home. With multinational companies (MNCs) outsourcing to the South to find cheap labour, with tax-exemption schemes for MNC production in developing countries, with goods paid for in the world's reserve currency and with Southern world savings invested in US bonds, the international monetary and trading systems have underpinned *a contradiction-ridden system of economic hegemony based on US private and public debt.*

On the basis, therefore, of both intra-country and inter-country statistics on private capital flows, profits, income distribution and debt, the Marxist argument against cosmopolitan universalism appears rather powerful.

3.3 The cosmopolitan substitution of ethics for politics

Unable to move beyond the surface of economic force, cosmopolitanism fails, from a Marxist perspective, to find enough critical distance towards the 'new liberal cosmopolitanism'. Without this critical distance, it replaces politics *with* ethics. For Gowan, Brennan and Calhoun, the project of cosmopolitan democracy ends up, for example, *moralizing politics* for not confronting the issue of power (in, respectively, Archibugi, 2003, pp. 64, 48, 112–33). We saw that the legal cosmopolitan response to this Realist criticism emphasizes the Habermasian distinction between an unmediated relation between morality and politics and a mediated relation through law. For Marxism, legal cosmopolitanism does not advance the argument, however. As I argued at the beginning of this chapter, this is a crucial Marxist point (whether it is correct or not). As Brennan and Gowan both argue, attention to the normative principles and institutional evolution of cosmopolitan law tends to mistake where power lies. It confuses juridical form with social substance and believes, wrongly, that legal remedy can effect social change in an economic force-field (compare 'On the Jewish Question', Marx, 1843/1992, pp. 230–2). For Brennan, legal cosmopolitanism ends up necessarily ratifying *Pax Americana*. For both Brennan and Gowan, it consequently diverts attention from, and commitment to, concrete forms of social solidarity and political resistance to government-framed market forces (respectively, Archibugi, 2003, pp. 48, 60–4; Gowan, 2003b, p. 23). Political, legal and institutional modalities of cosmopolitanism evacuate, as a result, the space of political struggle and wash over this space with normative prescription. For Marxists, political cosmopolitanism reverts to moral cosmopolitanism all the while believing that it is engaging in politics. The danger is global elitism.

In this important deliberation on the relation between justice, law and social life and agency, Gowan's argument goes one step further. I tracked earlier his interest in the cosmopolitan norm of global governance. For Gowan, without the social actors being there to sustain it, this norm will automatically regress to something close to the new liberal cosmopolitan norm of 'regulation'. As with the missed historical opportunities of 1944–5 and 1989–91, the norm folds back, as it were, into its lesser half because the economic and social actors do not yet exist that can articulate it as a concrete legal and political project. This is why, although desirable per se, the cosmopolitan norm, necessarily unfulfilled, cannot be used strategically. Structural complicity between neo-liberalism and the cosmopolitan political project can be seen best in their mutual concerns with 'regulatory' capitalism. Despite the differences in the weight of regulation between them, the normative concept of 'regulation' crosses the divide between neo-liberalism and cosmopolitan democracy. Their differences turn, that is, on 'a rather rudderless discussion of "how much" and "what kind" of regulation would set matters straight' (Gowan, 2003b, p. 20). From the Marxist perspective, this discussion is not interesting, because of its second assumption: the tendential fall in the rate of profit and the freeing of finance capital. Given the present forms of capitalist crisis, regulation of capitalist excess is not enough. A fundamentally new paradigm of capital investment and industrial policy are needed, one that returns financial capital to the real economy and creates a new production-led model of growth that does not compromise future generations (ibid., pp. 21–3). The capitalist system must, in other words, be fundamentally reorganized, and not simply 'regulated', in order for cosmopolitan norms of equity to make any concrete sense. This reorganization is an issue of economic production and political power.

3.4 Nation-state particularity contra cosmopolitan universality: the Marxist response to globalization

For Gowan, the reorganization of the capitalist system can only be achieved through organizing social forces at the nation-state level. Otherwise, public control of macroeconomic policy cannot be regained. Multilateral cooperation is certainly needed (comparable to that before 1971 and the collapse of the Bretton Woods system), but, via these arrangements, the major actors in this political struggle against neo-liberalism remain nation-states (see Gowan, 2009, pp. 21–9). Despite all the reversals of the past 25 years, it is only the state that has the power to introduce post-neo-liberal alternatives. For Gowan, this power returned with the 2007–8 economic crisis, as is evident in the (partial) renationalization programmes initiated by a number of countries (ibid., p. 19). Cosmopolitan arguments for regulation, whether it is made from an internationalist or critical cosmopolitan position, are therefore 'beside the point' (ibid., p. 21). The question is one of reorganizing the investment model of financial capital in the first place so that a cartel of bankers with direct relation to government is made impossible. Nation-state sovereignty still provides the right set of tools to do this, in both the developed and the developing world. This is not only because states have the sovereign power to arrest capital mobility and direct investment into the production process based on public-utility credit systems (ibid., pp. 21–5); it is mainly because this sovereign power remains based on the mandate of organized social forces. The Marxist argument for national sovereignty and equality of nations (as against cosmopolitan concern with moral equivalence of persons) is critical here.

As I argued in chapter 2, following Jean Cohen, the equality of nations is a post-Second World War achievement that is not part of the Westphalian system of nation-states (J. Cohen, 2004). Marxism shows how important this observation is economically. For, to wish to transcend this equality, as cosmopolitanism does when criticizing the Westphalian system, ignores the only present effective means that people have to reorganize the capitalist model of economic cosmopolitanism. Economic events in 2008 are grist to the Marxist mill: the series of government interventions to prop up the market confirms the continuing normative and political strength of national sovereignty.

The move against economic hegemony is therefore not to universalize further, but to *particularize*; not to aspire to supranational regulation, but to move back down to national agreement and consolidate regional resistance. Both the Realist and Marxist critiques of cosmopolitanism end up again in similar positions, but for different reasons. Realists turn to particular strategies because, given anarchy and the aporia of global government, the interests of the units of political power must be effectively coordinated and balanced as far as possible. *This is a moral argument about political prudence and a politics of limits.* For Marxists, the turn to the particular (the national and the regional) constitutes the only effective response possible to the necessarily imperial dimension of universalism due to the economic reality of power in the first place. *This is a strategic argument about political possibility.* Only once power has become relatively equal between economic actors can universalist arguments for global governance not revert to domination, but make concrete political democratic sense. The shift of economic power from the G8 to the G20 and the G2, consequent upon the current financial and economic crisis, would seem to confirm the materialist point. Until that shift has a levelling consequence, ethically minded aspiration for universal regulation is either shouting in the wind or abetting the powers that be.

4 Conclusion

In the context of a finance-based economic world order, skewed to Western interests in general and US power in particular, cosmopolitan arguments for a new political and legal global architecture do not wash. They perpetuate the skewed system of global capitalism and end up, at best, in ethics, at worst, in moralizing discourse. Institutional cosmopolitan arguments for global justice and democracy need to work at the level of contemporary power relations to make effective argument. Controls on cross-border capital flows and greater autonomy with regard to the setting of exchange and interest rates require holding to national sovereignty, and, where deficient, call for regional arrangements that permit trade and financial policies that are independent of the dollar. Rather than imposing uniformity from global governance regimes, different standards and rules are necessary throughout the world economy. Achieving greater income equality and social protection will be predicated on such particularist arrangements. Any call to democracy must begin with the latter, not with universalist pretension.

Following the divorce between economic and political spheres put in place by classical liberal thought and its neo-liberal legacy, cosmopolitanism does not allow one to diagnose political reality, power and innovation in the correct way and at the correct level. Realism argues that cosmopolitan support for humanitarian intervention risks ending up complicit with the neo-conservative triumphalism of the invasion of Iraq for lack of an analysis of borders and their limits on international policy. In a structurally similar argument, Marxism argues that normative and political modalities of cosmopolitanism risk complicity with the neo-liberal model of globalized finance and regulatory capitalism for lack of an objective analysis of practical economic reality. In this context normative cosmopolitanism is strategically wrong to maintain the horizons of universal rule and individual human life. Both a critique of universalism (as the necessary expression of particular interest given an uneven playing-field) and attention to state forms of institutional power are required in order that, precisely, social forces can gain control over macroeconomic policy. On legal, normative, institutional and political levels, cosmopolitanism offers, therefore, an inadequate ideological response to globalization, however well intentioned its moral vision may be.

Let me now turn to a cosmopolitan response to this set of hard-headed criticisms, focused on economic power.

5

A Cosmopolitan Response to Marxism

The debate between Marxism and contemporary cosmopolitanism lies in the response to global capitalism and to its systemic effects. The Marxist critique argues that cosmopolitanism is unable to sustain a progressive position regarding the world economy, remaining complicit with the 'new liberal cosmopolitanism' of regulatory global governance. Its failure to offer a critical alternative to the latter is, the last chapter argued, due to (i) its lack of analysis of the economic system as a whole and of economic power subtending it – its norms and institutional arrangements are therefore abstract and ethical only; (ii) its inability to provide social agents of transformation – its focus on institutional arrangements risks, accordingly, elitism; and (iii) its disregard of the nation-state and of the norm of nation-state equality to effect, under conditions of global capitalism, the very moral commitments in which cosmopolitanism is interested – its focus on the moral equivalence of people is thereby practically ineffective.

This chapter meets these criticisms, straightforwardly, by arguing for a reformist cosmopolitanism and, more importantly, for the *critical* pertinence of this cosmopolitanism. As I suggested in the introduction to the previous chapter, I am less concerned with precise principles of justice or equality in the debate between Marxism and cosmopolitanism than I am with the institutional effects to which loose principles of equality and equity redound. Quite simply, if at the level of the economy, there is no growth, then there are no questions of distributive justice in the first place (compare Risse, 2005, pp. 86–7). Bureaucratic communism failed partly because a planned economy undermined conditions of growth (Desai, 2002; Kornai, 1992). In response to Marxist critique and its focus on the economic system and economic power, I stress that normative and empirical questions are necessarily interrelated. It is therefore important, when responding specifically to this critique, that cosmopolitanism pitches the debate at the appropriate theoretical level and argues for the efficacy of particular institutional effects in order to achieve its normative goals. Any discussion of interdependence in terms of global capitalism must, consequently, address basic economic theory, since economic consequences are complex and affect normative positions (see, again, Risse, 2005).[1] This chapter's cosmopolitan response to Marxist critique is accordingly broken down into the following arguments.

The two parts of section 1 consider cosmopolitanism's relation to the capitalist system in general; they argue, from a cosmopolitan viewpoint, why global capitalism is open to effective reform, why capitalism and cosmopolitanism are necessarily related and why different forms of institutional-building are crucial for the 're-embedding' of economic liberalism today. Section 1 makes, therefore, a theoretical case for a progressive liberal cosmopolitanism *given* the nature of the capitalist system. Marxism and cosmopolitanism simply do not agree on this nature: a cosmopolitan response to the Marxist critique should make this line of division clear.

With this line drawn, section 2 then looks at the work of a prominent progressive cosmopolitan: David Held. Held is one of the few cosmopolitans to address the economy systematically and work with the critical distinction between progressive cosmopolitan liberalism and international neo-liberalism (Held, 2004, 2005a). Gowan's respective critique of the 'rudderless discussion' of regulation (2003b, p. 20) and of the complicity between cosmopolitanism and liberal global governance takes aim, precisely, at Held, Archibugi and 'Third Way' thinking of capitalism in general (see Giddens, 1998).[2] It is therefore important, in response to the Marxist critique, to see what work Held's notion of 'global social democracy' is trying to do. My argument is that it consists basically in an argument for a 're-embedded liberalism' and for a 'differentiated universalism' that, under conditions of interdependence, marry efficiency and equity and refuse the distinction between particularist and universalist strategies. The Marxist critique of cosmopolitan ethics in the name of the political equality of states seems, as a result, precipitate. Marxist argument for the political valence of the state remains strong; but the cosmopolitan response for a differentiated universalism between national, regional and global actors is also strong given the global dimension of the problems that an integrated world economy throws up. In line with my argument in chapter 3 on subsidiarity, cosmopolitan economic reformism therefore looks, necessarily, to an integration of national, regional and global governance structures that fosters sub-global development and community under universal constraints. This progressive liberal approach to efficiency and equity can be clearly distinguished from neo-liberalism and is not fated to become ethics alone. It anticipates, rather, new forms of international political theory and practice given economic interdependence.

Section 3 considers this cosmopolitan 'logic' in relation to the regulation of trade and finance and expounds, in the light of this, what a differentiated universalism concretely means. The argument is for increasing *complexity* of response with regard to global capitalism and its futures; resort to nation-state sovereignty is considered too simple in this context. Section 3 leads, inevitably, to a detailed debate with institutionalists in IR theory and international political economy (Barnett and Finnemore, 2004; Mattli and Woods, 2009; Simmons, 1999; compare, Koenig-Archibugi, 2003). Since my purpose here is to give a pertinent cosmopolitan response to the Marxist critique of universalism, I must leave a debate on 'rules' for elsewhere. This debate is nevertheless crucial.

Section 4 reconsiders the Marxist emphasis on economic production (rather than regulation) in the context of global warming and climate change mitigation. It argues that, on questions of energy and environment policy, the Marxist critique of regulatory capitalism remains highly relevant: regulation of the market system is not enough; large transfer of resources and of production methods from the developed to the developing countries is needed, if the challenge of climate change mitigation is to be met. I argue, here, following the implications of the debate with Realist critique, that exemplary and global state leadership is required to address the environmental consequences of global capitalism: progressive liberal cosmopolitanism here redounds to cosmopolitan realism.

The conclusion reiterates that a cosmopolitan response to the Marxist critique of cosmopolitan universalism depends on *how* the global capitalist system is theoretically addressed and *how*, then, this system is empirically embedded in institutional oversight. My response is a self-consciously progressive liberal cosmopolitan argument for a differentiated universalism, which looks to empirical ways to redress radical inequality of life-expectations and promote progressive change in a highly turbulent world. The overall argument leads to three important research agendas for cosmopolitanism.

1 Cosmopolitan Reformism

1.1 Cosmopolitanism and the capitalist system

If, as we saw at the end of the last chapter, Marxists accept that economic power is now shifting toward Southeast Asia, the economic system called capitalism remains, as Marx the dialectician first argued, a complex beast that resists unilateral affirmation or negation (Marx and Engels, 1848; Marx, 1867; Wood, 1972). Contemporary Marxism shows well that tendential decline in the rate of profit explains post-1970s finance-led growth. It also pinpoints the paradox of this form of growth in terms of the structural logic of capitalist crisis. The last chapter rehearsed how finance-led growth has not only compensated wage stagnation and dulled conflict between capital and labour; more generally, it has constituted a 'negentropic' way of deferring the industrial decline of the West. This Marxist account is important and dramatic. To consider, as Peter Gowan does, American economic hegemony in the 1980s and 1990s to be a way of preventing others from rising to rival terms of power suggests that development catch-up was explicitly hindered by the US and its allies. As we saw in the last chapter, for Gowan and other Marxists, liberal global governance shaped global power relations through international capital mobility and capital volatility (exchange-rate crises). This argument addresses the ambivalent nature of capitalism. I would simply argue that it does not interrogate it enough.

The past 30 years of neo-liberalism have not been all bad for the developing countries (see, particularly, Wolf, 2004). Not only did Southeast Asian countries and Brazil fare rather well (as the Northwest is now fully aware), globalization has also produced economic 'winners and losers' *among* the poor (see Harrison, 2007). The empirical outcomes of global capitalism defy, that is, easy generalization. These empirical outcomes have normative consequences for how interdependence is theoretically addressed. Let me take one example. Export-led growth was encouraged by the West when neo-liberal doctrine took over the Bretton Woods institutions from the mid-1980s (see Rodrik, 1997; Williamson, 1993). This export-led growth has now led to massive imbalances of trade between Asia and the Northwest, particularly the US. As the world reserve currency, the US dollar has certainly mitigated the effects of these imbalances by bringing external savings home to boost domestic consumption. In the end, however, the consequence of being the world's reserve currency has *not* been in the long-term interest of the US (Eichengreen, 2008; Gamble, 2009). It has made the US financially dependent on surplus countries, and it has stalled the much-needed reorganization of the American economy and implementation of industrial policy (Gamble, 2009). The neo-liberal doctrine of export-led growth has not therefore been in the *long-term* interest of Western hegemony; but it has been in the interest of China and its rise to global economic power (Jacques, 2010; Lampton, 2008). From the very beginning, export-led growth has, in empirical fact, *both* deferred the end of Western economic hegemony *and* helped bring this hegemony to an end. The neo-liberal doctrine of export-led growth shows the structural ambivalence of the capitalist system. Consistent neo-liberals, like Martin Wolf, rightly focus, therefore, on the long-term levelling aspect of international trade (Wolf, 2004, pp. 173–219). One could say something similar about the long-term effects of international financial liberalization: the sub-prime crisis in the US undid the logic of finance-led growth that underpinned American power from the 1980s and, what with the trade imbalance, thereby abetted the increasing power of Asian financial centres. The era of Anglo-American global financial hegemony is over (Artus and Virard, 2008, pp. 95–115; D. Cohen, 2009, pp. 243–60).

Marxists can of course argue that this ambivalence of capitalism precisely reveals the temporary nature of any solution to the deep, structural contradictions of capitalism: the decline in the rate of profit and the autonomy of finance capital (Harvey, 2010, pp. 1–39, 184–214; Ramonet, 2009; Stiegler, 2009). Despite its interest for understanding capital-labour dynamics, this account is, however, unconvincing, when one can, *at the same time*, persuasively argue that sub-Saharan Africa suffers from too little, not too much, foreign direct investment (for example, Wolf, 2004, pp. 139, 233; and Sachs, 2005, pp. 188, 208). The cosmopolitan would certainly agree that capitalism is crisis-prone (who today does not?). That said, the dynamic of capital accumulation has never been one way: as if, since the 1980s, it has been to the advantage alone of the Northwest, the wealthy and the financiers (Gowan, 1999). The ambivalence of capitalist dynamics means that there are always other undercurrents going on in the capitalist system, the outcomes of which are necessarily uncertain and, as the economists put it, 'perverse' with regard to original policy intention. This is again why there is interdisciplinary need to relate the normative to the empirical when theorizing economic globalization. Capitalist crisis in one area of capital accumulation reveals tension, not contradiction. The point has important theoretical and political consequences.

Tension means that capitalism is open to effective reform, even at the global level where there is no monopoly of violence and no clear sense of legitimacy, as there was at the domestic level in the successful social politics of the twentieth century. For, more players are always involved in the dynamics of capitalism than those who gain or lose present economic power; and these players may play a critical role in the system as a whole. I would argue that, in this respect, for cosmopolitans, a 'relatively equal playing-field' is not, as for Marxist critique, a necessary condition of economic reform, as my examples in this chapter will amply show. Short-term and mid-term strategies should consequently not renounce universalism to prefer particularist pragmatism and mandate given lack of social agency (Brenner, 2006; Chandler, 2003; Calhoun, 2003; Gowan, 1999 and 2003a). To make this cosmopolitan counter-argument solid, one must nevertheless affirm what I am calling a 'differentiated universalism'. In response to the tensions of economic globalization, cosmopolitanism must think global politics in ways that make possible *new* balances between capitalism and democracy at *various* levels of social organization; otherwise, the reorientation of an integrated world economy towards greater relative equality and equity is institutionally less likely.

On the basis of this reading of capitalist ambivalence, the cosmopolitan response to Marxism argues, therefore, for a clear distinction between the 'new global liberalism' of neo-liberalism and 'progressive liberal cosmopolitanism', one that is focused on institution-building and policy mixes that balance growth and social justice, efficiency and equity. Rather, therefore, than replacing politics with ethics in the context of economic power for lack of a social agent, this form of cosmopolitanism advances incremental global changes within an *uncertain* ideological and governance environment and future. The cosmopolitan response to Marxism is theoretically coherent and overtly reformist in this sense. Marxism argues that cosmopolitanism's response to globalization is wholly inadequate because it ignores capitalist economic power. My response suggests, conversely, that cosmopolitanism may be most interesting, as a body of thought in IR, when it is related to the political economy of a system of interdependence, the dynamics of which are *essentially* uncertain.

1.2 Cosmopolitan reflection on the market and regulation

To argue for the political appropriation of economic globalization in progressive liberal terms relies on an important assumption. The institution of the market is not simply a stop-gap arrangement, for want of a better form of social and economic coordination after the twentieth-century failures of the planned economy. The institution of the market is to be affirmed as an important social good as such; or rather, it is to be affirmed as a 'lesser bad' (since market incentives inevitably lead to the underproduction of public goods). This cosmopolitan affirmation of the market and of its incentives should be understood in both *historical* and *institu-*

tional terms. I consider the argument important for understanding the relation between cosmopolitanism and capitalism in general. This sub-section amplifies, accordingly, the concerns of section 1.1; it also dovetails with my historical reading of the 'normative' in chapter 1, section 2.3, and with my use of this argument in response to Realist critique in chapter 3, section 1.

The historical argument concerns the cosmopolitan attitude towards the economic system of capitalism in general. With its emphasis on the moral equivalence of people and individual moral worth, contemporary cosmo-politanism is fundamentally indebted to the capitalist evolution of society. As historical sociology informs us, the institution of the market system began in earnest in sixteenth-century Western Europe (Braudel, 1993; Polanyi, 1944; Tilly, 1990; Wallerstein, 1980–1). Placing the individual on the market as an owner of capital or as a wage-labourer, capitalism breaks the social bond between the individual and the community and promotes the process of individualization that becomes the leitmotif of the Enlightenment and the post-Enlightenment liberal age. As Marx was the first to argue, the paradigm of the 'naturally free individual' in modern political thought is simply unthinkable *without* the underpinnings of the economization of society (Marx, 1939/1973, pp. 157–60). To one side of their debts to natural law theory and to Stoic cosmopolitanism, both Locke's individual bearer of the natural right to possession and the Kantian person of moral dignity operate *from within* these economic underpin-nings. Thus, the very principle of modern moral cosmopolitanism – focus on the individual as the primary unit of concern – is historically and socially rooted in the evolution of capitalism. A materialist reading of cosmopolitanism is accordingly important: a necessary condition of the modern individual is economic. Since no modality of contemporary cos-mopolitanism argues against moral egalitarianism, a *comprehensive* cos-mopolitan critique of capitalism would be utterly self-defeating. In this respect, Marxist critique of cosmopolitan ambition is absolutely correct to focus on the *liberal* dimension of contemporary cosmopolitanism. The latter affirms individualization and the modernization processes that promote it. But, *contra* Marxist critique, this historical complicity does not make cosmopolitanism complicit with unfettered capitalism or with the lean regulation of it. In this theoretical context, Marxism's conflation of institutional and political cosmopolitanism with the 'economic cosmopoli-tanism' of neo-liberal global governance is too quick. For, it declines to countenance the *long-term* possibility of 're-embedded liberalism'.

This refusal is due, theoretically, both to its bleak appraisal of interna-tional markets outside the framework of legally *enforced* macroeconomic policy and to a residual ontology of 'species-being' that places community and self-fulfilment outside market mechanisms (Marx, 1844; Tucker, 1969; M Mészáros, 1975). The cosmopolitan disposition does not agree with these Marxist assumptions. First, international law must be thought differently from domestic law (see chapter 3, section 3.3). Second, the individual and community are necessarily interrelated, but also separate entities; the institution of the market aids this separation, but must be framed itself institutionally so that collective life and individual life work together. The point takes us from the historical affirmation of capitalism to that of its institutional framing and 'taming' (Held and Koenig-Archibugi, 2003).

As we saw in the last chapter, the modern institutional framing of the market is both domestic and international from the gold standard onwards. I consider the two levels in turn. Like reformist Marxism, cosmopolitanism accepts that the modern collective response to the contradictions of capitalism (socialization of the means of production) brought an end to economic and political individual life. Following classical liberal thought, it therefore reaffirms the market as an institution that promotes, at the domestic level, individual rationality, self-interest and risk. It affirms these principles not in their own right (as does liberal individualism), but as necessary, although not sufficient, conditions of economic growth and individual self-fulfilment. Since economic growth constitutes the necessary condition, in turn, of *any* (re-)distribution of goods or income, a modern society of equality of opportunity and welfare *requires* the institution of the market. I would therefore argue that contemporary cosmopolitanism must agree with classical liberal thought that: (i) the price mechanism organizes best the laws of supply and demand (in distinction to planned economies); and (ii) when price *can* reflect the laws of supply and demand, market mechanisms best decide the distribution of resources under conditions of scarcity (see Gregory and Stuart, 1995, pp. 91–112). Since the political equality particular to democracy is only realizable through generalizable conditions of wealth, economic growth forms the precondition of democracy in modern complex societies. This liberal argument is, I believe, domestically incontrovertible.

It is a commonplace, nevertheless, that this classical liberal thesis oversteps itself in two ways: (i) when it minimizes the prior institutional arrangements upon which efficient market distribution of resources depends; and/or when (ii), detached from the polity, the market replaces society on issues of common interest and collective life. If either tendency informs public policy, *unnecessary* inequality and social injustice occur. In the terms of rational choice theory, there are a certain number of goods that the market institution is unable to provide by itself: its agents (individuals and firms) are either not yet in place or, once in place, they have little incentive to provide them (Shepsle and Bonchek, 1997, pp. 260–1).

Here, in the context of framing global markets, it is theoretically important to understand what one means by 'public goods' in order to have purchase on Marxist rejection of the efficacy of 'regulation' and 'governance' at post-national levels.

Rational choice theory considers public goods predominantly in terms of goods that are non-excluding and non-rivalrous, like parks, libraries or (large) beaches. My use of a park does not exclude others from the same use of it (non-excluding), at the same time (non-rivalrous). These goods are normally provided by government, through tax-financing, due to 'free-rider' problems: the ability for one 'consumer' to free-ride on the private provision of another given the lack of exclusionary mechanisms (tickets, tolls, etc.) (see, for example, Shepsle and Bonchek, 1977, pp. 260–96; Sandler, 2004, pp. 45–74). In modern societies, it is government that resolves the problem of the under-provision of collective goods.

'Public goods' consist, second, in substantial and regulatory frameworks that allow a competitive market to function in the first place: functional infrastructure, external security, the right of property, the rule of law and anti-trust law. Now, these frameworks *precede* the question of 'market failure', since the market is founded upon them. As is well known, after the 1990s demise of the Russian planned economy, the 1970s–1980s neo-liberal ideology of *laissez-faire* capitalism forgets this point (Stiglitz, 2002). These substantial and regulatory frameworks are not, however, interventionist. They do not aspire to social goals like equity, a goal that requires government redistribution of national income. They lay down constitutive public 'rules' by which private markets run efficiently (see Cerny, 2008).

'Public goods' consist, third, in *outcomes* of public policy that balance the self-interest of the individual with the members of the collective as a whole: social insurance, universal health coverage, universal education, full employment and equal opportunity of access to public office. These public goods are not pre-existing regulatory frameworks that allow the market to function efficiently, but constitute *the result of normative social policies instituted by the public instance of government*. They ensue, therefore, from heavy framing by government of economic civil society. The post-1945 compromise between labour and capital in the northwest of the world was achieved, for example, through this type of heavy regulation: for example, 'neo-corporatist' wage negotiations and progressive taxation policies (Pierson, 1991).

Now, it is well known that neo-liberalism endorses the option of public policy providing a lean set of regulatory frameworks at the domestic level in the name of individual freedom, while progressive liberalism endorses the option of a heavy regulatory set of policies that provides, in the name of social justice, an institutional level playing-field within which the market is 'embedded'. The domestic distinction between neo-liberalism and progressive liberalism is therefore straightforward: they constitute two different ways of thinking and providing public goods (compare Gregory and Stuart, 1995, pp. 89–111, 136–47). For Marxist critiques of capitalism, this distinction is, however, wholly ineffective at the international/global level *without legitimate coercive force to curb economic power*: hence its reduction of cosmopolitan critique to complicity with a light neo-liberal regulation, which went global from the early 1980s. A cosmopolitan response to the Marxist critique of cosmopolitanism must disagree precisely here.

Let me appraise the disagreement through the problem that the international model of 'embedded liberalism' met from the 1970s onwards. As the political economist Benjamin Cohen and the IR theorist John Ruggie both argue, it is not possible to maintain, at one and the same time, a fixed exchange rate between national currencies (to ensure international price stability and, therefore, international trade), capital mobility (to secure movements in trade and investment) *and* autonomous national macroeconomic policy (control of money supply and interest rates to maintain social goals and values like full employment) (see B. Cohen, 1995; Ruggie, 2003). Economists call this essential incompatibility of goals 'the impossible trinity' (B. Cohen, 1995; Helleiner, 2005). Ruggie argues that the post-Second World War compromise between international/global capitalism and nation-state democracy was founded on the international policy choice of two of the above three possibilities: capital controls were effected nationally, with fixed exchange rates and national monetary policy (Ruggie, 1982, pp. 393–8). Domestic capital controls were, in other words, accepted by the leading nation-states *so that* international trade and nation-state democracy *worked together*. This 'mixed-policy' choice directly responded, as Eichengreen suggests, to the social and political costs of the era of the gold standard, theorized by Karl Polanyi in the last chapter, and to the ideological threat of communism (Eichengreen, 1998, pp. 3–4; see, also, Palan, 2003, pp. 63–82). With the internationalization of finance and the expansion of transnational corporations from the 1970s, however, the above solution to this 'impossible trinity' came apart (Ruggie, 1982, pp. 340ff.). Renewed capital mobility (first, movement of capital to the 'offshore world'; second, financial investment underpinning increasing international trade) required that national governments abandoned the fixed exchange-rate system. Ralph Bryant shows in detail that this shift in the level of capital flows necessarily created financial turbulence in the world economy because it promoted speculation on exchange-rate differences (Bryant, 2003). If economic globalization is often perceived in terms of the recent and contemporary sways in international capital movements, it is because, *without capital controls*, international finance capital and international industrial capital are drawn into conflict with each other. The large theoretical question of 'taming globalization' becomes, therefore, the following institutional question at the global level: *how* does one frame/regulate financial capitalist markets anew so that both trade and financial markets help produce, with governance mechanisms, market efficiency (growth) and the public good of equity?

Now, we have seen, Marxism is absolutely clear regarding this question. First, the post-Second World War compromise between capital and labour may well have fallen apart under conditions of finance-driven growth, but it was already detrimental to the underdeveloped/developing countries (Baran, 1976; Frank, 1971). Second, embedded capitalism in a world economy is not possible on a universal scale until there is 'a level playing-field' (Gowan, 1999). To attempt, therefore, to 'frame' contemporary global capitalism through regulation remains complicit with the lean regulatory regime of neo-liberalism that went global from the 1980s and replaced embedded liberalism. Institutional and political cosmopolitanisms revert, as a result, to ethical intention alone. Despite a relatively sparse economic literature within cosmopolitanism, I would suggest that the cosmopolitan rejoinder to this argument implies, in essence, the following kind of argument (see Cabrera, 2004, 2005; Held, 2004 and 2005b; Pogge, 2008).

It is not a question today of embedding international markets in the way in which they were embedded post-1945, unless one opts again for national controls. This option is neither politically feasible nor politically attractive given the contemporary extent of capital mobility and the possible consequences of economic nationalism under conditions of interdependence (compare Palan, 2003, pp. 180–91). Due, on the one hand, to the multiple nature of transborder flows, and, on the other, to the aporia of world government, nation-states must, consequently, look to a *new* mix of 'rule-making' institutions in the world economy in order to achieve, both domestically and internationally, a better balance between growth and equity. For the cosmopolitan, the regulation of global capitalism must, therefore, be practised in diverse ways depending on the specific issue being addressed (see, in particular, Held and Koenig-Archibugi, 2003).

This institutional policy mix could be argued as follows. At the high end, supranational regulatory regimes must be invented that come close to the force of domestic government intervention without the power of enforcement (see Cabrera, 2005). The absolute need for global taxation of speculative capital movements is the clearest example to date (Eichengreen et al., 1995; Patomäki, 2001); Thomas Pogge's even more ambitious idea of a global resources tax also fits into this supranational model (chapter 1, section 2.4). At the low end, intra-firm practices of conduct are required that invite, through network pressure, market self-regulation. The present example is corporate social responsibility (Ruggie, 2003, pp. 106–16). Between these two extremes, various forms of national and international regulatory regimes exist. There are those that turn to the regulatory frameworks of neo-liberalism that *precede* markets: market regulation, for example, of carbon credits on the basis of government-prescribed permit ceilings and rules of inter-firm conduct. This was a clear option open to the UN after the Kyoto protocol of 1992: it looked to a global market of carbon credits that, through market mechanisms, would encourage technology transfers to the developing countries (De Perthius, 2009, pp. 15–95). There are those that work through international coordination of sub-global actors: the Basel II regulation of the reserve ratios of central banks would, perhaps, be the most obvious example at present (see Simmons, 2006).

I have kept my examples to international trade and finance. It is nevertheless clear that this reformist argument for different degrees of regulation of global capitalism responds, in David Held's words, to an increasingly flexible, 'multi-level, multi-agent and multi-tool' environment (2004, pp. 13–15; and see Slaughter, 2004).[3] What I wish to stress is that within this environment, each type of regulation (from heavy to light) responds to the specific policy at issue. In other words, in a world in which both international trade and international finance markets are irreducible, the source and weight of international macroeconomic policy, *tuned to helping the achievement of national social goals*, must vary according to the issue at hand (see, also, Sandler, 2004, pp. 212–34). Interdependence is now simply too complex to allow for unilateral responses to the crises of capitalism. One major political challenge of the future is, therefore, that of finding sets of policy mixes and levels of application (municipal, national, regional, global) that can best embed markets within institutional frameworks informed by progressive goals. I consider that a clear cosmopolitan response to the Marxist critique of contemporary cosmopolitanism follows from these comments on regulation, even if this response cannot be entirely satisfactory (with respect to enforcement mechanisms).

The post-Second World War compromise between labour and capital and between working democracies and a capitalist world economy has to be re-thought and re-practised in something like universally coordinated, differentiated terms of 'governance'. Differentiation requires coordination between national polities and regional and global institutions, and it assumes, given the complexity of market interdependence, the political integrity of the tool of regulation between governance mechanisms and markets. It therefore endorses the concepts of 'regulation' and 'governance', since embedding can no longer be achieved, in a complex environment of capital flows, through the legitimate monopoly of violence: that is, nation-state government on the basis of national democratic mandate. (The difference between governance and government hinges on this relation to legitimate enforcement mechanisms.) As argued in the cosmopolitan response to Realism, from a cosmopolitan perspective *both* domestic *and* global modes of governance need, therefore, to reinvent themselves in order to realign global markets with sub-global political communities. The question is, again, one of *reinvention* in the context of emerging practical realities. This means, for cosmopolitanism, that a reformist, institutional agenda constitutes the correct horizon for a progressive liberal vision of the world. A clear distinction can now be made between neo-liberalism and cosmopolitan progressive liberalism.

The vision of the first focuses immediately on the prerequisites of growth for general welfare; the vision of the second focuses, at one and the same time, on growth and equity. The institutional means to achieve the first is formally universal (like practices for unlike contexts – the universal prescriptions of free trade, deregulation, tax reform, capital liberalization: Stiglitz, 2002); the institutional means to achieve the second vision is differentiated and context-bound. In contrast to the formal universalism of neo-liberal practices, cosmopolitan progressive liberalism endorses, therefore, a differentiated universalism, one which refuses either strategic or categorical separations between the practices of the nation-state and those of international institution.

2 'Global Social Democracy': What Can This Concept Mean? Re-embedded Liberalism

David Held's *Global Covenant* (2004) works, I would argue, with both the historical and the institutional assumptions of the above theoretical argument. The book – together with the subsequent debate it provoked (Held et al., 2005) – argues for an extension of the concept of 'social democracy' to the global level in contradistinction to the post-1970s neo-liberalization of international relations, on the one hand, and the 1990s anti-globalization movements, on the other. Held thereby makes two moves: (i) he puts the issue of economic power on the agenda of institutional and political cosmopolitanism in terms of 're-embedding liberalism'; and (ii) he argues for this re-embedding through normative social vision, institutional practice and context-bound policy. At the beginning of his *Global Covenant*, Held writes, for example:

> While the values of social democracy – the rule of law, political equality, democratic politics, social justice, social solidarity and economic

efficiency – are of enduring significance, the key challenge today is to elaborate their meaning, and to re-examine the conditions of their entrenchment, against the background of the changing global constellation of politics and economics. (2004, p. 16)

To this purpose he suggests that the 'lens' of these values can serve as 'social democratic tests' (ibid., p. 17) that evaluate competing political programmes and policies at all levels of political organization from the municipal to the global. This 'filter mechanism' (ibid.) is set explicitly against the outcomes of neo-liberal international policy: the 1990s 'Washington Consensus' and the 1990s structural adjustment programmes of the IMF and the WB (ibid., p. 57ff.). Held understands 'global' social democracy in these terms. The book therefore focuses its engagements on the political value of *coordination* and *regulation* and the political site of *institution*.

I am unconvinced that the universalization of the domestic political regime of social democracy is helpful for the argument (hence my work on the principle of subsidiarity in chapter 3). In principle, as this book has intimated several times, it allows weak cosmopolitans like David Miller or Thomas Nagel to redirect our attention to the hitherto material preconditions of socioeconomic redistribution and thereby question extensions of the notion of social justice to the global sphere (my chapter 2, section 2.2). That said, it seems to me that the concept of 'global social democracy' appears most effective in Held's work when considered as a loose normative framework within which institution-building can be rethought in opposition to neo-liberalism. The concept is, in other words, used by him as part of a *strategic* argument against both neo-liberal and anti-globalization arguments. I therefore suggest that, while the concept of 'global social democracy' is too large to mean anything concrete for the world as a whole, it can be understood as making political argument for a new era of 're-embedded liberalism'. Re-embedded liberalism seeks balances between efficiency and equity for all countries within the world. Most of the empirical work of the *Global Covenant* and the subsequent debate bear out these last observations, offering thereby an institutional response to the previous Marxist critique.

In the sections on economics (Held, 2004, pp. 23–70; Held et al., 2005, pp. 31–6), Held specifically analyses, for example, the terms of trade, the finance and production flows and the regional income gaps between developed and developing countries. On all scores, he notes structural or systemic disadvantage to developing countries. He also notes changes in terms of trade and patterns of production that are moving to the advantage of Southeast Asia (2004, pp. 34–46). It is the implications that he draws that are important to me here in the context of the goal-driven value of regulation and the political site of institution.

First, given the lag between developed and developing countries, Held argues that any straightforward integration of national economies into the world economy cannot be 'adequate medicine for low-income countries to escape a development trap [sic]' (ibid., p. 48). Neo-liberal policy advanced by the IMF and the WB during the 1980s and 1990s is considered inadequate, not because of its market-oriented policies per se, but because it created no institutional depth from out of which a country could emerge in the first place in order to compete, industrially and financially, with developed economies. The use of capital controls and public coordination between finance and industrial capital by both China and South Korea since the 1980s proves this developmentalist point. The regulatory framework of international neo-liberalism was, in other words, minimal and geared to 'negative freedom' from government interference and government corruption (to use Isaiah Berlin's terms). In such ideological circumstances, the trap of poverty remained, with the exception of India and China, and inequality increased: as the last chapter documented, international trade and international capital mobility created, on average, more losers than winners (see pp. 135–6). For Held, therefore, free trade and capital mobility are, in principle, good for economic development. But, without complementary policies, they turn bad (2004, pp. 50–2). It is the *minimal regulatory framework* of neo-liberal international public policy that makes economic globalization bad; *not* liberal capitalism as such.

Second, the integration of emerging economies into the world economy must be staggered, incremental and constantly supplemented by policies that allow poor countries to adjust to open markets. Free-trade theorists like Jagdish Bhagwati and Ann Krueger (the long-time American 'voice' of the IMF) focus too much on trade policy and the abundant factor of unskilled labour in developing countries in order to reduce poverty (Bhagwati, 2004). Here, Held follows the thinking of developmental theorists like Geoff Garrett and Robert Wade and the trade-reform policies of the economist Dani Rodrik (Held, 2004, pp. 48–52). Given that the world economy is not an even playing field, globalization must be shaped for different countries at different phases of development (ibid., p. 47). Poor countries lack, for example, the basic infrastructure for worker mobility (the movement from one non-competitive sector of the economy to a more competitive one), the development of human capital (education and credit) and physical infrastructure in general (the ability to move goods to market). It is in these circumstances of *given* poverty that trade liberalization creates *further* poverty: that is, mass unemployment in the sector hit by competing imports without social security networks. Classical liberal arguments concerning free trade do not, therefore, work for poor countries (see also Chang, 2002, 2007). A heavy regulatory regime is needed at the domestic level to kick-start a country out of poverty. Since, further, poor countries lack at the same time financial markets, capital investment from abroad *necessarily* creates instability and social crisis if this capital is only placed in the short term (Krugman, 2008; Stiglitz, 2002; Sachs, 2005). If there is a run on the home currency, financial capital will pull out, leaving the country without resort to other private creditors. In poor countries, government policies that are *complementary* with the horizon of international market integration are therefore an institutional requirement in order to provide basic education, credit and capital development. Otherwise, the 'losers' of international trade will not be in a position to find jobs elsewhere (see also Harrison, 2007, pp. 1–38).

Held argues, persuasively, that global trade and finance markets are therefore beneficial to all countries on condition that coherent poverty reduction strategies are *already* in place at the domestic level before liberalization begins (2004, p. 52). Complementarity requires a staggered order of policy prescriptions that entail, as Robert Wade (2003) and Ha-Joon Chang (2002) have demonstrated, protective tariffs for targeted industries. In order for globalization to create general wealth, annul absolute poverty and, gradually, increase equality, emerging countries must be 'internally integrated' prior to becoming externally integrated into the world economy (Held, 2004, p. 49). *Contra* the neo-liberal world economic integration of the 1980s and 1990s, Held argues that emerging countries must have ownership of their industrial policy in order to become viable players in the world economy. Within this perspective, national economic policy constitutes a necessary *condition* of any future economic cosmopolitanism, *not an alternative* to it.

In contrast to neo-liberal and anti-globalization ideologies, what exactly does 'global social democracy' mean here? It comprises, I would claim, a loose normative argument for institution-building that is founded, concretely, on a mix of market, government and post-national governance policies. This mix can be understood in two senses:

1 Policies need to be complementary and integrated: an open-trade policy can only be effective for an emerging country if it is simultaneously supplemented by a social security policy, an educational policy and an infrastructure policy. When an open-trade policy in a particular industrial sector is not yet considered appropriate, protection of the nascent sector is required. This flexible set of policies is, for Held, the hallmark of progressive liberalism in the economic field.

2 Complementary and staggered policy-making works between national integration and global coordination and cooperation. The timing of integration into the world economy, together with the possible fall-outs of integration, requires careful cooperation and assistance. These can only be provided by international-level institutions, like the IMF and the WB, in coordination with regional and national arrangements like development and commercial banks. Working together, they have both the widest outlook on the relations between national, regional and world economies and the most international legitimacy, compared to private markets. Held's 'policy mix' is therefore neither exclusively national nor exclusively global. It is this potential coordination among nation, region and world, I suggest, that makes the mix 'progressively cosmopolitan'.[4]

If, to follow the trade example, there is a clear domestic integration strategy, gradual reduction of trade barriers between trading partners is more rather than less likely to promote national growth with general wealth. To follow the development angle, if a poor country is to escape the poverty trap through staggered integration into the world economy, large amounts of portfolio investment and aid from developed countries *are* required so that a complementary policy strategy is possible in the first place. *On this condition alone is endogenous development at the national level possible in a world economy.* The Marxist critique of cosmopolitanism does not address this institutional complexity; nor does it address the fact that institutional and political cosmopolitanisms are focused on national development for greater equality and equity to be possible in the first place. It would also seem to me slightly unfair in this context to accuse cosmopolitan progressive liberals of wrongly extending the domestic concerns of social justice to the global level, as David Miller's arguments on the distinction between social and global justice suggest. Held, at least, is seeking policies for fostering *endogenous* development under conditions of interdependence.

Held's sophisticated argument works towards a differentiated notion of governance that requires sustained cooperation between national, regional and global institutions. It is not complicit, therefore, with the formal universalism of neo-liberal prescriptions. Nor is it complicit with either nationalist protectionism, resisting the 'neo-imperialism' of international organizations, or regionalism, as distinct from (or as a replacement of) global coordination. Rather, to counter the formalism of universal neo-liberalism, Held makes the case for the coordination of policy within and between national, regional and global institutions of governance under the umbrella of social democratic values. His cosmopolitanism in the economic sphere argues for social democratic goals of policy (efficiency, solidarity, equity) and emphasizes a differentiated, but coordinated, governance structure by which these goals are more rather than less likely to be attained. Again, I am unconvinced by the global use of the term 'social democracy': but I hope to have made clear how the term *functions* as a filter-test for empirical 'mixed-policy' analysis.

This 'policy mix' points to the positive role of international institutions in squaring the field between developed and developing countries. A final comment regarding Held's line of argument is important here. Marxism argues that intergovernmental institutions have been subordinate to American hegemony since the 1980s and that the ideology of neo-liberalism serves as cover for the power of the US and its allies. Held's cosmopolitan response *qua* 'global social democracy' implies, rather, that neo-liberal policy at the international institutional level has probably been as much a mistake in policy as a strategy of domination (compare Stiglitz, 2002). Theorists of trade and finance liberalization have ignored (arrogantly or not) the material conditions of development. In this sense, in liberal vein, political cosmopolitanism regarding economic power is not conspiratorial. The danger of a non-conspiratorial position is, of course, the risk of naivety. In the context, however, of present policy-shifts in international institutions, the cosmopolitan position seems rather convincing. In committing major errors of policy, international institutions have been very harmful: which proves their potential power when harnessed to state leadership. But harbouring such power, together with error in policy, means that *reform* of institutional policies can *also* have large effects – as long as these institutions continue to have the backing of leading states. The issue, then, is not to displace neo-liberalism, or think it completely anew (Cerny, 2008). The question is rather to align the neo-liberal commitment to market growth and international trade and finance with developmental strategies attuned to the particular case. With both the ongoing shift of economic power to Asia and a global focal point like climate change, this reform to something like more 'social democratic' policies constitutes a clear political challenge for the future. Marxism's charge that cosmopolitanism replaces politics with ethics underestimates, I am arguing, the institutional complexity of this reformist agenda. This complexity may well fall foul of the realist consequences of climate change and the trade-offs that these consequences demand. It may fall foul of an emerging Chinese regional hegemon and of a regionalist division of the world that lessens the power of international organizations. These are questions to be debated theoretically and empirically in the coming years. Held's normative vision of the world economy – together with the type of institutional and policy flexibility which is required to bring it about – remains nevertheless highly consistent. More importantly, here, the Marxist critique of cosmopolitanism does not offer either a better or more effective *comprehensive* economic alternative under conditions of interdependence.

3 The Cosmopolitan Logic of Re-embedded Liberalism

The last section focused on Held's understanding of global social democracy in the area of development and ended on a non-conspiratorial note. The bad influence of neo-liberalism should be considered, perhaps, as much a journey of mistakes and unintended consequences as one of intentional domination over the developing world. It is worth, in this context, emphasizing further the kind of universalism with which cosmopolitan progressive liberalism is concerned. This section takes brief examples from international trade and finance, which serve to reinforce the theoretical argument for 're-embedded' global capitalism.

My first example returns to the issue of trade theory. Classical liberal thought argues that international trade is not a 'zero-sum' game. There are net gains from trade. In the last chapter (section 3.2), we saw that Marxists argue that the neo-liberalization of international trade policy has led to enormous polarization of wealth (see pp. 135–6). The fact that figures for global poverty have declined from 40 per cent of the world's population to 18 per cent since the 1980s, while global inequality has increased, with just under half the world's population now living on less than $2 a day, suggests that a much more *messy* account is necessary (World Bank, 2009). Again, one needs to address, theoretically and empirically, the ambivalence of capitalism in order to propose progressive agendas.

As economists rightly argue, the benefits of international trade can only be evaluated in the long term. The integration of a national set of markets into the world economy takes time and is necessarily painful. Moreover, in any international trade relation, there are those who immediately benefit from trade and those who pay the costs. International trade appears to be, in this short-term respect, a 'zero-sum game'. As the trade economist Ann Harrison has recently argued, the 'winners' and 'losers' of international trade are not simply to be found in different sectors of the economy (importers on the one hand, exporters on the other in an import-competing sector); they are often of the same income-class (2007, pp. 8–10). Now, my theoretical point is this. If both long-term and 'sector' analysis are needed to assess the benefits and costs of international trade, aggregate evaluations of poverty and inequality can only serve as general guides to a global problem. To argue so is not to deny the devastating consequences that trade and finance liberalization can have on a developing country: half the world's population is very poor; this is intolerable from several moral perspectives. The point is rather that the effects of trade liberalization on each sector of a national economy need to be carefully analysed *before* one can decide what 'complementary policies' are required to ensure social and economic adjustment to the world economy. The general theoretical point follows.

The universalism of cosmopolitan progressive liberalism must remain normative. It can *argue*, morally and politically, *for* efficiency and equity; it can *advocate*, in general, staggered and complementary polices for integration into the world economy. But it will wish to leave both the nature of the policy itself and the specific form of regulation required to particular, empirical analysis. The top-down international neo-liberalism that has come into being since the 1980s has been the *very opposite* of this approach! Regulatory frameworks for market efficiency have simply been imposed prior to market consolidation. The difference between the two kinds of universalism is, consequently, important: one is normative and commutative; the other is prescriptive and formal. Marxism's critique of cosmopolitanism shuns these distinctions.

My second example involves a progressive liberal approach to global finance and entails a much more prescriptive understanding of universal regulation. I will again speak broadly. The major culprit of bad globalization has been speculation on international capital flows and global capital volatility. It is now an accepted commonplace that international currency crises since the 1980s (speculative attacks on devaluing currencies; capital exit from countries at risk) have led to increasing poverty in the countries concerned: Mexico (1994–5), Southeast Asia (1997–8), Russia (1998) Argentina (2002) (see Stiglitz, 2002; Soros, 2002; Wolf, 2008; World Bank, 2009). A distinction needs to be made, therefore, between speculative capital and investment capital.

While many companies have outsourced their production facilities abroad to keep wages down and profit margins up (as Marxist analysis emphasizes), capital flows *also* alleviate poverty. Despite homeward-bound return on the capital invested, a country's openness to capital investment (FDI) promotes transfers in technology and skills. It also increases the money supply in the country, allowing access to credit, the condition of economic development (Prasad et al., 2007). That sub-Saharan Africa has had negative growth since the 1980s and also little financial investment seems to bear this causal relationship out negatively (Sachs, 2005). Global financial integration is, quite simply, *ambivalent*. It can underwrite the movement of international trade and assist economic development. In doing so, the liberals are correct to say that it helps growth (which, carefully managed, may lead to overall poverty reduction). Conversely, turned towards speculation, it fosters crisis and increases poverty. In this last respect, as the financial crisis of 2007–8 showed for the first time in history, global financial integration fosters contagion throughout the financial system. *The universal reach of financial capital is consequently a very mixed blessing.*

The question of the regulation of finance capital seems at least twofold. With regard to capital investment, capital controls should be placed on the borders of nation-states and highly targeted: they should serve to keep inward-bound capital, precisely, *invested* (Strange, 1998; Palan, 2003). With regard to speculative capital movements, given the universal reach of contagion in a globalized system, they *must* be universal and cosmopolitan. And given the goal of speculative capital to profit from differences in the value of a domestic currency, in an exchange-rate value between domestic currencies, and/or in domestic tax rates (for foreign capital), they need to be imposing (Eichengreen et al., 1995). Otherwise speculative capital will simply move elsewhere to make its profits: to tax havens that move ahead of regulation, to countries whose tax rate for foreign investment aims to be competitive in distinction to the other countries, etc. Such cosmopolitan imposition is a tall order without global coercive force, but it is the only one feasible that can embed global capitalism without either reversion to protectionism or the risk of greater regional conflict. Cession to supranational governance on this specific issue constitutes, therefore, a precondition of it.[5]

Since the flows of speculative capital work globally, their regulation and reduction must be *formally* universal in order to be effective. The cosmopolitan argument for universal financial regulation is straightforward given the nature of the speculative capitalist beast and the logic of competition. To tame this logic as much as possible, regulation of speculative capital has to be applied equally: like application of the same rules. This is true irrespective of the substantive content of the regulation itself: a global Tobin tax on short-term capital movements or domestic controls on capital flight to tax havens (see, respectively, Eichengreen et al., 1995 and Patomäki, 2001; Palan, 2003). In the example of international finance – in contrast to that of international trade – formal universality prior to regard for particular substantive issues is therefore a necessary condition of effective 'embedding' in the pursuit of progressive social and political goals.

My two examples of international trade and finance show that universalist responses to economic globalization must be differentiated. The mode of *universalist* argument depends, first, on the type of capital movement considered and, second, on the issue at hand. The most appropriate type of regulation follows. Strong forms of global regulation are required if the question is one of formal universality (e.g. when addressing the side-stepping behaviour of speculative capital). Weak forms of regulation are required if market competition is considered an effective tool to change behaviour (e.g. the price principle of carbon markets or the 'branding' logic of corporate social responsibility). These distinctions are critical for any consequent universalism today. A critique of cosmopolitanism that does not address these differences misses the fundamental ambivalence of capitalist accumulation, the diversity of issues it throws up and the complexity of its re-embedding in contemporary circumstances.

From a Marxist perspective, cosmopolitanism ends up complicit with neo-liberal practices for lack of social agency. Its reformism is ideologically stagnant: its purchase is only ethical and normative, not political and practical. It pushes universalism at a moment of needed particularism. In cosmopolitan response, I am arguing that this critique of cosmopolitanism avoids the substantive interest of the market, the range of issues to be addressed within the system of capitalism and the increasing array of 'regulatory' tools at one's disposal to embed the dysfunctional aspects of the system. From the cosmopolitan perspective, it is not that Marxism is wrong. It has critical things to say regarding power, capitalist crisis, structural dissymmetry, class antagonism and finance-led growth with its private debt regime. It is, rather – to employ the language of Kenneth Waltz (1954) – that its 'image' of international politics is over-simplifying. This over-simplification begins with deep-seated distrust of market mechanisms. In response, the cosmopolitan move to re-embedded liberalism – regulatory regimes and a discourse of governance together with the moral compass of a basic normative vision – suggests a more multilayered response to contemporary capitalism than that of economic nationalism and/or regionalism. Its most important counter-argument to Marxist strategy is the following: in conditions of world capital, only effective coordination between national, regional and international institutions will allow for endogenous development.

4 Global Energy Futures: Economic Dilemma and State Leadership

The Marxist critique of all forms of regulatory capitalism remains, nevertheless, telling with regard to the future of global energy policy and requires a cosmopolitan response to the institutional need for large resource transfers between the developed and developing world. This final section considers the cosmopolitan response to the Marxist critique of cosmopolitan reformism in the context of climate change mitigation. I analyse a couple of important dilemmas in the future of sustainable development and suggest a cosmopolitan argument that is focused less on the agency of world citizenship and more on that of exemplary state leadership. The final part of this chapter's response to Marxism dovetails in this respect with my response to Realism. Having discussed in the context of the world economy different 'universalist' strategies of cosmopolitan progressive liberalism, I conclude with a more modest argument for cosmopolitan realism given the intractable problems of developing a global energy policy. In so doing, I nevertheless continue to argue (*contra* Marxism) for the distinction between the universalism of cosmopolitanism, on the one hand, and the universalism of neo-liberalism, on the other.

It is now clear that the new energy markets provide the major site of long-term future capital investment (see, in particular, Chevalier, 2009). They thereby offer the US and other developed countries of the world the opportunity to redirect financial capital to the real economy and restructure their economies after a period of unilateral finance-led growth. Given the increasing connection between energy markets, regulation and climate change mitigation, this site also provides a 'cosmopolitan' focal point for solidarity between nations, peoples and citizens. The cosmopolitan Patrick Hayden stresses, for example, that environmental degradation 'must be addressed by the world community', and that 'environmental justice' provides a decisive object for cosmopolitan political analysis and proposal (Hayden, 2005, pp. 131, 133–40). 'World environmental citizenship can be viewed', he concludes, 'as a component of the more general cosmopolitan conception of world citizenship' (ibid., p. 147). That said, there are immense practical problems with this emerging discourse of cosmopolitan environmental solidarity and justice (on the normative level, see Caney, 2009a). The material interests of states play a large role in these problems. The reduction of poverty is linked to increasing access to energy resources. Reduction of poverty in India is, for example, severely hampered by the fact that only 58 per cent of the population have access to electricity (IEA, 2007, p. 46). The International Energy Agency (IEA) has estimated that for the whole population to have access to it, India's energy demand will need to double by 2030 (ibid., p. 49). Greenhouse gas emissions will jump by 57 per cent if this demand is in large part met by India's biggest natural resource, coal (coal-fired power stations). With India and China emerging as giants of the world economy, such an increase would be unsustainable for the planet as a whole. My point is this: a cosmopolitan global perspective on human and planetary sustainability is riven with major dilemmas of interest, given, precisely, the need on the part of developing countries to exit poverty. Let me exposit this general problem in the context of future energy investment: here the Marxist critique of capitalist globalization is very telling with regard to the insufficient nature of non-enforced regulation. The problem is that a nation-state response is equally insufficient.

It is now a given of the global public domain that the average temperature of the planet will rise by 6 degrees by the end of the twenty-first century if world production and consumption patterns continue as usual (IPCC, 2007). This rise is unsustainable for life on the planet; a rise of only 2 degrees by 2050 is, however, deemed sustainable. The scientific community has now established direct causality between human energy use and global temperatures: 60 per cent of greenhouse gases (GHG) are attributable to CO_2 emissions, and 60 per cent of these emissions are attributable to power, industry and transport uses of energy (IEA, 2008, p. 397; see, also, De Perthius, 2009, pp. 13–50). The IEA has estimated that an 80 per cent reduction of carbon emissions (on the baseline of 1990) is required by 2050 if this target of 2 degrees is to be achieved (2008, p. 381). A radical shift in the way in which the planet as a whole supplies and uses energy is obviously necessary. The shift to a low-carbon economy presents, indeed, an extraordinary challenge for the world as a whole. As suggested by cosmopolitan analysis (Held, 2004; Hayden 2005; Caney, 2009c), the challenge would appear to elicit *par excellence* a cosmopolitan response. The challenge is to solve a world problem and to manage the global public good of planetary sustainability by, and for, a world community that comes together on a specific issue. For, it does not matter from what nation CO_2 emissions come; one ton of CO_2 has the same effect on the planetary environment, whatever its source. A collective response on the part of all nations would seem, therefore, rational given the interdependence of interests (compare my response to Realism in chapter 3, section 2). The two major dilemmas that block the emergence of this response arise, however, from the *unprecedented* level of cooperation needed between the developed and developing countries for it to be possible. For these dilemmas to be addressed, major transfers of technology would seem necessary (Chevalier, 2009; Zhao, 2007). The Realist and Marxist critiques of cosmopolitanism dovetail here. Without the force of supranational government is this intervention in the world economy feasible?

The first dilemma is clothed in historical irony. Returning to the example of India above, it is estimated that over 85 per cent of the increase in global energy demand will come from non-OECD countries between 2005 and 2030 (IEA, 2008, p. 400). This means that by 2050 developing countries will constitute over 65 per cent of the demand in world primary energy, the largest part of which will be represented by China and India (ibid., p. 418). Most of the effective shift to a low-carbon economy is therefore required of the developing countries. The energy economist Jean-Marie Chevalier notes in this context: 'If the Chinese had today the same standard of living as developed countries they would have 700 million cars, implying an annual gasoline consumption equivalent to the entire annual oil production of the Middle East. This is just impossible. Two other planets would be needed' (2009, p. 1). The irony is clear. The developing countries – notably China and India – must forgo the development path of Northwestern production and consumption at the precise moment that they are catching up with the developed countries. The Western economic model of modernization is not generalizable. The irony has not been lost on India, which has stated that the problem of climate change is a Western-induced problem and, therefore, to be resolved by the West.[6] China appears more amenable to cooperation given its own immediate interest in reducing domestic pollution, although it equally blamed the West at the Copenhagen summit.[7] But the dilemma remains huge. Not simply does the 'American way of life' have to change; developing countries will become those primarily concerned with this change. Cosmopolitan solidarity and management of the global public good of sustainability seem, precisely, necessary, but impractical given who the major agents of change are.

The second dilemma follows from the role of energy in economic development (see Chevalier, 2009, pp. 115–44, to which the following analysis is indebted). In all, 108 poor countries, including India and China – that is, 4.7 billion people of a total world population of 6.9 billion – have an average income per capita between $900 and $3,500 a year (2008 World Bank Development Indicators, cited in Chevalier, ibid., p. 116). A minority of these countries have access to scarce resources like fossil fuels. China, with a population of 1.6 billion people, has, for example, 1 per cent of gas and 1.2 per cent of oil world reserves; its neighbour, Russia, with a population of 143 million, has 25 per cent of proven gas and 6.3 per cent of proven oil world reserves (British Petroleum, 2008/9). If poor countries in the majority have little access to modern sources of energy, then they cannot exit the poverty trap by themselves. Poor and situated in the most volatile regions of the world, they are, precisely, the most vulnerable to climate change *and* increasing poverty. These facts mean that, presently, the majority of the world's population faces a straightforward choice between exit from poverty on the one hand and CO_2 abatement on the other. It is understandable if they choose the former.

If they do, the choice will exasperate tensions between resource-rich and resource-poor countries, as in the potential case of a conflict between China and Russia (Itoh, 2007). The risk of armed conflict resulting from both regional concentration of natural resources and powerful weather events could be devastating in Latin America, Africa, the Middle East and Asia (D. Smith, 2008, p. 116). It is also estimated that these very regions of the world will make up just less than 90 per cent of the population of the world by 2050 (Population Reference Bureau, 2010; UN Population Division, 2008).

My point is the following: the risk of world instability consequent upon climate change lies in the very parts of the world where access to electricity and climate change mitigation are *necessary* but *opposing policies*. This second dilemma invites, I would have thought, a large dose of cosmopolitan pessimism. Marxist concern with material interest and economic power is again helpful in this context. It suggests that the dilemmas of interest between the developed and developing worlds, the present shift of economic power to Asia, together with the large increase in population in the south of the world, will all serve to undermine global collective action, *at the precise moment* when a cosmopolitan approach to global energy policy is needed. I suggest, here, two cosmopolitan responses to this scepticism: the first works with the previous affirmation of different regimes of regulation; the second requires a cosmopolitan politics of intervention that is state-led.

Recent policy literature coming from the IEA, the UN International Panel on Climate Change and energy experts affirms a global diversity of energies and a mix of market and state tools. This double 'policy mix' can, it is argued, promote cooperation between the developing and developed countries (IEA, 2008, pp. 51–4). There is, for example, a strong commitment on the part of developed countries to participate in the market diffusion of clean energy technologies to the developing world ('clean development mechanisms'). The IEA estimates that, as a result of this diffusion, energy demand in the developing world could increasingly switch to non-fossil fuels (an estimated one half of world energy demand by 2050: IEA, 2008, p. 418). This switch will *only* be possible, it is argued, with increasing use of nuclear power: something with which anti-nuclear environmentalists need to come to terms (Zaleski, quoted in Chevalier, 2009, pp. 266–8). The drawing-up of regulatory frameworks that commit countries to specific CO_2 emission ceilings and the concomitant use of market mechanisms like cap-and-trade systems to implement these targets can also be gradually globalized, using market tools (De Perthius, 2009, pp. 77–133). Regulated global energy markets have, therefore, a major role to play in promoting global cooperation.

But they are clearly not sufficient alone. I here extend David Held's understanding of complementary policies to climate change mitigation. Markets need to be increasingly complemented by massive public and private investment in low-carbon technologies and by strategic reorganization of economic activity. The US and the EU may take the global lead here (Chevalier and Meritet, 2009; Meritet, 2009). Responses to the two dilemmas will increasingly work, therefore, at two levels: use of the self-interested nature of the market to coordinate technology diffusion and CO_2 emissions reduction, given an increasing price of carbon; use of the state to direct financial investment and international trade towards energy priorities. We are only at the very beginning of this new period of the world economy (Helm, 2007). One can nevertheless say the following in the context of the previous Marxist critique of cosmopolitanism.

To one side of the 2007–9 crises, the model of finance-led growth will likely mutate with the emergence of the energy economy. This mutation will probably accompany regulation of global finance and reorient financial capital back to the real economy. Capitalism is consequently reorganizing its next stage of accumulation in response to the challenge of planetary sustainability. This capitalist scenario of the future will work in general *towards*, not against, catch-up between developing and developed states. The Marxist critique of global capitalism does not address this scenario. Crucial to the above 'policy mix' are three things that, acting together, would seem to cut across any national or regional resistance to international coordination: (i) an open, but regulated global financial system; (ii) an open international trading system; and (iii) proactive state policy. Without international finance and trade flows *and* state autonomy on specific issues of industrial coordination, the shared responsibilities of sustainable development between the developing and the developed world will not be possible. Marxism's concern with material interest and economic power is telling when addressing the potential conflicts between the various players of the future world economy: these conflicts are likely, and undermine cosmopolitan vision. But, economic nationalism and/or regionalism, advocated by Marxism for the sake of development, would be precisely the *wrong* way to forestall or contain these conflicts. For, they would prevent the *positive* effects of market interdependence: the future transfer to the developing world of technology and skills for a low-carbon economy; the use of the market to drive down emissions while maintaining growth; and the need for global collective agreement on CO_2 emission ceilings (De Perthius, 2009, p. 207). Marxism's lack of attention to the positive effects of market mechanisms undermines, in turn, its own critique of more universalist strategies. A differentiated universalist and mixed-policy approach would seem much more appropriate.

But regulation is not enough. The dramatic nature of the second dilemma implies that major action is needed by the international community (as was confirmed by the failures of the UN Copenhagen summit). I have argued strongly for regulation and governance up to this point in my cosmopolitan response to Marxism. As with universal control of speculative capital, investment in a new energy economy (in the context of climate change) requires strong intervention by international authorities. Otherwise, it is more than likely that the dilemma between climate change and development will not be alleviated quickly enough (IEA, 2008, Introduction). At the end of his important book *The New Energy Crisis*, Jean-Marie Chevalier proposes 'a New Marshall Plan' for the developing world in the context of the 'explosive interaction between population growth and a world of scarce resources' (2009, p. 142). For him, the order of problems the world faces today is similar to that which Americans and Europeans faced in post-Second World War Europe: 'to fight against hunger, poverty, desperation and chaos' (ibid.). The intervention of the Marshall Fund was possible due to the preponderance of American economic and military power: American dollars were exchanged for American goods. The intervention also took place in the ideological context of the Cold War and the spur of the communist challenge (Ikenberry, 2006, pp. 21–50). From the Marxist perspective, a new 'social-democratic' Marshall Fund is not possible without the material weight of ideological difference. It is this Schmittian condition – the intensification of difference through selection of an enemy – that is missing today (see, for example, Gowan, 2003b, p. 49).

The second dilemma of climate change mitigation makes the cosmopolitan response to sustainable development very difficult. But it also points up the only answer possible once both market and state tools have been accorded their place. The normative behaviour of states and peoples needs to change so that transfers of aid become a political possibility. This change in normative behaviour requires, without doubt, intense citizenship pressure on states (to return to Patrick Hayden's point). But it *also* requires leadership on the part of the major players involved. Without such leadership, collective action with regard to climate change will be stymied by the above dilemmas. Given the present shifts in economic power and the lack of an economic hegemon, it is argued that the four most important players will probably be the US, China, Brazil and the EU (Chevalier, 2009). The incentive to lead will be both domestic and international. China needs to reduce domestic pollution and wishes an increasing role in global governance despite its non-democratic colours (Zhao, 2007). The US seeks greater energy independence and wishes to maintain world power (Meritet, 2009). Brazil is highly endowed with fossil fuels, is a leader in biofuels, and wishes to lead the Southern hemisphere on energy issues (Pinto, 2010). The EU is the present leader in climate change mitigation, wishes to propose a model of an integrated energy market, and aspires to normative power at the global level (Keppler, 2009). There is therefore enough to suggest, from a rational choice perspective, that the promotion of global collective action on climate change *is* possible given these four players and their special incentives to lead. The UN meeting in Copenhagen 2009 did not make major steps in CO_2 emission reductions precisely because of the difference of interest between development and climate change mitigation. It nevertheless created a new dynamic and forum for state-leadership and cooperation.

Climate change mitigation presents, therefore, an important example of a normative cosmopolitan concern, one informed by the broad 'social democratic' values of efficiency, solidarity between nations, equity and sustainability. Given the above dilemmas, it can ultimately only be put in place, however, through the example of major power leadership. Whatever else it may advocate, a progressive liberal cosmopolitanism must assume, at this moment of history, the mantle of *cosmopolitan realism*. This mantle nevertheless undercuts the Marxist focus on nation-state development that refuses to articulate global cooperation.

5 Conclusion

Marxist critique charged cosmopolitanism with replacing politics by ethics. Given the lack of material conditions to effect substantial global change in the economy, reformist proposals reproduce the status quo (Northwestern hegemony) and only work normatively. Marxist critique is accordingly concerned to analyse the distinction between proposed norms and the reality of economic power behind those norms. In this sense we saw in the last chapter that legal cosmopolitanism for Marxism runs the risk of being a red herring, diverting attention from material modalities of power and interest to legal formality. We also saw that, for Marxists, the cosmopolitan norms of the post-Second World War international economic set-up were immediately undermined by the forces of economic power (the hegemony of the US and its allies). Contemporary cosmopolitanism is reducible to the new liberal cosmopolitanism of global elites. The cosmopolitan response to the Marxist distinction between cosmopolitan norm and the empirical reality of power focuses on the relation between norm and institution under conditions of economic interdependence. In sum, it redounds to the following.

The economic reality of contemporary capitalist interdependence is so complex today that a multilayered and multi-tooled approach to governance is necessary. Economic poverty and inequality can only be redressed through a combination of market, state and international policies at domestic, regional and global levels. *Contra* fragmentation of the world economy, coordination between these levels must be maintained. There is no one formula to the reduction of poverty or the institutionalization of social justice, but general principles (social democratic 'tests' in Held's terms) can help inform multilevel policy-making in response to socioeconomic needs. These principles are not simply normative: in a complex reality, they have empirical effects through a normative shift in public policy. The agenda for progressive politics, together with a bottom-up and top-down approach to it, do not replace politics with ethics: they look to the reinvention of politics in an uncertain global environment. This politics embraces the diverse tools of market, state and regulatory mechanisms and advocates at domestic and international levels complementary 'policy-mixes' to further progressive liberal values.

The universalism of cosmopolitanism should, perhaps, be considered in more Hegelian than Kantian terms. Hegel considered the universal as a differentiated whole, not as an imposition of the universal upon the particular (Hegel, 1831). This 'whole' at a global level is an extraordinary challenge, and we have little idea how it would look concretely. Held's flexible model of multilayered and multi-tooled governance underpinned by specific principles does however suggest, I would argue, imaginative ways of thinking it that are *rooted* in material, economic tendencies. It does not promote common rules for all. I have argued this most clearly concerning the difference of 'universal' regulation for international trade and international finance. The one requires context-based analysis under general principle; the other, the universal application of formal rules. Neo-liberal universalism is, in contrast, unilaterally 'Kantian': it has fostered a formal culture of 'one peg fits all', with bad social consequences. Without global regulation, domestic regulation is impossible in today's economy; but without domestic and regional regulation, global regulation is doctrinaire and intolerant, except in the case of speculative capital. The universalist discourse of cosmopolitanism in the economic context should be understood in these differentiated terms: these terms distinguish it from the 'new global liberalism' to which Marxism reduces it.

Regulatory regimes of the world economy are, however, unsatisfactory, particularly concerning global movements of speculative capital and the particular issue of climate change mitigation. Both require supranational governance. With regard to the dilemmas of cooperation between developed and developing countries on climate change, strong policies are needed. Without a world economic hegemon, the only possible solution to these dilemmas will come from the major economic regions of the world and their state leaders: the US, China, Brazil and the supranational organization of the EU. In conjunction with markets, on the one hand, and international organizations, on the other, these entities should lead the world on environmental solidarity between states, peoples and citizens. Cession of national sovereignty on specific issues of concern should follow.

Marxist critique argues that cosmopolitanism fails as a political response to economic globalization. I suggest, on the contrary, that cosmopolitanism is potentially most powerful when addressing present and future relations between politics and economics. Cosmopolitan universalism may well, in time, be best understood economically. For this potential to be realized, several aspects of the world economy need to be considered by cosmopolitans:

1 An in-depth analysis of the distinction between institutionalism and cosmopolitanism should be made regarding global regulatory regimes. This agenda would complement in the domain of political economy that of the reinvention of democracy highlighted at the end of chapter 3.
2 More concrete analysis of the distinction between cosmopolitan global public policy and emerging global governance policy issues would be helpful.
3 Interdisciplinary work is required between political theory, political science and international economics that promotes cosmopolitan-type strategies of cooperation between the developed and developing world in the context of climate change (especially in the context of regionalization).

Without this research, the Marxist critique that cosmopolitanism is abstract may prove telling during the next decades of world-political turbulence. This would be unfortunate given the deep need for cosmopolitan-inspired public policy on specific, but interrelated issues in the world economy.

Cosmopolitanism presents itself wilfully as a modernist discourse. It inherits the liberal emphasis on the individual; its concerns with justice are rooted in modern progressive ideology; its commitment to the positive effects of globalization and climate change mitigation connotes world economic practices. It is not modern in IR theory terms when it foregrounds the supranational since the modern is related to the nation-state (Ruggie, 1993). The universalism of cosmopolitan discourse remains fundamentally modern, however, when it explicitly assumes the heritage of Enlightenment and post-Enlightenment rationalism. This heritage has been challenged by 'postmodernism'. Postmodernism is not mainstream in IR theory, although its influence is growing and its non-universalist colours have gained sympathy on the Left, particularly after 9/11 and its geopolitical consequences. A book that emphasizes the complex strategies of cosmopolitan universalism in the context of globalization should, I believe, contain a debate between postmodernism and cosmopolitanism. The last two chapters are devoted to it.

6

The Postmodern Critique of Cosmopolitanism

In contrast to liberalism, Realism and Marxism in IR, postmodernism does not constitute a school of thought. No postmodernist accepts the term uncritically ('poststructuralism' is often preferred), and a variety of practices are covered by it (Campbell, 1998). Its arguments contain, nevertheless, a basic 'family resemblance' (in Wittgensteinian terms). This resemblance has allowed postmodern argument in IR to acquire intellectual consistency since the 1990s and increasingly designate a specific approach to world politics (see, for example, Edkins and Vaughan-Williams, 2009; Edkins and Zehfuss, 2008). The approach is epistemological, ethical and political. It aims epistemologically to test the assumptions and limits of any knowledge of the political as opposed to the rational empiricist method of mainstream international relations theory (Ashley and Walker, 1990; Walker, 1993; see recently Burke, 2008). With its concomitant focus on contingency, uncertainty and plurality, it aims, ethically and politically, to promote non-normative understandings of justice, and to anticipate a political agency outside the terms of modern subjectivity and rationalism (Der Derian, 1997; Devetak, 2008; Edkins et al., 2004; Lawler, 2008). Given this engagement with contingency and difference, postmodernism considers itself an appropriate form of critical thought for a globalized world of dissymmetry and hierarchy (Walker, 2003). The postmodern approach in IR goes at times too fast for its own good, but it would also be impatient to deny it theoretical rigour from the perspective of the heuristic method (for example, Katzenstein et al., 1998; Keohane, 1986). It has recently acquired more support in IR as a result of the perceived consequences of, on the one hand, neo-liberal international economics and, on the other, post-1990 interventionism and post-9/11 domestic and international practices of security and surveillance. Indeed, postmodernism in IR can be considered to have taken up the gauntlet of a post-Marxist non-economic critique of liberalism and its international avatars.

Cosmopolitanism does not, understandably, fair well from this critique. Although it has made little sustained analysis of the former, postmodernism's deconstruction of modernity, together with its general approach to universalist strategies of thought and practice, necessarily indicate strong resistance to the contemporary cosmopolitan disposition. It is considered naive, theoretically unsophisticated or practically dangerous: complicit, in the last, with global liberal governance (a critique which obviously dovetails with that of Marxism analysed in chapter 4). This chapter shows how these judgements work; the next chapter offers a strong cosmopolitan response. As with the chapters on Realism and Marxism, one important aim of this 'debate' is to disentangle cosmopolitan progressive liberalism from conflation between the cosmopolitan dimension of liberalism and recent practices of universalism. Although postmodernism is not mainstream in IR, the stakes of this debate are important concerning the specificity of the political domain and the handling of political violence.

Given the recent emergence of postmodern thought in IR, this chapter differs slightly in form from chapters 2 and 4 since the postmodern arguments need themselves to be made in more detail. Section 1 analyses the major constants of postmodernism in the context of modernity, with general regard to IR; section 2 focuses on Michel Foucault and Giorgio Agamben's respective criticisms of political modernity given their specific importance to postmodern IR; section 3 rehearses three IR postmodern critiques of global liberal governance indebted to them and the consequences of these critiques for cosmopolitanism; section 4 considers the work of Jacques Derrida in the context of cosmopolitan liberalism, his non-normative emphasis on ethico-political responsibility, together with the way this emphasis has been assumed in postmodern IR regarding universalism. The conclusion summarizes the postmodern critique of contemporary cosmopolitanism from these various criticisms. Despite more exposition, the overall architecture of analysis (of the postmodern) and consequent diagnosis (of the cosmopolitan) is therefore held to.

1 Postmodernism, Modernity and IR

The postmodern approach to IR, together with its concomitant critique of cosmopolitanism, is to be understood in the context of modernity. This section analyses briefly the major traits of modernity, the French critique of these traits that shaped postmodernism and the overall consequences of this critique for IR (Beardsworth, 2009).

There is a wide variety of description of modernity in political theory, political sociology and political science (see, for example, Beck, 1992; Connolly, 1988; Giddens, 1990; Habermas, 1987; Rengger, 1995; Rose, 1981; Ruggie, 1993). On the back of the last two chapters, I will define it here as a *reflective* response to the material processes of modernization: institution of the market economy, urbanization, industrialization and rationalization. This reflective response takes place in two waves: first, in the liberal thought of the European Enlightenment (from Locke to Rousseau and Kant); second, in the post-Enlightenment thought of Georg Hegel, Karl Marx and lesser continental critics of liberalism. The late nineteenth-century/early twentieth-century sociology of Emile Durkheim, Georg Simmel and Max Weber prolongs this second wave. It is continued, with methodological ambivalence, by the Frankfurt School of political sociology (Horkheimer, Herbert Marcuse, Theodor Adorno and Jürgen Habermas). These writers emphasize, to a greater or lesser degree, the following traits of modernity:

1 The emancipating power of the faculty of reason: that is, a strong commitment to both rationalism and the practical effects of rationalism (freedom). The character of what is rational differs immensely from one author to the next, but all place thought within the confines of reason (however understood). All are equally concerned with freedom as the horizon of the political (however differently they think it): that is, each deduces the possibility of freedom from rational capacity.
2 Commitments to truth and to the possibility of historical progress. Over the progressive waves of modernity, these commitments change. For Locke, for instance, the truth of society lies in a contract of exchange between individuals while, for Hegel, it lies in the precedence of the state and war. For both, however, the fundamental mechanisms of society can be analysed truthfully. Knowledge of these mechanisms promotes progressive change. This theoretical and practical framework grounds 'social science' at its best.
3 The political centrality of the subject. Again, despite differences in how the subject is conceived, modernity places the notion of an autonomous, self-determining subject (individual, nation, supranational institution) at the centre of political consideration. The norm of autonomy is universal.
4 A universalist approach to ethics and politics: a major ethical or political norm is considered in general terms.

These commitments lead advocates of modernity to the following second-order concerns:

1 To affirm a certain exemplarity of Western processes of modernization. The West does not present the only path of economic and political development for the rest of the world (clearly not, given the causal relation between capitalism and global warming). Rather, the major institutions that the West has put in place over the last 300 years (from the market to the initial organization of world governance – the UN) set a good example.
2 To distinguish normatively and institutionally between religion and the state, the state and civil society, rights and responsibilities and a liberal commitment to democracy and the rule of law.

The general axiomatic underpinning these foundational concepts of political modernity is freedom through reason. This axiomatic is at once epistemological, ethical, political and aesthetic. From the 1960s onwards, French thought criticizes this axiomatic of modernity in the humanities and social sciences. Using the tools of Saussurean linguistics, Heideggerian phenomenology and Freudian psychoanalytic discourse, writers like Jacques Derrida, Gilles Deleuze, Michel Foucault, Jacques Lacan, Jean-Francois Lyotard, Julia Kristeva and Roland Barthes argue the following:

1 There is no simple correspondence between the rational knowing subject and the known object. No representative theory of reality is therefore possible: its truths are always already interpretations.
2 The rational modern subject, grounding the fields of knowledge, ethics, politics and culture, is a decentred effect of symbolic and structural processes that are in principle multiple and unmasterable. Ethical and political autonomy are fictions.
3 Reason and law are consequently strategies of violence (whether in liberal or anti-liberal form). Freedom cannot therefore be deduced from reason.
4 Critical attention should be given accordingly to context, singularity and difference. Deep suspicion towards Western rationalism and practices of freedom is a precondition of this attention.

This postmodern approach to modernity neither transcends modernity nor opposes it unilaterally. It is intent, rather, on circumscribing the violence of modern categories with regard to the complexity of the real – *contra* claims to the universal, the true and the progressive – and on looking to non-universal ways of thinking and practising freedom and justice. In the contemporary political field, these claims are made by liberalism. Postmodern thought constitutes, accordingly, a critical disposition towards domestic and global variants of liberalism: one that anticipates, from out of modern assemblages of power, new practices of political agency.

The implications of postmodernism for IR should be clear from the above.

1 Postmodernists within IR deconstruct the empirico-rationalist model of social science and consider both the categories and reality of international politics in interpretive terms (respectively Walker, 1993; Campbell, 1992 and 1998).
2 They emphasize the 'normalizing' strategies of liberal rationality and law, considering them practices of power at both the domestic and international level. Global liberal governance is theorized as a new practice of domination and exception (Aradau, 2007 and 2008; Bigo and Tsoukala, 2008; Dillon and Reid, 2009; Edkins et al., 2004).
3 They foreground the place of ethics in international politics, but, crucially, approach questions of justice and responsibility in non-universalist terms (Der Derian, 1997; Edkins, 2000; Vaughan-Williams, 2007; Zehfuss, 2002 and 2009). Alone, ethical and political norms and rules close down articulation of the differences of the world.
4 And, consequently, postmodern political agency is considered in terms of theoretical and practical resistance to rule. Recent postmodern IR has predominantly resorted to the theoretical groundwork of Michel Foucault, Giorgio Agamben and Jacques Derrida to rehearse these concerns.[1] The next two sections look at Foucault and Agamben and their IR legacy in the context of cosmopolitanism. Section 4 then considers Derrida in this context.

2 Foucault and Agamben: The Biopolitical Fate of Liberal Governmentality

From his modern histories of insanity, psychiatry and penal reform (Foucault, 1965, 1973, 1977) to his later reflections on sexuality and ethical life (Foucault, 1988–90), Foucault's genealogical critiques of modernity congregate around three major concerns: the regime of *knowledge-power* and modern processes of *normalization*; the transformation of state power into the art of *governmentality*; and the general *biopoliticization* of modern politics. I look briefly at each.

For Foucault, the specificity of modern power cannot be adequately understood either in terms of legislative sovereignty and juridico-institutional structures (liberalism) or in centralized terms of the state apparatus (Marxism). Modern power constitutes a 'disciplinary grid', made up of forms of knowledge, institutions, technologies and practices, which individualizes people in such a manner that, at the same time, they remain 'significant elements' of the state (Foucault, 2000, p. 413). The modern discourses of psychiatry, medicine, criminal reform, sexuality, population studies and neo-liberal economics are all considered by Foucault as practices of individualization, to one side of the law, which links these individuals to the state (Foucault, 1965, 1977, 1988–90, 2007, 2008). Modernity is therefore characterized in terms of two movements: (i) knowledge becomes power; and (ii) power comes to work, not through imposition or repression, but through processes of 'normalisation' (Foucault, 1977, pp. 183ff.). These processes – the disciplinary mechanisms of modern life – are productive. But they constitute subjects as disciplined 'objects-and-subjects' as distinct from those whose behaviour remains 'undisciplined' (ibid.). Becoming-a-subject (what Foucault calls 'subjectivation') is neither an affair of reason and of impartial law nor a process of repression and submission: it is the result of disciplinary individualization. Linked to the state, individualization works for the power of the latter and is mapped out in contrast to others. In other words, the modern liberal state exercises power through the 'individualizing tactics' of 'normalization' and 'differentiation' (2000, pp. 329, 335). Crucially, for Foucault, the liberal discourse of individual rights and constitutional government form part of this process of normalization. He comments: 'Right should be viewed . . . not in terms of a legitimacy to be established, but in terms of the methods of subjectivation that it instigates' (1980, p. 97). The regime of rights cannot therefore be opposed to normalization procedures since it underpins the new economy of disciplinary power in the first place (ibid., p. 106).

Modern disciplinary mechanisms of power alter the parameters and function of the state. State rationality works now less through the visible exercise of power than through the modern 'art of government' (Foucault, 2000, p. 322). The aim of this art – in the increasingly 'regulated' domains of illness, crime, sexuality, health and economic behaviour – is 'to develop those elements constitutive of individual lives in such a way that their development also fosters the strength of the state' (ibid.). In *Discipline and Punish* (1977), modern penal reform – together with the practices that work with it: the technico-medical model of the hospital, commissions of surveillance, the modern organization of prisons and the factory, penitentiary education and the military order – form part of the division and hierarchization of individuals that frame the terms in which they act. State power dissolves into a general art of government of behaviour. In Foucault's terms, 'governmentality . . . structures the possible field of action of others' (2000, p. 341). Following Bentham's penal project of the panopticon,

Foucault calls this art of government 'panopticism' (1977, pp. 196–7). Transgressors of the law (criminals, delinquents) become the exception against which, but also through which, the actions of 'normal' rule-abiding citizens are understood. Rather than considering the exception as an extra-judiciary case, Foucault's focus on the discursive practices of power makes the exception 'the key to understanding the law's normal functioning' (Bigo and Tsoukala, 2008, p. 33). This governmentalization of the state turns it into an instance increasingly concerned with people and their things (Foucault, 1980, p. 220). Foucault also calls this concern 'govern-mentality' and its practice either 'the art of government' or 'governance' (ibid., p. 221).

Ultimately, for the state to survive in its modern form, it is not simply the actions of the mind or the body, but life itself, which becomes the object of politics. Political modernity is the age of 'biopolitics': the state wields its power over living beings *as* living beings. The life of individuals becomes an issue and outcome of power (ibid., pp. 121–2; Foucault, 2000, pp. 412–16). Individuals are thereby normalized through the governmental techniques of statistics, population studies, health and family policies, and welfare policy (Foucault, 2007). The rights, for example, to life and to health provide the opportunity for the modern subject to be regulated by political rationality and distinguished from those who fail such policies. For Foucault, refusal to address this double-edged nature of governmental society ignores the fundamental transformation of political modernity: state rationality has become the normalization of life (1980, pp. 139–43). Power has therefore become pervasive under the name of the governance of life and its utility – behind and beyond surface distinctions between market freedom and government intervention (Foucault, 2008).

Under these three traits of Foucauldian thought – power/knowledge and normalization; governmentality; biopoliticization of politics – Foucault distanced himself in the 1970s and 1980s from the emerging model of domestic and international liberal rule: governance (ibid.). Liberal questions of the legitimacy and legality of authority are placed within technologies of normalization; governance orders society in terms of normal and abnormal behaviour; and *contra* liberal ideology, the individual and its rights are not the site of free political agency, but reinforce the power of seeping governmentality. Individual autonomy must, therefore, be sought to one side of the modern liberal subject in resistance to normalizing distinctions that make us who we are: what Foucault calls 'the undefined work of freedom' (1984, p. 46).

Giorgio Agamben has become important in recent political and post-modern IR theory given his radicalization of Foucault's critique of political modernity and the global nature of this radicalization. In this respect, his most important work is *Homo Sacer: Sovereign Power and Bare Life* (Agamben, 1998). I focus on five of its arguments: the modern state of exception; 'bare life' and *homo sacer*; the complicity of liberalism and fascism; the camp and de-politicization; and the biopoliticization of contemporary governance.

Unlike Foucault, Agamben connects the biopolitical order of power with the juridico-institutional structure of law. He does this in two steps: (i) following Carl Schmitt (Schmitt, 1927), the political order is equated with the sovereign decision and situated in the structure of exception; and (ii) this structure is founded, not on the Schmittian distinction of 'friend/ enemy', but on that between natural and political life. Sovereign is he who does not simply legally place himself outside the law in order to suspend it (the state of emergency, martial law). Sovereign power is founded in the first place on the structure of exception. The space of juridico-political validity lies, in other words, in what is *excluded* from it. The excluded is abandoned outside the rule's validity and internalized within the law as the very exception to its rule (Agamben, 1998, p. 180). For Agamben, sovereign power lies in this double structure of exception, where rule and exception, law and violence, right and fact enter into what he calls 'a zone of indistinction' (ibid., p. 19). In contrast to Schmittian analysis, however, the sovereign decision is founded on the line that it draws between natural and political life.

Here Agamben generalizes – in Heideggerian vein – the Foucauldian understanding of biopolitics. Western politics as a whole is grounded in the sway that sovereign power holds over determinations of life. Aristotle's founding distinction for Western politics between natural life and political life depends on the exclusion of simple life from the *polis*. Through the sovereign distinction between *bios* (a qualified life) and *zoe* (natural life), natural life is excluded from the *polis*. The *polis* only functions as specifically political through this exclusion (ibid., p. 106). Agamben calls life that is banned from the *polis*, but simultaneously captured by it (as what is 'excepted' from its rule) 'bare life' or 'naked life' (ibid., pp. 28, 52). Bare life, that is, emerges on the border of the *polis*. It is neither natural life nor political life, but the result of the exclusion of the one (*zoe*) from the other (*bios*) (ibid., pp. 83, 107). The archaic Roman legal figure of the *homo sacer* (sacred man) describes the legal exceptionality of this bare life (ibid., pp. 71–4). Sacred man is excluded in Roman law from both profane and religious spheres, human jurisdiction and divine law (ibid., p. 82). Since its killing is neither a murder nor subject to ritual, *homo sacer* is 'a life that can be killed without being sacrificed'. 'Bare life' is accordingly the life that cannot be sacrificed and yet may be killed. For Agamben, the production of bare life as sacred life constitutes the original activity of sovereignty. He writes: 'The sovereign sphere is the sphere in which it is permitted to kill without committing homicide and without celebrating a sacrifice, and sacred life – that is, life that may be killed but not sacrificed – is the life that has been captured in this sphere' (ibid., p. 83). The foundation of political life is consequently not only the exception of natural life as 'bare life', but the circumscription of this life as a life that may be killed. The original Aristotelian demarcation of political life from natural life condemns biopolitics at the same time to be a politics of death, a 'thano-politics' (ibid., p. 160).

According to Agamben, political modernity brings a crucial twist to this argument. The modern *polis* rests upon the rights regime as articulated in the 1789 French 'Declaration of the Rights of Man and the Citizen'. This regime makes gains against arbitrary and selective power. Framed, however, in the constitutional order of national sovereignty (Article 3: 'The principle of all sovereignty resides essentially in the nation') the rights regime now permits, for Agamben, the inscription of natural life (*zoe*) within the state order (ibid., p. 121). Drawing natural life into the order of the national citizen, the doctrine of rights comes to make life the very issue of the modern *polis*. Agamben writes:

> What lies at the basis [of the national and biopolitical development of the modern state] is not man as a free and conscious political subject, but above all, man's bare life, the [pure fact of] birth that as such is, in the passage of subject to citizen, invested with the principle of sovereignty. . . . *Birth* becomes nation such that there can be no interval between the two terms. (Ibid., p. 128)

The implications of this inscription are, for Agamben, profound.

Life (*zoe*) is now 'politicized', not as opposed to juridical structures (as Foucault argues), but precisely because it has acquired the status of a right. Since all life is politicized as Right, all life is potentially 'depoliticized' at one and the same time. For, once *zoe* is drawn into the *polis*, 'citizenship can be constantly called into question', and the line is redrawn between the life that has political value and the naked life that has none (ibid., pp. 131–2). Drawn, redrawn and withdrawn, the modern regime of rights will recurrently, if paradoxically, produce 'bare life'. For Agamben, the line of decision between life and death moves *inwards* into the modern polity and makes impossible any hard normative distinction between liberalism and fascism, between the discourse of rights and that of eugenics (ibid., p. 127). The modern politicization of *zoe* leads to its virtual depoliticization as 'bare life'. As 'citizens' we are all potentially *homines sacri*. 'Only because politics in our age had been entirely transformed into biopolitics', concludes Agamben, 'was it possible for politics to be constituted as totalitarian politics to a degree hitherto unknown' (ibid., p. 120).

Since biopolitics provides this general space within which both liberalism and also Nazism and fascism can be understood, one cannot *oppose* the former to the latter. National Socialist ideology, with its emphasis on 'blood and soil', emerged after the crisis of identity between birth and nation following the First World War. For Agamben, this disjuncture between life and citizenship does not, however, allow one to look to the 'Rights of Man' as the answer to renationalization and genocide. The regime of rights produced this situation in the first place, allowing for the constant possibility that rights are abrogated for particular citizens against others, and bare life is reproduced. In this production, the sovereign space of exception becomes the norm, and the worst can happen again.

It is not therefore the *polis* that is the site of biopolitical modernity, but the *camp* (ibid., p. 181). In the camp, constitutional liberties are suspended indefinitely, and the exception to the rule becomes the rule. The juridical procedures by which the Nazis deprived Jews, gypsies, the handicapped and political prisoners of their rights so that 'no act committed against them could appear as a crime' do not present, for Agamben, an exceptional moment in history (ibid., p. 175). Rather, the camp has become the very paradigm of political space when '*homo sacer* is virtually confused with the citizen' as such (ibid., p. 171). When, with globalization processes, this dissociation between birth and nation becomes ever-more important, it is the camp that resolves the disjunction. No longer able successfully to order *zoe* in a determinate space, the nation-state opens at its very centre 'a dislocating localization called camp' in which 'every form of life and every rule can be virtually taken' (ibid., p. 175). For Agamben, reflection on world politics needs to recognize this *illiberal structure of liberalism* that the camp symbolizes. The riotous suburbs, holding stations for migrants at airports and off-shore, the 'ethnic rape camps' of former Yugoslavia, even the international humanitarian camps of the contemporary global order – all testify to the modern (de-)politicization of *zoe* (ibid., pp. 132–4). The argument is totalizing, but the last point is highly important for postmodern IR.

For Agamben, humanitarianism remains deeply complicit with that to which it is opposed: the state order. Humanitarian intervention works on the distinction between human rights ('the rights of Man') and political and civil rights ('rights of the citizen'). This distinction simply confirms the modern separation of the rights-bearing individual from political empowerment. Humanitarianism ends up considering human life 'exclusively as bare life' and depoliticizes its refugee objects in an inverse but symmetrical manner to the way in which the state excludes its subjects of suspicion. As Agamben puts it: 'A humanitarianism separated from politics *cannot fail* to reproduce the isolation of sacred life at the basis of sovereignty; and the camp . . . is the biopolitical paradigm that it cannot master' (ibid., p. 133, my emphasis). The development project of liberal democracies to eliminate poverty and help redress global inequality reproduces, ironically, this same complicity between internationalism and nation-state order. Object of the cosmopolitan conscience of humanity, the people of the Third World have become 'the exception of the world' (ibid., pp. 179–81). In their misery and exclusion, they are turned into depoliticized objects of the global liberal gaze and governance. *Homo Sacer* concludes with a sombre remark: 'an unprecedented biopolitical catastrophe' lies on the horizon 'unless life can be re-politicized without resort to the relation between politics, medicine, and jurisprudence' (ibid., p. 188).

Let me now look at the application of these two postmodern critiques of political modernity and liberalism in contemporary IR theory and its self-evident implications for cosmopolitanism. Given liberal interventionism and the security outcomes of 9/11, there is an increasing volume of IR scholarship working with these postmodern assumptions. I focus on three paradigmatic examples: the recent work of Didier Bigo, of Michael Dillon and Julian Reid, and of Jenny Edkins.

3 The Illiberal Practices of Global Liberal Governance

3.1 The politics of security

The French political sociologist Didier Bigo seeks to transform traditional IR security studies by an interdisciplinary approach that links IR, political sociology and criminology (Bigo, 2004; Bigo and Tsoukala, 2008). He places questions of security and insecurity, specific to a global age of uncertainty and risk and that intensified with the 'Global War on Terror', within a sociology of the 'transnationalization of bureaucracies of surveillance' (Bigo and Tsoukala, 2008, p. 14). The contemporary age is one of 'governmentality by unease' (ibid.). Amalgamating Foucault and Agamben, Bigo proposes the concept of 'the ban-opticon' (2004; Bigo and Tsoukala, 2008, pp. 31–8) to specify the 'illiberal practices at the heart of liberalism' (Bigo and Tsoukala, 2008, p. 35). The 'ban-opticon' describes the operation of surveillance technologies and their social agents in the face of structurally limitless threats. It is 'characterized by the exceptionalism of power (rules of emergency and their tendency to become permanent), by the way it excludes certain groups in the name of their future potential behaviour (profiling), and by the way it normalizes the non-excluded through its production of normative imperatives, the most important of which is free movement' (ibid., p. 32). Contemporary practices of surveillance and security pinpoint, therefore, how liberalism works through norm and exception (at the level of the use of technologies, juridical practices and culture). Bigo is rightly critical of Agamben's propensity to centralize the exception on the sovereign decision (ibid., p. 46, n.45): the exceptionalism of liberalism tends to be in specific cases of the suspension of the law and targets a small number of people. But, for Bigo, following both Foucault and Agamben, the creation of special laws of emergency gives sense to the overall reconfiguration of normal behaviour for the majority. Detention of terrorist suspects without trial, evacuation of suspect asylum-seekers, retention of refugees in 'waiting-zones' at international airports – this general use of 'special laws' heightens the sense of uncertainty and risk in a globalized world and, at the same time, engenders the liberal sense of the norm. This norm is the mobility of citizens, under general conditions of surveillance, to which normal citizens are subject, without being excluded. The surveillance of everyone is, therefore, not on the agenda, but the surveillance of a minority 'who are trapped into the imperative of mobility' is, while the majority is normalized as regular free movement. This form of 'ban-panoptical' governmentality appears to be, for Bigo, 'the main tendency of the policing of the global age' (ibid., p. 32).

A cosmopolitan perspective on globalization in an age of insecurity would seem, from this perspective, sociologically impertinent. Bigo's reflection on the 'ban-opticon' obviously pre-dates the present move on the part of the American administration to annul the exceptional categories of the 'Global War on Terror', 'enemy combatant' and 'international police operations', and to abide by international law. I presume that, for Bigo, such adjustments to international law are important, but do not change the *fundamental* practice of contemporary liberal power: governmentality by unease. New configurations of norm and exception will necessarily emerge. Distinguishing between normal and suspicious life, global governance will always instrumentalize the juridical inventions of cosmopolitanism in order to fill the global holes of uncertainty and doubt. Legal cosmopolitanism is thereby complicit with liberal domination, uncoupled from state-form and class.

3.2 The liberal way of war

In *The Liberal Way of War: Killing to Make Life Live* (2009), Michael Dillon and Julian Reid present the logics of norm/exception and biopolitics in the context of contemporary interventionism. They argue that war is 'specific to liberal rule' (ibid., p. 8) and that the 'liberal way of war' is not one of geopolitics, as for the Realist school, but that of biopolitics (ibid., p. 127). Indeed, 'what distinguishes liberal imperialism has always been its biopolitics rather than its geopolitics' (ibid.). From this postmodern perspective, they thereby disagree with Realism that liberalism is inadequate to international reality. Global governance goes to war in the name of life. For Dillon and Reid, it is the life sciences that provide liberalism with the biopolitical terms of its power (ibid., pp. 45–8). Following Agamben's thesis, liberal politics and global liberal governance do not take the sovereign individual or nation as their 'referent object of power', but 'species life' as such (ibid., p. 39). Globalization, in other words, provides liberal power with the new virtual territory of human life and it wages war in its name.

Dillon and Reid go into detail regarding the life sciences and their place in this liberal regime of power, particularly the transformation of military discourse and practice through the amalgamation of cognitive and information sciences and molecular biology (ibid., pp. 51–80). They argue that liberal governance turns around the definition of the properties of species existence and the consequent *demarcation* between 'good life' and 'bad life'. This 'truth-regime' of life leads to a form of governance in the name of contingency, not of liberal freedom (ibid., p. 83). Since the 1990s military and humanitarian interventions in 'failed' or 'rogue' states, war is declared against state structures that endanger life's capacity to live what they call 'the emergency of its emergence' (ibid., p. 85). The latter is life's ability to emerge against dangers to it and so organize itself in adaptation to its hostile environment (ibid., pp. 69–71, 83–7).

'Making life live' by promoting bio-humanity is dangerous. For the authors – contradicting Realism – it is the global regime of biopolitics that leads to the contemporary paradoxes of intervention. Advancing the cause of peace and prosperity through wars of life requires the rational calculation of life that instrumentalizes the latter and depoliticizes it (ibid., pp. 40, 87). War declared against danger to life is, furthermore, virtually 'limitless and uncontrollable' (ibid., p. 107). In Agamben's terms, the line between *bios* and *zoe* is increasingly drawn within global society, promoting ever-newly imposed distinctions between a life worthy of living and one that is not. Once life becomes the object of power, the global liberal elites live 'in a permanent state of emergency', since 'there is no immanent limit to war-making in the name of life' (ibid.). Exception to life becomes, therefore, the rule of liberal rule. Finally, the liberal way of war ends up 'lethal' (ibid., p. 88), since war in the name of life inverts into the recurrent production of bare life (the refugee and internment camps, poverty: apolitical life). This production is, at one and the same time, unable to control the limits of death. The killing of innocent civilians by 'rational' cybernetic drones in Afghanistan and Iraq would be one clear example of this runaway logic. In view of these irresolvable paradoxes, it is, for the authors, the biopoliticization of international politics that creates the limitless fear and need for security that characterizes globalization (ibid., p. 33). The present blurring of distinctions between the military and the police, and between military policy and civil development strategies, testifies to a global state of 'permanent danger'. It reduces the human to the bio-human and forecloses classical avenues of emancipation from domination (ibid., pp. 36–40).

For Dillon and Reid, international law and the evolution of the human rights regime are subsidiary to the global 'auditing' and 'ordering of bio-humanity' (ibid., p. 92). In Foucauldian language, the cosmopolitan dimension to the Universal Declaration of Human Rights and the UN Charter, together with subsequent 1970s rights covenants, are considered a normative reduction of 'difference to the same' (ibid., p. 48). 'The liberal subject', they continue 'died with the divinity that endowed it, in the sense that hardly anyone seriously believes in [this subject's "rights and reason"] but one is nevertheless ritually compelled to invoke them since they remain the burnt-out horizon of the modern' (ibid., p. 45). Without transcendental foundation, liberal subjectivity disappears into the 'governmental mechanism' of life, subject to the normalizing descriptions of the properties of species existence (ibid., pp. 81, 121).

In a structurally necessary turn in this overall argument, Dillon and Reid consider international terrorism in terms of 'resistance' to the global liberal regime of life (ibid., pp. 127–46). Their account of terrorism is not its apology, although it cannot, I believe, avoid ambivalence. Their major points are the following.

First, the recent 'Global War on Terror' forms an essential part of the liberal way of war. Post-9/11 terrorist events and counter-terrorist measures of surveillance and security have exacerbated the form of contemporary liberal governance, but they have not fundamentally changed its regime (ibid., p. 130). This regime is based on the protection of infrastructure (transport, energy, security, food, water) that makes life possible, rather than the actual human beings that inhabit it (ibid., p. 130). Recent forms of terrorism – Al Qaeda and Islamist groups – are not new, as Jean Elshtain argues, because of the fanatical religious terms in which their hatred of the West is couched (Elshtain, 2004). Nor are they new, as Michael Ignatieff (2005) argues, because of their suicidal means. What makes them distinct from previous terrorism is their 'exposure of, and hostility to, the *reduction of the human to the biohuman* on which the liberal project depends' (Dillon and Reid, 2009, p. 131, my emphasis). Al Qaeda specifically seeks to destroy the infrastructures fundamental to the capacities of liberal regimes and global liberal governance. It is thereby 'mocking [liberal] strategy by mimicking it' (ibid., p. 138), contesting the global biopolitical order by revealing its infrastructure's 'fundamental vulnerability' (ibid., p. 138). For Dillon and Reid, the symmetry of concern with infrastructure works with the dissymmetry between them. This dissymmetry is not the liberal one of a commitment to civic freedom, on the one hand, and ideological prohibition and repression, on the other. Rather, it is 'a conflict *between* regimes empowered by their control and regulation of life properties and processes [*and*] political movements opposed to the biospheric hubris on which liberal politics is based' (ibid., p. 132). The authors' attention is therefore focused not on the methods and values of terrorist organizations as such (they never define terrorism for this reason), but on the biopolitical order in which both liberal and terrorist are considered to work. Liberal distinction between the two – one recalls Agamben's thesis on the biopolitical nature of liberalism and fascism – is subsidiary to this fundamental articulation.

Dillon and Reid's book works with texts and statements from the previous Bush administration (notably Rumsfeld's paranoid *National Plan for Research and Development in Critical Infrastructure Protection*). One may wonder – much more so than with Didier Bigo, given the focus on a general state of exception – to what extent its reading is determined by a disastrous moment of American global leadership. The thesis wishes to address, that said, the globalization of political modernity as a whole. The liberal way of war is a necessary symptom of the modern biopoliticization of politics. Given transnationalization processes, it is now the trait of global liberal governance.

The implications of Dillon and Reid's analysis of the liberal way of war for cosmopolitanism are clear. In my terms, legal and normative forms of cosmopolitanism hold on to a 'burnt-out model' of liberal subjectivity that prevents it from analysing the power structure of bio-human liberal governance. Lack of such analysis makes both these forms of cosmopolitanism and the desire to politicize international institutions in political cosmopolitanism complicit with the power-structure of global governmentality, however good their intentions. The critique is structurally close to that of Marxism. To 'repoliticize' world politics requires addressing the biopolitical aporias of global liberal governance, not transcending them through cosmopolitan principle based on the global extension of classical sovereign subjects. Contemporary forms of terrorism do not offer an alternative, but they are, in the meanwhile, to be understood as 'agents of resistance' to the domination of the bio-human order. Cosmopolitan liberalism will not constrain, therefore, the violence of power under global legal form; with

God dead, it could further contemporary violence under an even greater veil of species life.

3.3 Depoliticization of the victim

My third example of postmodern IR theory is Jenny Edkins's *Whose Hunger? Concepts of Famine, Practices of Aid* (2000). The book presents a complex negotiation with international strategies of famine relief and the contemporary practices of humanitarian intervention that have evolved out of them. It is another provocative thesis. Because of lack of space, I will be brief, since Edkins's argument would ultimately need to be worked out through her overall engagements with sovereignty, ethical subjectivity and alternative forms of political empowerment (Edkins et al., 1999; Edkins et al., 2004).

Following Foucauldian analysis, Edkins argues that modernity is distinguished by the technologization of life, consequent upon the foregrounding of natural science as the solution to lack of human progress. The technologization of life is underpinned by 'certainty' in scientific solutions to 'human failure' (2000, pp. 15–18): science-oriented approaches to premodern situations of destitution privilege programmatic prescriptions rooted in in-depth knowledge of the causes of suffering and their effects (ibid., pp. 41, 53–5). Both famine relief, in particular, and humanitarian action, in general, are 'centrally located' in this disposition of modernity (ibid., p. xvii).

> Preventing famine, as a technical malfunction, favors expert knowledge and expensive (and profitable) technological solutions. It is linked with the centralization of power in international organizations or research institutes. In Foucauldian terms, the science of famine produces the starving subject as a subject of knowledge within a regime of truth produced by the institutions and practices of development studies. (Ibid., p. 54)

Edkins is concerned with two approaches to famine in particular. The first response to famine, as a natural catastrophe conceives extreme hunger and starving subjects as a 'neutral, blame-free event' following Malthusian conditions of scarcity (ibid., p. 26). Experts of developmental and agro-economic studies are then called in to determine the exact cause of starvation and prescribe remedial action (ibid., pp. 28–37). The second response – that of Amartya Sen – considers famine to be the break-down in legally-sanctioned economic entitlements to food, its production and exchange. This approach was applauded by international institutions in the

1990s. Famine tends not to be caused by a shortage of food-supply in general, but more by a relative rise in food prices, by inefficient production systems, and by local withdrawal from market-systems of exchange that leave specific groups vulnerable to starvation. Remedies should be found in warning systems that indicate immanent collapse in entitlement systems and/or in public food policy and re-entitlement initiatives. Edkins appreciates Sen's approach, but finds its rationalist assumptions highly problematic (ibid., pp. 45–9). 'Despite his challenge to Malthusian approaches to famine,' she comments, 'Sen remains within its central assumptions – those of the modern episteme' (ibid., p. 54). A technological response to famine as failure is sought. Sen also fails to acknowledge the 'violence of law' (ibid., pp. 60, 80): an economic-system-based analysis, even if tied to specific social and legal reforms, can depoliticize famine as such by not attending to the violence of patterns of economic distribution (ibid., pp. xviii, 55–8). Both modern approaches end up, therefore, 'reproducing famine', because, obsessed by causes, they do not consider the *political* conflicts in which famines are implicated and the ways in which consequent humanitarian intervention is necessarily instrumentalized by these strategies of power on the ground (ibid., p. 66). Edkins's recurrent example is that of the Ethiopian/Eritrean famine of 1984 and the way in which the Ethiopian government used famine relief to resettle populations (ibid., pp. 6, 9, 14, 75–8).

The modern techno-scientific disposition to famine 'bio-humanizes' individuals; through exclusive attention to their biological needs, it takes them out of the power relations in which they are inscribed as victims of famine in the first place. Subject to relief, they are structurally not empowered to resist *as* political subjects. For Edkins, modern approaches to famine produce 'bare life'. They therefore intensify the problem that they sought to resolve. Or rather, in a strident opening formulation, 'modern politics' does not mitigate famine; 'it causes famine in the first place' (ibid., p. xviii). Distinctions between minimal human rights, on the one hand, and citizenship, on the other, between politico-military intervention and neutral human aid (provided by NGOs and international institutions), are therefore misconceived and dangerous: they allow for scientism, disempowerment and the continuing domination of the West over the South.

Edkins's argument is quite complex, and she shuns easy answers. One cannot argue against cosmopolitan moral compassion for the world's starving subjects: they are in the immediate gaze of the world's rich (ibid., pp. 116–27). But one cannot argue for famine relief either, given the immediate technologization of our compassion and its consequences for the suffering. Caught in this double bind, Edkins seeks to underscore the difficulty, by stressing 'responsibility' and the need to make 'ethico-political decisions'. This responsibility would shun knowledge in advance and the programmatic 'certainty' and 'closure' of international policy prescriptions and attend to the local, historico-political contexts (ibid., pp. 147–8). These last two arguments (the double bind; the refusal of closure and ethico-political responsibility) are explicitly informed by the philosophy of Jacques Derrida. Before turning to it, I summarize Edkin's implicit criticisms of contemporary cosmopolitanism within, and at the end of, her analysis of famine.

First, modernity is necessarily objectifying and disempowering. Since humanitarianism remains within modernity, cosmopolitan commitments to the former are therefore caught up in the search for certainty of the latter. These commitments end up in biopolitical programmes of closure that end up imposing abstract solutions upon recalcitrant politically determined problems. The cosmopolitan rights discourse of humanitarianism does not give rise to a legal subject that can contest arbitrary power; it disempowers the individual and abandons it to the naked life of the 'camp'. Imposition ends up in the production of bare life and the depoliticization of its starving bearers. Moral cosmopolitan calls to the end of famine (for example: Singer, Nussbaum and O'Neill, as expounded in chapter 1) are thereby likely to end up 'enact[ing] imperial sovereignty' and robbing victims of 'political refusal' (Edkins et al., 2004, p. 12). In this postmodern analysis of famine and its modernist remedy, the contemporary cosmopolitan disposition is either moral, but politically naive, or lethally obsessed with deducing life from knowledge of the causes that destroy it.

For all four authors discussed, cosmopolitanism remains therefore irreducibly complicit with the dominating practices of global liberal governance.

4 Jacques Derrida: Law, Democracy-to-come and Ethico-political Responsibility

The effect of Jacques Derrida's thought in social science has been less than that of Foucault and immediate followers like Agamben. Despite important works of deconstruction in the 1990s by Robert Walker (1993) and David Campbell (1992 and 1998), Derrida's legacy in IR theory may be just emerging (see, for example, Fagan et al., 2007). Jenny Edkins's turn to Derrida in her paradoxical analysis of famine and humanitarian aid works with a context-bound understanding of ethico-political responsibility that derives from Derrida's conceptual framework (Edkins, 2000, pp. 116–21). As she puts it, 'a Derridean approach argues that whether or not to respond in situations of human suffering is a decision that has to be made in a particular instance. No abstract knowledge can avoid the ethical and political responsibility involved' (ibid., p. 106). Similar 'anti-scientist' commitments to Derrida that think through the irreducible risk of decision in the international political field are made by an emerging 'poststructuralist' wave of IR scholars, who accordingly eschew the cosmopolitan project (Bulley, Vaughan-Williams, Zehfuss). Their presence is marked in the UK, but much less in the US, partly because deconstruction entered the US through comparative literature departments and was considered neither theoretically nor politically rigorous (Beardsworth, 1996). Mainstream political science has left deconstruction to the humanities or to normative political theory. In light of the above postmodern IR focus on judgement, I consider here three aspects of Derrida's later work in the general context of cosmopolitanism: (i) his understanding of law; (ii) his concept of 'democracy-to-come'; and (iii) his rehearsal of ethico-political decision-making. These three concerns are inextricably linked. I do not consider Derrida's specific engagement with cosmopolitan hospitality until the next chapter (see Derrida, 2001; compare G. W. Brown, 2010). This chapter is concerned with the general problematic of his thinking on the 'non-normative', one that leads his legacy in IR to eschew cosmopolitan ideals or projects in the name of judgement and singularity.

Political and legal scholars inspired by Derrida turn to his essay 'Force of law' (1990) to rehearse his understanding of law. I prefer to do so through Derrida's reading of the American Declaration of Independence, 'Declarations of independence' (1986). It plays out the concerns of 'Force of law' in tangible form and is focused on a primary document of political modernity. The American Declaration of Independence is the first political enactment of modern sovereignty and the modern subject. Natural equality and the 'inalienable rights' of life, liberty and happiness are presented as 'self-evident truths', ones that authorize, and legitimate, the separation of the 13 American colonies from British colonial rule. Their bearers, the American people, ground the anticipated institution of representative democratic government, the American Republic. While admiring the modern logic of the Declaration, Derrida problematizes its natural law assumptions by examining the linguistic register of its performance. This linguistic reading opens up the terms of his subsequent engagement with the relation between ethics and politics. His analysis focuses on the final paragraph of the declaration, which reads:

> We therefore, the Representatives of the united States of America, in General Congress, Assembled, appealing to the Supreme Judge of the world for the rectitude of our intentions, do, in the Name, and by Authority of the good People of these Colonies, solemnly publish and declare, That these united

Colonies are, and of Right ought to be, Free and Independent States . . . and that all political connection between them and the State of Great Britain, is and ought to be totally dissolved.[2]

This sentence oscillates, for Derrida, between a descriptive ratification of the American people and the very performance of this people through the act of its representative signatories (Jefferson, Franklin, Penn, etc.). He writes:

> This people do not exist before this declaration, not as such. If it is the case that the people are born as a free and independent subject, as a possible signatory, [their independence] can only be achieved through the act of signature. The signature invents the signatory. The signatory is only authorized to sign the declaration once it has reached, as it were, the end of its signature, in a sort of fabulous retroactivity. (1986, p. 10, translation modified)

The goodness of the American people – the foundation of the act's legitimacy – is only invented through the act of declaration, and the historical signatories are only legitimated to free this people, to act as its 'representatives' once they have already freed them, after the event. The disjuncture between 'is' and 'ought' ('these Colonies are, and of Right ought to be, Free and Independent States') is testimony to the fact that the self-determination of the American people is impossible as a simple present. The name of 'God' – that is, the divinely endowed inalienable rights of the modern subject, the divine protection of the rectitude of both people and signatory – closes this 'inadequation of the present to itself' (ibid.) and hides the necessary disjuncture between the descriptive and normative modalities of the declared autonomy. As Derrida tersely puts it, ' "Are and ought to be", fact and right. "And" is God' (ibid., p. 27). Without this 'simulacrum of the present' produced by the name of God, there would be no American people in the first place. The homology between representative and represented would be impossible. 'God' is indeed nothing in this founding text of modernity but the impossible present of self-determination, of popular sovereignty. Several conclusions can be drawn from 'Declarations of independence' that pertain to the axiomatic of political modernity as a whole.

First, any act of democratic sovereignty is, strictly speaking, impossible. The law that represents a people and is legitimated by it (in distinction to pre-modern power) institutes this people at one and the same time. This 'impossibility' is not, however, negative; it is a productive impossibility. The 'inadequation' of the political present to itself constitutes the condition of the act of American independence, but it simultaneously reveals it to be a fiction. Impossibility is the condition of possibility of x, not x's constitutive negation. The necessary lag between governing and governed means that the *demos* of political modernity cannot legitimate the founding law that represents it until the law will have been passed. Democratic legitimacy is always retrospectively configured, but smuggled into a sovereign present by reference to God. Secular autonomy is therefore an important, but impossible norm of modernity.[3]

Second, the abyss of authority – covered over by transcendent principle – means that all law is, structurally speaking, violent. Qualitative distinctions between pre-modern and modern articulations of law are consequently not possible. To recognize the founding violence of law in modernity is important, for Derrida, precisely because individual and collective notions of sovereignty aspire to self-grounding and, in doing so, seek universality and non-violence, under law, in the public domain. Liberal tenets of self-determination and non-violence disavow the structural violence of modern law. The point here is not simply the Kantian argument that law must be enforced to be law: liberals are well aware of the violence of law (I return to this point in the next chapter). Rather, for Derrida, the founding violence of the law implies that political legitimacy is structurally in abeyance and needs therefore to be constantly reconstructed. The abyss of the authority of law, hidden and disclosed in political modernity, connotes constant political struggle and judgement at the heart of democracy. The point makes it understandable why scholars and practitioners on the centre-left or left of the political spectrum turned to Derrida in the 1990s for a theorization of the limits of liberal institutional politics (Beardsworth, 1996; Campbell, 1998; Mouffe, 2000). The founding violence of law necessarily creates exceptions to the law – however universal its intention. Given the necessary disjuncture between governing and governed, the law 'always already' (in Derridean language) withdraws from some bodies as it represents others. In 1776 particular Americans are represented, universally, but not the indigenous peoples of American and non-American territories, African slaves or women. Their subsequent Americanization will result retroactively from struggle and judgement in the political domain. For Derrida, exception and law must be thought *together* in the founding violence of any law. In contrast to Foucault, Agamben and their postmodern legacy, Derrida does not emphasize, however, the normalization processes of law. He is too aware of the necessary fictions of sovereignty to cast modern law in the simple lot of disciplinary coercion. This is a crucial difference between Derridean and Foucauldian analyses of the subject, the consequences of which are not yet assumed in postmodern IR theory.

Third, given the aporetic nature of modern law, critical attention must be given to singularity below and above law's normative aspiration. Since an act of universal ambition ('the American People') must fall short of the universality it declares *as* it declares it, there can be no reconciliation between political universality (the universal formality of law) and individuality (civil and non-civil lives). The necessary disjuncture between 'is and ought' means, for Derrida, that individuals will always fall short of their mediation through legal universality. In this deconstruction of liberalism, Derrida turns to the ethical philosophy of Emmanuel Levinas (Levinas, 1969). Like Levinas, Derrida calls these unmediated particulars 'singularities'. Singularity constitutes the remainder of the attempt to conjoin 'ought' and 'is', law and fact, norm and concrete life. Singularities mark the excess of the modern subject (universally mediated individuality through law). From the 1990s onwards, singularity is thought by Derrida in terms of 'hyper-ethical justice' (Derrida, 1994). This notion of justice is not the institutional outcome of legal and political struggle (liberal justice, proletarian justice, Third World justice, global justice, etc.). It is the necessary excess of all legal, political and even moral determinations to which judgement must recurrently attend in distinction to ethical and political programmes. 'Declarations of independence' leads to Derrida's articulation of 'democracy-to-come' and ethico-political decision-making.

In respect of globalization processes and world politics, the concept of 'democracy-to-come' is most interestingly rehearsed in Derrida's *Specters of Marx* (1994) and *Rogues* (2005). The two works straddle the period of economic neo-liberalism and political neo-conservatism. Here I focus on *Rogues* alone, referring to *Specters of Marx* when apposite. *Rogues* is an indicting critique of leading democratic states after 9/11: there is no more rogue a state, for Derrida, than the US. Since this historical period of indictment is over, I focus on Derrida's theoretical moves. Western hypocrisy and the 2003 invasion of Iraq are symptoms of the problem of the contemporary world order. Sovereign decisions of regional and global import are made by the oligarchic 'dictatorship' (ibid., p. 98) of the five permanent members of the UNSC (ibid., pp. 95–102). When these decisions are blocked under the anachronistic procedure of the security council veto, a coalition of the world powers refuses international law and institutes states of exception. There is no exploration in the text between the disorder of contemporary historical events and immanent critical attempts to change it from the existing state of affairs (compare Beardsworth, 2007). Rather than expositing normative remedy, as legal and political cosmopolitan arguments seek to do, Derrida instead inscribes the empirical hypocrisy of Western democracies and the structural problem of the UNSC *within* the aporetic structure of democracy as such. In the 2003 international context of general roguery, he thereby aims to account, at one and the same time, for the norm of democracy, the desired extension of more democratic accountability to the global level, and their necessary perversions. The concept and practice of 'democracy-to-come' emerges from this deconstruction of empirical reality and (cosmopolitan) normative response to it.

What, then, is the aporia of democracy, whether one thinks or practises democracy locally or globally? For Derrida, democracy is characterized by two major aporias.

The first is the irreducible tension between the two principle democratic values of freedom and equality. Derrida returns to Aristotle's exposition of it in his *Politics* (Aristotle, 1984b, VI, 1, 1317a–b). For Aristotle, the basis of the constitution of democracy is liberty. This requires the application of the numerical equality of rule, 'one principle of liberty is for all to rule and be ruled . . . and for the will of the majority to be supreme' (ibid.). But it also requires the proportionate equality of individual whim, 'that a man should live as he likes . . . whence has arisen the claim of men to be ruled by none' (ibid.). The tension is settled by Aristotle through revolving public office. In modern liberalism, it leads to the two avenues of libertarian and social democratic versions of democracy. The greater the freedom of each member, the less equal democratic society becomes as a whole; the greater the equality of society as a whole, the less free are its individual members. This tension of democracy is well known to political theory (Kymlicka, 2005, pp. 53–101). So, why does Derrida make it the overall framework for his consideration of recent international affairs? For Derrida, the aporetic nature of the tension has profound consequences at all levels of political thought and practice. To show this, Derrida transcribes the Aristotelian dilemma into a Levinasian one between the 'incalculable singularity' of each individual and the 'calculable equality' of individuals (2005, pp. 24–5). *Specters of Marx* already speaks about the impossibility of democracy in these terms: democracy calls for 'the infinite respect of the singularity *and* infinite alterity of the other as much as for the respect of the countable, calculable, subjectal equality between anonymous singularities' (1994, p. 65). *Rogues* places this account explicitly next to Aristotle's, but reverses the order: the second liberty is 'by essence the unconditional, immeasurable, indivisible, and heterogeneous to calculation and measure', whereas the first liberty, 'equality[,] tends to introduce measure and calculation (and thus conditionality)' (2005, p. 48). The democratic relation between incalculable freedom and calculable equality is aporetic because the relation between the two, while necessary, is *itself* incalculable. In other words, it is not simply that singularity will always fail to be mediated by legal calculation (as 'Declarations of independence' makes clear). The necessary relation between singularity and law must be calculated for democratic society to exist, but it resists calculation. Law is necessary: without law, there is no possibility of either 'access to' absolute singularity (ibid., p. 52) or the democratic equality of singularities. But with law, absolute singularity is at the same time reduced since it is incalculable. Democracy is in this sense impossible: it is always 'to come'. For Derrida, this impossibility undermines a priori any normative horizon of democracy (compare chapter 2, section 2.3), but it defines its recurrent 'promise' (Thomson, 2007).

In *Specters of Marx* Derrida speculates upon the impossible 'holding together' of heterogeneous singularities. With a deconstructionist eye to the *Communist Manifesto*, he calls it 'the alliance of a *rejoining* without conjoined mate, without organization, without party, without State, without property (the communism that we . . . nickname the "New International"' (1994, p. 28), a link, as he puts it later, 'of affinity, suffering and hope' but without 'common belonging' to any determination, humanity, class or other (ibid., pp. 85–6). Following Jean-Luc Nancy, Vaughan-Williams has in turn called this bond 'a community of singularities' as distinct from the Kantian 'cosmopolitan ideal and its ethics and politics' (Vaughan-Williams, 2007, p. 115). More sensitive to the necessity of political choice and political limits, the later *Rogues* is, however, not concerned with this bond of absolute singularities. The 'link' that concerns him is that between singularity, on the one hand, and determination, on the other. It is this relation that underpins the notion of democracy-to-come, since freedom and justice are made impossible through that which makes them, precisely, possible (law). This is the first aporia of democracy. It is also this relation, as incalculable, that makes ethico-political judgement all the more necessary and difficult in the international political field. For Derrida, one cannot postulate a purely ethical community of singularities in the political field, in the very name of singularity.

Making clear this aporia leads to the second. It is familiar in republican literature. For Derrida, it is a necessary consequence of the impossibility of modern sovereignty. Democracy concerns deliberation and decision under the rule of the majority. The moment of deliberation is a moment of inclusion; the moment of decision is a moment of exclusion (2005, p. 102). This moment comes to a head in the necessary 'indivisibility' of sovereign power (ibid.). For law to be made, discussion must come to an end. For law to have effect, it must have force. The indivisible nature of sovereign authority is what brings law into actuality, but in doing so, such authority risks abusing its power by making itself an exception. Although regular elections present the democratic safeguard against the corruption of government, the overall deconstructive point is outstanding. The abuse of power is constitutive of democracy because democratic law must be actualized and enforced. The aporia between freedom and calculation returns at the precise site of sovereign execution. Derrida calls this aporetic logic the 'autoimmunity' of democracy: the means by which democracy defends itself against the threat of pre-modern forms of sovereign power risks destroying this defence and reintroducing selective power (ibid., pp. 25, 36, 52). Recent Western democratic hypocrisy, the democratic abomination of the present UNSC (ibid., pp. 98–107), and normative democratic responses to them are all inscribed within this aporia. The inscription does not qualify the urgent need to reform radically the UN system in the name of greater democratic accountability to the world's peoples. Derrida is neither anti-universalist nor anti-cosmopolitan. It implies, rather, that the cosmopolitan concept of world democracy cannot function as a norm for global democratic thought *without* attention to democracy's constitutive aporias. In this context, for Derrida, 'the question of a universal, international, interstate, and especially trans-state democratization remains an utterly obscure question of the future' (ibid., p. 81).

Unlike cosmopolitan accounts of post-national democracy like those of Jürgen Habermas, David Held and Daniele Archibugi, *Rogues* refuses to envisage a cosmopolitan project under the regulative idea or norm of the sovereign dignity of the individual or of democratic equality, since each idea is necessarily undercut by the other. These aporias make democracy impossible as such, but they equally allow for the possibility of a singularity that is always to come (Derrida's deconstructed notion of democracy). This means, for Derrida, that democratic reason must therefore open itself out to the 'incalculable effects' of democratic aporia, to the 'weak force' of absolute singularity and to 'the eventfulness of the event' that cuts across programmatic anticipations (ibid., pp. 128, 135, 144). This democratic reason implies a double strategy at the international level. On the one hand, one affirms the human rights regime, evolution of international law and the attempted reform of the UN Security Council and General Assembly. On the other hand, and at the same time, one is attentive to the hyper-ethical values of singularity and justice and to the singular context of one's actions, both of which lie beyond democratic sovereignty and equality. This double strategy is what Derrida considers 'ethico-political responsibility' in the political field; it requires constant and vigilant judgement.

This double strategy regarding world politics and contemporary military and humanitarian interventions constitutes one powerful example of deconstructive ethico-political responsibility which Edkins uses in her *Whose Hunger? Conceptions of Famine, Practices of Aid*. Edkins's use of Derrida in the context of her own argument against the political technologization of famine and the depoliticization of starving subjects constitutes, in turn, a strong and forceful critique of an internationalism that pays little attention to local political conflict (compare Mamdani, 2009). For postmodern scholars in IR in general, Derrida offers consequently a theoretical framework through which to exercise a responsibility of decision that is adverse to ethical and political programmes, globally modest, and locally repoliticizing. What some of these writings tend to forget, nevertheless, is the importance of choice and limit for Derrida *within* the aporia of democracy. The next chapter turns to the implications of this point through a renewed analysis of liberal law. Before moving to the next chapter, I conclude this section and the chapter as a whole.

5 Conclusion

Postmodern thought is complex: it is neither for nor against the Enlightenment. That said, informed particularly by the intellectual strategies of Foucault, Agamben and Derrida, postmodern IR theory situates the cosmopolitan disposition in the political logic of modernity and liberal universalism. At worst, this disposition does not offer an effective alternative to international public policy and remains complicit with the 'technologizing' strategies of global liberal governance (more Foucault/Agamben-inspired scholarship); at best, it fails to address the aporias of democracy and runs the risk of political *hubris*, a technology of political judgement and prescriptive closure to the event (more Derrida-inspired scholarship). The postmodern critique of cosmopolitanism is often implicit, but its problematization of domestic and international liberal regimes and criticisms of humanitarianism necessarily imply a critical approach to cosmopolitan ambition. This approach tends to focus on the double-edged nature of modern rights and their extension to the international human rights regime. At worst, moral, normative and legal cosmopolitanisms depoliticize subjects of suffering and reinforce Western imperialism by extending minimal rights to subjects; at best, they can end up offering remedies to world politics that disenfranchise the very individuals they wish to free. Foucauldian and Agamben-inspired IR scholarship looks to one side of the normalization processes of liberal norm and rule for political alternatives, seeking ultimately new categories of autonomy and freedom to one side of the rights regime. Derridean-inspired scholarship remains attentive to the paradoxes of norm and rule and seeks an ethico-political responsibility that works between singularity and political determination. Postmodern approaches to cosmopolitanism differ, therefore, in their degrees of critique, and such differences lie, ultimately, in the place accorded to law in the political sphere. Radical postmodern IR thought (exemplified here by the work of Dillon and Reid) maintains a strongly critical position with regard to international variants of liberalism. 'Weaker' forms of postmodernism (exemplified by authors like Campbell, Edkins and Walker) remain ambivalent towards these variants and vigilant of their vulnerabilities. Given constraints of space I have not considered the influential work of James Der Derian that brings the work of the French political theorist Paul Virilio to bear upon contemporary strategies of war. I would locate him in the 'weaker' variant of postmodern critique. All these authorships are nevertheless agreed on one point: the normalization and juridification of world politics is likely, to a greater or lesser extent, to separate the legal from the political and thereby remove the very possibility of political counter-power. As a result, cosmopolitanism cannot achieve critical normative status, in contrast to contemporary practices of international liberalism, without falling back into the programmatic. This fall encourages the accusation of complicity with imperial sovereignty: here, postmodernism remains close to the axiomatic of Marxism. Cosmopolitanism does not distinguish itself in this respect from the problematic tenets of state sovereignty; it unwittingly repeats them at a higher level. In Derridean terms, a Janus-faced thinking and practice – open to the unconditional 'weak force' of singularity, but aware of the necessity of decision – presents something like the best alternative to contemporary world order. Therefore, from a Derridean perspective, postmodern IR necessarily looks forward to responsible judgement in the international sphere.

I now turn to what I consider the most effective cosmopolitan response to this scale of criticisms.

7

A Cosmopolitan Response to Postmodernism

In the cosmopolitan responses to Realism and Marxism, I have attempted to disentangle progressive cosmopolitan liberalism from contemporary conflations of (i) cosmopolitanism and neo-conservatism and (ii) cosmopolitan liberalism and neo-liberalism. A progressive politics, suitable to a globalized world, can only be retrieved if such conflations end. Scholarship must find analogies between ideologies; but intellectual and political force requires breaking these analogies at the price of scholarly simplification. This disentanglement is also important regarding the postmodern IR critique of cosmopolitanism. The cosmopolitan disposition is, in overall outlook, modernist: it is committed to reason, to the modern liberal subject, to universalism; it works with the rationalist assumption that knowledge empowers. The postmodern critique of political modernity deconstructs these commitments. There is force in its criticisms of the structural limits and unintended consequences of the liberal order. But these criticisms – ironically given the underlying philosophy of context, singularity and politicization – generalize too much and reduce effective political agency. With respect to international relations the latter point is important. Politics is about making decisions and setting limits. The postmodern critique misunderstands the specificity of politics if it does not squarely address the positive consequences of 'drawing the line' (for the opposite viewpoint, see Edkins et al., 2004, pp. 14– 18). Drawing the line, making distinctions does not foreclose possibility and deny political life. It is their very condition. The point does not simply constitute a liberal-style argument for the lesser violence against the classical substantial end of the collective good (Rawls, 1993; Ignatieff, 2005). Following strong Hegelianism, it suggests that 'drawing-the-line' *opens up* difference and singularity in the first place (Rose, 1981). Large political projects foster progressive transformation; they do not flirt with imperialism. Given the nature of the problems besetting the states, peoples and individuals of the world, these projects are needed – whatever the risks, the unintended consequences, the possible complicities. 'Good' politics is, by nature, both ambitious and messy. In the force-field of the political domain, it could not be otherwise, as Realists teach us (although they remain in my opinion too modest). Radical versions of political thought must address this point squarely. Younger generations unhappy with the liberal order require proper framing of the political to adapt responsibly to an increasingly complex, difficult environment. This chapter rehearses a cosmopolitan response to the postmodern critique of universalism in light of this overall point. It is divided into four sections.

Section 1 reconsiders the structure of liberal law with regard to Foucault's, Agamben's and Derrida's ambivalence towards law. Section 2 responds to each position from a limited progressive cosmopolitan perspective. The specificity of the political is circumscribed by this response. Section 3 then makes an argument for a cosmopolitan politics of the lesser violence and a cosmopolitan sense of decision that responds to Derridean concerns with the ethico-political nature of the decision-making process. Section 4 makes it clear, however, that this response is not Derridean and does not accept the deconstruction of cosmopolitan norm as the condition of cosmopolitan invention and judgement. Comparison with Realist prudence is again made and dovetails with the concerns outlined in chapter 3, section 2.4, on a cosmopolitan political ethics of limitation. The conclusion reiterates that, rather than closing difference down in a globalized world, cosmopolitan political argument opens this world up to the future.

1 The Logic of Liberal Law I: What Is Liberal Law?

Foucault's and Agamben's problematizations of modernity exposit, respectively, decentralized technologies of power and the operations of sovereign power. Despite the difference in attention to liberal law, both consider law as an integral part of the normalizing process of biopolitics. Within this process, there can be no normative opposition between legal rule and coercive practices of behaviour, between, at worst, liberalism and totalitarianism. Aspiration to autonomous subjectivity is therefore placed outside legislation, legal entitlements and juridico-political institutions: hence

Foucault's concern with the way in which exception determines norm and Agamben's metaphysical focus on a globalized state of exception that increasingly produces the situation of bare life. Political empowerment and agency are thereby removed from the legal domain; law depoliticizes. We have seen how this approach to political modernity has had considerable effects on postmodern IR theorization of domestic government and inter-national liberal regimes, particularly on the contemporary problematic of military and humanitarian intervention. Derrida's engagement with the status of law in modernity is more patient and subtle: he does not untie the postmodern value of singular lives from legal determination. That said, couching the democratic trade-off between liberty and equality in terms of an aporetic relation between unconditional singularity and alterity and the measurable equality of singularities, he downgrades the role of law. Derrida stresses that law 'gives access' to singularity (Derrida, 2005, p. 52), but he never considers the former a background condition of the latter under modern conditions of life. As the profound reading of 'Declarations of independence' makes clear, singularity always already exceeds modern commitments to sovereign measure. As *Rogues* later puts it, the uncondi-tional lies in the 'weak force' of singularity; not in the strong force of executive power (ibid., p. 150). The risk of liberal law for all three author-ships, despite these critical differences, is depoliticization. The liberal policy-maker technologizes power relations and offers – on the bases of scientific and political rationalisms – prescriptive principle blind to local specificity. Under the sameness of universal remedy, the global victim (the starving; economic, political and environmental refugees) is wrenched from out of the political context in which his or her suffering carries meaning, and to which his or her own agency should respond. For Foucault and Agamben, this biopolitical fate of law requires a concept of citizenship separate from the legal regime; for Derrida, the aporia of universalism requires the supplement of an ethico-political judgement that opens free space to incalculable singularity.

I wish to make a cosmopolitan response to each position in turn through first rehearsing the logic of liberal law. As we saw in chapter 1, the tenets of modern liberalism are based, from Hobbes and Locke onwards, on the paradigm of the 'state of nature'. Law effects the passage from nature to political society. For pre-Enlightenment and Enlightenment thought, the state of nature is a heuristic tool that allows one to circumscribe the speci-ficity of political society in contrast to pre-political life. The passage from one to the other is the social contract. From Hobbes onwards, the unit of analysis within the mechanism of the contract is the individual. From Locke onwards, this individual must be an outcome of the contract. The passage from the state of nature to political society becomes that from *arbitrary* freedom (arbitrary in the sense of singular life, but also in the sense of liable to contestation by a freedom that is stronger) to *relational* freedom (freedom that is only possible by including the freedom of others). The modern liberal subject constrains its own singularity in order to be free, given plurality. As article 4 of 1789 'Declaration of Rights of Man and the Citizen' puts it, liberty 'consists in the power to do anything that does not injure others; accordingly, the exercise of the rights of each man has no limits except those that secure the enjoyment of these same rights to the other members of society'.[1] As I argued in chapter 1 with respect to Kantian liberal republicanism, this self-limitation of relational freedom constitutes the major political construct of modern liberalism (compare Swift, 2006, p. 154). Its structure underpins the concepts and values of individual autonomy, public law and popular sovereignty. Freedom is only possible from the liberal perspective 'under the rule of law' because each and every individual can only be free in relation to the freedom of others. Kant makes the point precisely:

> The whole of concept of external right [public law] is derived from the concept of freedom in the mutual external relationships of human beings, and has nothing to do with the end which all men have of nature (i.e., the aim of achieving happiness). . . . *Right* is the restriction of each individual's freedom so that it harmonizes with the freedom of everyone else in so far as this is possible within the terms of a general law. And *public right* is the distinctive quality of the *external laws* which make this constant harmony possible. Since every restriction of freedom through the arbitrary will of another party is termed *coercion*, it follows that a civil constitution is a relationship among *free* men who are subject to coercive laws, while they retain their freedom *within* the general union with their fellows. (1793/1991, p. 73, emphasis in original)

One form of freedom and coercion – the force-field of arbitrary wills – is replaced by another form of coercion and freedom – the force of public law, condition of the freedom of many within a polity. Postmodern thought is right to critique this force when it becomes arbitrary and selective, when legal determination of the limits of modern persons' rights becomes unduly exceptional. The end of article 4 of the 1789 Declaration – 'These limits [to our rights] can be determined only by law' – allows at one and the same time for the rule of law to constrain power and to abuse its power. Derrida's aporetic understanding of democratic sovereignty high-lights this. Will Kymlicka's work on the right of minorities within liberal law seeks to differentiate the structure of relational freedom further given this very danger (Kymlicka, 2001). The structure of relational freedom resists, however, both Foucault's and Agamben's analyses and makes even

Derrida's Levinasian transposition of the dilemma of democracy in *Rogues* questionable. There are three outstanding points that ensue from this analysis of liberal law. They allow for a clear cosmopolitan response to postmodern criticisms of normative, legal and political modalities of cosmopolitanism.

1 The specificity of liberal law with regard to freedom lies in its understanding of law as empowerment in complex modern societies. Civil freedom – that is, the universal application of the same law to all citizens – differentiates individuals from each other in relating them to each other. There is nothing *essentially* 'normalizing' or 'dominating' about this principle of public law. On the contrary, it is the condition of difference, freedom, and empowerment in complex societies.

2 The sovereign individual of political modernity is a *juridical fiction*. No individual is an autonomous subject except through the law: otherwise, he or she is subject to the violence of others' arbitrary freedom. The modern subject is a legal fiction, not an existential fact or experience. Nobody – as psychoanalysis is the first to remind us *qua* the modern discipline of the dilemmas of modern individuality – has ever been a subject; nor will anyone ever be one. We become subjects through juridical fictionality. The application to the field of law, on the part of recent French thought, of criticisms of the modern subject through linguistics, modern phenomenology and psychoanalysis is therefore a 'category error' (to borrow the language of Realism). The individual's relation to law and modern polity is not the same as that to language, to time and space, or to desire. The postmodern generalization is flawed. Jacques Derrida is the one French thinker, I believe, squarely to resist this generalization, although I shall argue that his understanding of singularity and of political risk is still determined by it. The modern subject is an extraordinary legal and political fiction; but that fiction has massive effects for the differentiations of modern complex life.

3 Liberal freedom implies that the other is, in the language of deconstruction, 'always already' in the liberal self. In Hegelian terms, rights imply, from the first, responsibilities (Hegel, 1831; Franco, 1999; Rose, 1981). As republican liberals emphasize, given relational freedom, to have a right entails reciprocity and obligation (see Philip Pettit's instructive conclusion to his *Republicanism*, 1997, pp. 283–305). This means that, *contra* Aristotle's analysis of liberty in democracy cited in the last chapter (Aristotle, 1984b, VI, 1: 1317a–b; see above, p. 194), one cannot, in principle, separate freedom from equality in modern societies. Modern democracy does not function within two opposing values: individual liberty, on the one hand, and equality of individuals, on the

other. When freedom is posited through law as relational, the question of equality – though not its definition – is, in principle, *already* contained in the modern delimitation of freedom. Liberal individualism forgets this structure of liberal freedom and runs the risk of untying right from responsibility and allowing the individual to shirk the social consequences of its precondition (relational freedom). This is why the republican liberal argument is conceptually and politically tighter. I now address the implications of these points for Foucault, Agamben and Derrida from the perspective of progressive liberal cosmopolitanism.

2 The Logic of Liberal Law II: Cosmopolitan Response to Postmodern Reflection on Law

Foucault's reduction of law to a form of power is ambivalent: power is productive. The modern subject emerges through coercive disciplines, but those disciplines, including legal practices, individualize. Individualization is nevertheless always linked to state power. This overall framework for thinking law among modern state practices of normalization means, for Foucault, that rights cannot be opposed to power since they are complicit with it. Foucauldian analysis refuses thereby to consider the self-coercion of the individual in terms of freedom and empowerment. Since, however, the modern subject is a legal fiction, and since modern complex societies require law for differentiation among individuals to be possible in the first place, Foucault's notion of power cannot be held up consistently. What is power for Foucault is equally empowerment for individuals who wish to leave their pre-political condition by being recognized through constitutionally guaranteed rights. The practices of modern liberal society constitute as many constraints on the arbitrary use of power as opportunities for the state's increasing purchase on the behaviour of individuals. And the rights regime is one particular practice of self-discipline in relation to others that carries these constraints forward. Once one conflates law and power through the figures of normalization and exception, the 'panopticon' becomes all-pervasive in society, and little place is left for political agency. If one accepts the structure of liberal law in complex societies, the rights regime may be a powerful counter-tool to domination. Further freedoms can best be achieved, therefore, through expanding practices of law, not through side-stepping them.

To side-step modern law is to remain within the terms of Marx's critique of liberal law, which seeks social self-determination (Marx, 1843). Both the fate of communism and the contemporary complexity of singular lives no longer permit this recourse. To wish, therefore, to separate autonomy and freedom from their Enlightenment configuration makes no sense in terms of either domestic or international society. The common and harsh judgement that Foucault is a crypto-anarchist is understandable in this context. Anarchism presents a consistent political theory regarding the abuse of law and immediate sites of political agency; but it does not address the liberal problematic of relational freedom in complex societies. Since globalization implies an increasing blurring of the domestic/foreign borders, the complexity of social differentiation needs domestic and international public law *all the more* for the basic dignities of individual life to be possible within it. To recall Didier Bigo's provocative work on security studies, liberal regimes can always become illiberal. States of emergency with respect to internal or external 'enemies' are the extreme forms of reminder of the social nature of liberal freedom, and definitions of enemy and emergency are structurally open to abuse by particular interest or the politics of paranoia. But the best way to defend liberal society from illiberal states of exception is to work for a more inclusive, more accountable practice of law. With the shift of economic power to Southeast Asia, and the dilemmas of climate change, we are entering a new age of globalization. In this age, the case for greater individual freedom under the law at all levels of governance will be difficult and require careful political argument. Foucault and his legacy in IR remind us of liberal vulnerability, but practices of normalization do not put in question *the normative case for relational freedom*. Foucauldian analysis risks substituting eventuality for principle. Legal cosmopolitanism works, rightly, with the norm, but needs to reflect more, as I argued in chapter 3, on the relation between law and force in global processes of social differentiation.

The risk of mistaking eventuality for principle is fully run by Giorgio Agamben. His biopolitical generalization of the Aristotelian distinction between natural and political life loses the specificity of the political. His further reading of political modernity in terms of the biopoliticization of *zoe* does not stay with the paradox of modern law: coercion for freedom in complex society. Under the Heideggerian umbrella of Western 'enframing' (*Ge-stell*), crucial political distinctions become blurred.[2] As a result, Agamben leaves us in the political dead-end of the camp.

Agamben considers that Aristotle's distinction between natural and political life leads to the ban of natural life from the polity, a ban upon which sovereign power is founded. But the *polis* is defined as that organization which embodies the human capacity to transcend biological needs and identities and to distinguish between natural and political freedom (compare Hayden, 2008; Owens, 2009b), between, precisely, 'life' and 'the good life' (Morgenthau, 2004, p. 30). Losing this distinction, one loses the specificity of politics. Modern liberalism inherits this distinction and places it on the shoulders of the individual in its relations with other individuals, reorganizing collective life through the 'neutrality' of law. The concept of right offers prescribed entitlements, but, returning to the argument of chapter 1, it is only through posited law that these entitlements function. For Agamben, however, the rights-based inscription of natural life ('birth') into the modern polity makes us all virtually *homo sacri*. Both the stateless refugee and the domestic citizen are in the same potential lot because, once political identity is defined in terms of birth, all citizens can become victims of depoliticization. The line that draws the identity of the polity – citizens and non-citizens – becomes virtually limitless and therefore always exclusionary. With the break between nation and citizenship, rights are increasingly entitlements that produce bare life, rather than mitigating it. This argument must be countered.

Within a political community, reciprocal rights organize relational freedom. This freedom is effective because these rights function through the force of law. It is the political community of the nation that gives concrete content to abstract rights of security, property and freedom. When, as with the human rights regime, the 'rights of Man' operates in distinction to the rights of the nation-state citizen, they risk having no meaning. Subjects of such rights may be dealt with in a depoliticized manner as a result. Here the postmodern focus on the depoliticizing effects of the human rights regime is understandable. The question is, however, how to respond to these effects. The cosmopolitan response to this situation is twofold: (i) legal entitlements should be secured at the international level *so that* they function as well as possible as entitlements at the local level; (ii) such entitlements will themselves function politically only when communities at both the international and domestic levels embed these rights in a common sense of commitment to a specific group of values (the growing lock-in of domestic and international rights regimes under minimal political agreement). Whether one considers this horizon practical or not, whether one endorses weak or strong forms of cosmopolitanism, one can at least say this. The achievement of something like functional law at the international level does not constitute a horizon of domination that will produce political exclusion; it is the very condition of political inclusion in a globalized world. The argument, which seeks coordination of rights among national, regional and global entities, undermines the postmodern move. The alternative approaches are clear.

To place the international refugee camp on the same level as the Nazi concentration camp is, whatever else, generalizing metaphysics. The victims of the first await legal and political redress through law: this redress increasingly takes place, or not, through negotiation between domestic polities and international society; the second were the victims of a state of exception that targeted specific members of the polity on the basis of bio-logical and racial types, and those members were largely ignored by the international community of the day. The difference between the two camps is that between a renaturalized life seeking, through legal entitlement, transition to social dignity, and a political life reduced to naked life. This normative distinction stands even if the two camps appear the same (and, superficially, they may). It stands because of the logic of liberal law and the gradual reinventions of it beyond the nation-state.

That rights are only abstract without political community is not an argument *against* their role in mitigating suffering; but it is an argument for making sure that legal cosmopolitanism *is* complemented by the political cosmopolitanism of argument, judgement and justification. Those following Agamben are correct to claim that the political dimension of humanitarian disasters often redound to local context. But the legal and political status of the victims can only also be achieved at regional and global levels given the transnational nature of the problems and remedies involved: border-disputes, increasing migration following ethnic conflict, climate change; lock-in of rights regimes, economic investment and responsible government. More importantly, in complex modern societies repoliticization *follows* the constitutional inscription of rights. The franchise of the working class, women and African Americans in twentieth-century liberal polities was based on the universal right of civic freedom. Political struggle took place, in other words, *within* the liberal juridical fiction of institutionalized freedom, not against it. Universality is the condition of social differentiation, not its annulment. As Seyla Benhabib puts it, 'universalist norms are mediated with the self-understanding of local [and specific] communities. The availability of cosmopolitan norms increases the threshold of justification to which formerly exclusionary practices are now submitted' (2006, p. 71).

Agamben's argument for a common biopolitical space within which both liberalism and fascism are inscribed makes, consequently, short shrift of the empowering structure of liberal law and of its ongoing supranational reinventions. If one *denies* this structure in complex societies (and even a poor country is structurally complex if it functions in the world economy), one cannot argue either for sites of political subjectivity or for the productive outcome of drawing the line. Political agency is thereby reduced to the local and to exit options: which makes no political sense today. The nation-state and international organization are inextricably entangled: this entanglement should be politically appropriated in new ways, not denounced as annulling political recognition. The next section continues this reflection in terms of the lesser violence. I first end this section with a discussion on Jacques Derrida and the structure of liberal law.

I noted above that Derrida is the one French philosopher not to have generalized the logics of experience and desire across the social sciences and to have stayed with the ambivalent specificity of the modern subject and liberal law: freedom through coercion. Indeed, his less well-known book *Glas* (1974) – a sustained reflection on political philosophy and literature through readings of Georg Hegel and Jean Genet – specifically addresses this 'stricture' of law. Law does not reduce difference to the same; it opens and closes difference at one and the same time (see Beardsworth, 1996, pp. 46–97). For this very reason, Derrida is committed to supranational legal and political institutions. That said, his understanding of singularity, political risk and invention remain determined by the above generalization. This ultimately makes Derrida's understanding of possibility too formal.

I argued above that one cannot separate freedom from equality in the modern understanding of political freedom. If freedom is relational, the question of equality is *already* contained in the modern definition of freedom. The definition itself of equality is, however, left open: equality of opportunity, equality of reward, equality of outcomes, etc. Aristotle's understanding of the democratic dilemma is pre-modern. The point is not taken up in *Rogues* despite Derrida's previous (1974) analysis of the stricture of modern law. Aristotle should consequently not, I suggest, stand as a guiding definition of the aporias of democracy from out of which 'democracy-to-come' is thought. Liberalism does not say 'liberty is . . . that a man should live as he likes' (Aristotle, 1984b, VI, 1: 1317a). Liberty in modern complex societies reflects the ability to live as one likes insofar as this ability does not harm others' (reciprocal) abilities. Liberty is a political concept of self-restraining individuality in social plurality. The tension in Aristotle between liberty and equality is not modern. One should therefore not equate, as Derrida does, incalculable singularity with freedom, and moral, legal and political calculation with equality. Freedom and equality cannot be separated in republican liberalism. They cannot subsequently be re-related in aporetic manner as an irreducible paradox between 'the infinite respect of the singularity *and* infinite alterity of the other', on the one hand, and 'respect of the countable, calculable, subjectal equality between anonymous singularities', on the other (Derrida, 1994, p. 65). The liberal concept of freedom includes within it, again, reference to all other citizens. The force of law, that Derrida powerfully expounds in 'Declarations of independence', is unthinkable without this formal inclusion before determinant general rules. Law is force, before any executive order, because we must be coerced into freedom ('forced to be free', as Rousseau notoriously put it: 1762, Book 1, 7). The only consistent political theoretical response to this coercion is anarchism.

When *Rogues*, transcribing Aristotle into modern Levinasian terms, considers freedom in terms of 'singularity' and 'alterity', it is not rehearsing a modern political aporia. It is rehearsing an aporia between a hyperbolic understanding of ethics (unconditional singularity) and a specific understanding of politics (formal or numerical equality). As I stressed in the last chapter, Derrida emphasizes the incalculable nature of the *relation* between the two. This is important since it undermines the very thought of 'a community of singularities' in the political field (for example: Vaughan-Williams, 2007). I would suggest now, however, that the very possibility of this postmodern reflection is already the institution of modern law. In societies of wide social differentiation, law constitutes a background condition of 'incalculable singularity', it does not simply 'give access to it' (Derrida, 2005, p. 52). In contrast to Foucault and his legacy, Derrida is certainly committed to the necessity of determination for there to be singularity. But singularity still rides free of determination in his work. The relation between singularity and calculation is considered necessary, but it remains a relation between two analytically separated entities that are *then* brought back into relation with each other in aporetic mode. Of course singular lives precede law since life precedes law. But, under conditions of social plurality, law constitutes the background condition of singularity as well as the risk that it can be annulled. The aporia of modern democratic determination is to be situated, in other words, *within* the law of freedom and not between a 'free' (incalculable) singularity and all moral, legal and political laws. The problem lies in the modern liberal paradox of law and freedom and its futures in global social differentiation and staggered relations between law and force. The problem lies not, as it does in *Rogues*, in a general deconstructive metaphysics of singularity and calculation which is *then* applied to modern democracy and possible internationalizations of it. If one works with the first problem, one is more engaged in a politics of legal differentiation; if one works with the second problem, one is more engaged in a deconstruction of law and democracy as such. These are two different ways of responding critically to international actuality.

My different responses to Foucault, Agamben and Derrida suggest, overall, the following: (i) the regime of rights empowers and differentiates under the fiction of a sovereign subject; (ii) this subject is always already related to others through public law which empowers him or her; (iii) the risk of exceptions to the law *as* the law is built into this structure, but the latter equally offers normative remedies to it; (iv) in the present break-up between nationhood and citizenship, legal cosmopolitanism offers the right kind of perspective because it holds to the *structure* of liberal law with increasing social differentiation (now beyond the borders of the nation, not only within it); (v) in the name of difference and individuality, more invention of universal law is therefore required, not less; (vi) the risk of depoliticization must be addressed through a multilevel structure of governance, not against it, and this is the challenge of political cosmopolitanism and its differentiated universalism; (vii) it is within this structure that new modalities of the force of law will emerge (compare chapter 3). Given these points, I turn now to a reflection on the lesser violence and a cosmopolitan understanding of such politics.

3 A Politics of the Lesser Violence: Cosmopolitan Response to Illiberal Liberalism

The 2004 report, 'A more secure world: our shared responsibility', of the UN High-Level Panel on Threats, Challenges and Change (UN, 2004) adopts many of the recommendations of the International Commission on Intervention and State Sovereignty previously set up by the Canadian government in 2000 (ICISS, 2001). As Alex Bellamy emphasizes (2005 and 2008), the Canadian Commission was set up to reconsider humanitarian intervention after the Kosovo crisis and in response to General-Secretary Kofi Annan's call to the General Assembly to sort out tensions between state sovereignty and human rights (Annan, 1999). I am less concerned here with the Commission as such than with a series of distinctions it makes. I pursue these distinctions in order to address the question of the lesser violence in the context of 9/11 and its postmodern theoretical legacy in IR. The following commentary works with my response to Realism in chapter 3.

The Commission argues, first, for the 'responsibility to protect' (R2P) as against 'the right to intervene' in order to alleviate the UN Charter's tension between respect for human rights, on the one hand, and the principles of state sovereignty and non-intervention on the other. It argues that 'states have the responsibility to protect citizens from avoidable catastrophe' (ICISS, 2001, 2.29). This responsibility should take precedence over those of sovereignty and non-intervention in cases of state-related 'large scale loss of life, genocide or ethnic cleansing' (ibid., 4.19). For the judgement to be made, it must be established, therefore, beyond all reasonable doubt, that the large-scale loss of life is the consequence of government policy.

Second, state sovereignty comes to imply a dual responsibility with this judgement, one that is made the condition of UN membership of the international society of states. The responsibility to respect the sovereign right of states now implies state responsibility to respect the 'the basic rights of all people within the state' (ibid., 1.35). The right to become a member of the UN involves responsibility to one's own peoples. In the terms of this chapter, the domestic structure of rights and responsibilities under liberal law is here reinvented at the level of global society. I would argue that this society represents something like a republican contract between 'international order' and 'world society' (to use the language of Hedley Bull, 1977). The Canadian Commission emphasizes the order of states all the while making internal sovereignty a global issue of overview and citizenship: classic modern sovereignty is thereby undermined, but the 'disorder' of human rights in an international order of nation-states is contained by the principle of sovereign *legitimacy*. A shift is thereby made possible to a slightly more cosmopolitan world society that remains state-related: people's government leaders are not immune to international justice and jurisprudence. When the report remarks that 'universal agreement' on these two principles standing together was possible (ibid., Appendix B), a significant step towards minimum political global agreement is canvassed. That said, subsequent dilution of the report at the UN World Summit 2005 showed some disquiet that the R2P principle could justify non-consensual military intervention (see Bannon, 2006; Bellamy, 2008, pp. 615–18).

Third, the R2P principle was nevertheless ratified by the UN Security Council (UNSC) in 2006 and is considered a new legal norm of state legitimacy, involving economic, judicial, military and political commitments.[3] This norm could at some future point gain consensus and become international law: principles guaranteed by interstate treaty. In the meantime it is considered by its proponents as, 'on average', a growing international practice (1.25).

Fourth, the principle of 'responsibility to protect' negotiates carefully not only between state sovereignty and the sovereignty of the dignity of the person, but also between already existent violence (the conflict on the ground) and the violence of war that intends to bring peace. The key questions with regard to the use of force are therefore: (i) 'With what right?' and (ii) 'When is force permissible?' I have already responded to these questions in chapter 3 from a mid-term normative perspective that synthesizes the thoughts of cosmopolitanism and classical Realism. The Canadian Commission offers two sets of Realist guidelines from a short-term perspective given the present reality of power. From these constraints, it presents its ethico-political judgements. Given the present set-up, the UNSC is the realistic source of authority: it should not be replaced, but its membership should be improved to canvas wider international/global legitimacy. In the eventuality of conflict between the five permanent members, cases should be deferred to a two-thirds majority of the General Assembly and to regional associations, although it leaves ultimate authority, understandably if inconsistently, in the hands of the UNSC. The question of legitimacy is not resolved by the report, given its desire to reform the present situation. Use of force – military intervention and/or humanitarian intervention, secured by military force – is only considered the *extreme* form of the responsibility to protect. A line is drawn between legitimate and illegitimate use of force according to five precautionary criteria: the right authority (which can only be the least wrong authority in an unreformed UN system); just cause (large and systematic violations of human rights and/or extreme threats to international security and peace); right intentions (mixed motives of states are a political fact of life, but a clear distinction between these motives, double standards and consistent international concern is possible); last resort (use of military force after all diplomatic efforts are perceived internationally to have been exhausted); proportional means (the violence unleashed should not exceed, beyond all reasonable calculation, the violence to be mitigated); and reasonable prospects (the outcome of intervening must be seen, prior to the event, as more protective of the lives of those concerned than the outcomes of not intervening). The report concludes that the responsibility to intervene, if acted upon following these criteria, must be accompanied by the responsibility to rebuild. Conflict resolution that resorts to violence should work to a durable peace that mitigates the violent conditions under which intervention was deemed appropriate in the first place. It also remarks, *contra* the Realist argument of selectivity (all interventions are selective given the irreducibility of power and interest), that, with respect to right intentions, 'the reality that interventions may not be mounted in every case where there is justification for doing so, is no reason for them not be mounted in any case' (ibid., 4.2). In other words, the Commission is at one and the same time normative and prudent.

The UN report of 2004, 'A more secure world: our shared responsibility', takes up all these recommendations and makes them specific goals of international law regarding intervention. It endorses the principle of 'responsibility to protect' rather than the 'right to intervene' because the principle convincingly places the responsibility first with states. The use of force is equally carefully circumscribed, and the problem of legitimacy leads the panel to advocate in detail a recomposition of the Security Council (14.244–260). Kofi Annan hoped at the end of 2004 that the UN report 'Threats and challenges' would have effects in the following year.[4] On one level, this was clearly not the case. The report could be considered to have gone nowhere in terms of UN institutional reform and the evolution of international law. I would argue differently.

The intensity of the post-9/11 climate of security continued to muffle explicit attempts to reorganize that climate. The years 2004–6 were watershed years for changing perceptions around Iraq, especially after the US Congressional elections, and nervousness at the concept of non-consensual military intervention. Despite considerable watering-down at the 2005 World Summit, the R2P report continues to have effects: as Alex Bellamy, critical himself of its criteria-thresholds for intervention, argues, 'the endorsement of the R2P by the General Assembly and Security Council demonstrates a broad consensus that international society should be engaged in protecting populations from grave harm' (Bellamy, 2008, p. 630). Within a Habermasian-type perspective, my argument is that these reports form part of the gradual, messy, reversible evolution of international law with regard to states' international rights and domestic responsibilities towards their peoples. As I argued in chapter 3, such constraints will only gradually be accepted by the weaker states if the stronger states show leadership. For the moment, this example remains the overall prerogative of Northwestern democracies, although China is in agreement that 'massive humanitarian' disasters are the 'legitimate concerns of the international community'.[5] Simply put, this is the least violent alternative that international cooperation between states in conditions of increasing interdependence has. It nevertheless suggests possible international agreement on a minimal 'republican' contract of membership in the international community of states: if a state enjoys *rights in international society*, then this state has *responsibilities in domestic society*.

This alternative embodies, therefore, a universal norm of behaviour on the part of all states. It draws a normative line between 'poor leadership' and 'good leadership' founded on a common value of social life. And it sets out conditions for the justification and use of force on the basis of that line. As a principled argument, sensitive to power politics and instrumentalization, this alternative works within the logic of the lesser violence and theorizes, within the context of global 'threats and challenges', principles of action. Some of the threats referred to may be partly contrived (nuclear terrorist attack seems logistically impossible without state support), and there is an uncalled-for sense of emergency in the report that postmodern IR theory would rightly problematize. The cosmopolitan disposition should, nevertheless, endorse this alternative as a positive step towards less violence. No military or humanitarian intervention (with heavy military assistance) has yet lived up to these principles. They represent a large shift in international thinking, rooted to the reality of state-power politics, which will have normative effects on state behaviour. They suggest, rightly, that peremptory intervention in the name of genocide is counter-effective; conditions of bad government and civil conflict must be improved. The responsibility to rebuild must therefore be done in as localized a way as possible in order to rebuild the conditions of the victims' political agency;

and, from the first, the responsibility to prevent massive harm always precedes that of protecting peoples from harm undertaken.

All this presents a huge, practically impossible task. From the cosmopolitan perspective, it is nevertheless the right normative framework to think about and practise increasing commitments to peoples' vulnerabilities under conditions of state-interdependence. Postmodern argument does not undermine the empowering function of this framework. The above reports make careful distinctions and draw political limits, showing how reasoned calculation opens up the path to lesser violence. That one must predict that the outcomes of intervention are less violent than the outcomes of not intervening requires on-the-ground knowledge of a complex nature. *Contra* Edkins's overall take in *Whose Hunger?*, calculative science helps to determine the better knowledge and the better decision. She is right, nevertheless, to insist on active local participation in the mitigation and development process.

International organizations like the World Bank, the IMF and OECD have been gradually moving in this direction since 2002. Institutions take time to change direction. My point is not to underestimate the moral smugness and technical arrogance of some members of IGOs and NGOs. It is to argue, rather, for something like the right philosophical framework at a given moment of history. Such arrogance should not, in other words, undermine the case for progressive principle at the international level, a differentiated universalism, nation-state proactiveness and social scientific calculation. Edkins and Zehfuss are also right to argue for political responsibility and risk (Edkins, 2000; Zehfuss, 2002, pp. 254–5; 2009). But the political judgements involved are making global governance *reasoned*: sensitive to difference, operating within difference, and fostering difference through generally accepted norm and rule.

The 2004 UN report dedicates a sub-section to terrorism and counter-terrorist measures (6.145–64). I address its recommendations in order to respond, in the name of the lesser violence, to Dillon and Reid's (2009) account of the 'liberal way of war'.

The UN report recognizes that terrorism is a political issue 'concerning political grievances' (ibid., 6.145) and 'flourishes in contexts of regional conflict and foreign occupation' (ibid.). It is also aware, after wide consultation with governments in the North and South of the world, that 'approaches to terror focusing wholly on military, police and intelligence measures' have 'alienate[d] large parts of the world's population and thereby weaken[ed] the potential for effective collective action against terrorism' (ibid., 6.147). Its proposal for a broader-based approach, which encourages public support rather than opposition for all states that have active terrorist networks on their territory, includes attacking root economic, social and political causes and strengthening states' ability to counter terrorism 'within the framework of human rights' (ibid., 6.148–9). It condones the third UNDP *Arab Development Report*, 'Towards freedom', which catalyzed public debate within the Middle East 'on the need for gender empowerment, political freedom, rule of law and civil liberties' (ibid.). It argues for counter-terrorism measures that remain within a legal framework, respectful of rights and civil liberties, where and to the extent that this is possible. It therefore suggests that intelligence-gathering will overstep liberal legal frameworks, that the exception is inevitable regarding the prevention of mass loss of life. At no point does it condone, however, practices of torture for the greater good. It suggests that all member states of the UN should sign up to the various international conventions on anti-terrorism and terrorist financing and recommends that the UNSC's Counter-Terrorism Executive Directorate be widened in membership and extended in authority (6.154–5). Despite its insufferable name, this UN body prevents bilateral assistance that weakens a global approach to security, but its practices should be regularly reviewed.

Most importantly for my purposes, the panel realizes the importance, at a specific moment of alienation from the West, of heading this broad-based approach with a normative framework for defining terrorism. It stresses: 'Achieving a comprehensive convention on terrorism, including a clear definition, is a political imperative' (ibid., 6.159). Two issues have prevented this in their opinion: state terrorism and perceptions of terrorist legitimacy ('the terrorist as freedom-fighter'). Clearly, any comprehensive definition of terrorism should not override the right of resistance, but the report draws a line at the use of force against civilians: 'there is nothing in the fact of occupation that justifies the targeting and killing of civilians' (ibid., 6.160, 164a). Their definition of terrorism follows, based on Security Council Resolution 1566 in 2004. Terrorism is 'any action that is intended to cause death or serious bodily harm to civilians or non-combatants, when the purpose of such act, by its nature or context, is to intimidate a population or to compel a Government or an international organization to do or abstain from doing any act' (ibid., 6.164d). This last comment is ambiguous: the term 'any act' returns one to the state of natural freedom; in the public realm acts are legally circumscribed, and this is precisely what opposes them to terrorist action. That said, the normative framework is compelling on the condition that all states and non-state actors are inscribed within it (principle of reciprocity).

Out of the requirements of political realism, the report is not hard enough regarding Western double-standards. The cosmopolitan extension of this report's aspiration to a normative framework is, however, the right way forward (as distinct from postmodern retrenchment). The extension would argue that there can, in principle, be no exceptions to the persecution of civilian life for political ends, and that, if exceptions are made, they have to be accounted for by domestic governments according to democratic principles of governmental legitimacy. At the level of global collective security, a body should, therefore, be formed that is authorized by the General Assembly, assisted by the Executive Security Council and linked to the ICC, which monitors exceptions to the rule. This is not politically feasible at present, but it provides the 'compelling normative' and institutional framework to which a world politics of non-alienating counter-terrorist measures should tend. Again, instituted rights provide *the most appropriate response* to exceptions to the law.

Despite its 'best-practices' terminology, the report provides, then, as much resistance to normalization processes as it is part of them. It draws a clear line between terrorist life and other forms of life because it believes in the universal value of the right to life. This right does not foster normalization through the definition of non-legal exceptions (Foucault, Bigo); it fosters normative distinctions between what is 'tolerable' and what is not. In *The Liberal Way of War: Killing Life to Make Life Live*, Dillon and Reid argue that these very distinctions biopoliticize life and end up being lethal. They suggest, further, that such distinctions propagate liberal notions of tolerance that have their own intolerant limits, and are therefore implicitly or virtually imperial, or at the very least, impose Western categories of law and politics on non-Western states and populations (following Derrida, in Derrida and Habermas, 2003). The terrorist, I recall from chapter 6, is considered by Dillon and Reid to resist 'the reduction of the human to the biohuman' (2009, p. 131). By seeking to destroy the infrastructure fundamental to the capacities of liberal regimes and of global liberal governance, contemporary terrorism 'mocks [liberal] strategy by mimicking it' (ibid., p. 138). This argument should be met by the cosmopolitan politics of the lesser violence indicated above.[6]

First, Al Qaeda and associated terrorists target in a random manner innocent civilian life. That they target infrastructure that houses them is *secondary* to their strategy. Without the killing of innocent life, terrorists would not fulfil their aims: to put pressure on governments and international organizations (particularly its declared enemy, the UN) through the creation of fear amongst the population (see Ignatieff, 2005). Al Qaeda terrorists are not resisting the liberal 'reduction of the human to the biohuman'; they are instrumentalizing civilian life for political ends. These ends have been clear ever since Bin Laden publicized them after 9/11. They also have their own understandable and justifiable logic as ends: withdrawal of American troops from the holy land of Islam, withdrawal of state support from Israel and institution of a Palestinian state (see Rashid, 2008; Scheuer, 2008). What is not understandable is the means used to achieve this political end. If Al Qaeda wished to resist this reduction to the bio-human, I would argue that a more Gandhi-like approach of non-violent resistance would be both more attuned to the problem of biopoliticization and, possibly, more effective. They have not chosen that route: one that the Nelson Mandela-led ANC considered before deciding, in the balance of forces, to target, specifically, South African infrastructure (Mandela, 1994, pp. 107–62). Loss of life was always regretted by the ANC, at least when it was guided by the imprisoned Mandela. In contrast, radical Islamic forms of terrorism have little interest in complex modern life. They use modern and contemporary technologies, but refuse the general social consequences that accompany them.

Second, Dillon and Reid suggest that the suicide tactics of contemporary terrorism are not of interest. Following Agamben's Heideggerian reading of political modernity, they argue, rather, that the general biopolitical scenario underscoring it is alone of interest. But, the suicide tactics of Al Qaeda *are* interesting regarding life. The latter have no respect for Western civilian life, Muslim life or their own lives because they work within a fundamentalist normative framework. This framework radicalizes and instrumentalizes the Islamic concept of *jihad* ('spiritual struggle'), separates Muslim from Muslim as much as infidel from fidel and provides them with paradisiacal rewards for committing collective murder. To characterize in this context Al Qaeda and its associate groups as 'fundamentally resisting . . . the reduction of the human to the biohuman' (Dillon and Reid, 2009, pp. 144–5) is a totalizing judgement that remains, precisely, blind to distinctions of life. It is these distinctions that require definition and critical political appraisal. Despite the rigour of its polemic, Dillon and Reid's Agamben-inspired critique of liberal life risks theoretical complicity with the worst violence. It is critical to pursue the double standards and paradoxes of liberalism, but not at the cost of losing distinctions that permit life in the first place.

Third, and consequently, there is an important appraisal of difference that must be made prior to addressing Western democratic hypocrisy. To tar both liberalism and its enemies with the same biopolitical brush, in the name of difference, is not that appraisal. It prevents one from looking to required distinctions and limits and, subsequently, to political decisions which – while violent in their delimitation – make the difference over political time. To circumscribe terrorism and gain global consent to that circumscription is, as we saw in the UN 2004 panel argument above, a 'political imperative of the first order'. To make this possible is, without doubt, a political struggle, but one guided by a universalizing logic of agreement and reciprocity.

Fourth, Dillon and Reid not only fail to give an account of terrorism that permits better distinctions (they do not wish to, but my argument is that not to do so constitutes the very failure of their politics of difference), they make no consequent distinction between greater terrorists and lesser terrorists. As recent events in Afghanistan have shown, this distinction is, precisely, vital. One must not only distinguish a terrorist from the population, one must also distinguish terrorists who have a global/regional ambition (as Al Qaeda does) and those who have a local-national political end. Dillon and Reid argue in this context that contemporary forms of terror do not constitute 'a conflict about the coincidence of sovereign claims over a disputed territory' because 'they are not simply sovereign ... in those ways' (ibid., p. 131). The point is moot. Many Taliban fighters are fighting for their particular province as much as for Afghanistan: they are not fighting the West in the name of a pan-Islamism (Rashid, 2001 and 2008). If they commit terrorist acts, they are not of the same kind as those of Al Qaeda because their insurgent aims are related to the end of foreign occupation. At the time of writing, there is increasing resistance in the Northwest to a NATO presence in Afghanistan. The outcome remains unpredictable, but the Western powers in Afghanistan and Pakistan are attempting to bring the more local Taliban fighters into the political process and gradually leave the process of Afghan self-organization to the Afghans. Such co-option, if it remains possible, requires a 'compelling normative framework' of terrorism, political process, military procedure and long-term development that persuade angry civilian populations to move from terror to politics. It requires a general ethos of *ethical life* that is advocated by democratic example of the rule of law, by clearer separation between military and humanitarian intervention, rapid apology for collateral damage and visible indication of the sway of international law. This universalism requires, precisely, conceptual distinctions and ethically and politically defined limits.

In sum, can a biopolitical reading of contemporary forms of terrorism argue for these distinctions: distinctions of principle, of identity and of decision on which a less violent way of life for the Afghan people as a whole is predicated? Given its postmodern metaphysics, under which all liberal cows and all terrorist cows appear 'black' (Hegel 1807/1977, p. 9), it is, I fear, unlikely. It is more likely that a cosmopolitan perspective on the lesser violence, international rule of law and differentiated universalism may.

4 Political Judgement and Risk: A Cosmopolitan Response to Derrida and his IR Legacy

Departing from two international reports submitted in response to 9/11 and the subsequent invasion of Iraq, the previous section has made argument in favour of a cosmopolitan politics of the lesser violence. This politics is informed by the strong Hegelian understanding that conceptual limits provide for the possibility of difference, not its annulment. Jacques Derrida's early reading of Levinasian ethics, 'The violence of metaphysics' (1967) is more sympathetic to this understanding than is commonly understood (see Beardsworth, 1996, pp. 122–41). In that essay, he argues for a community of the 'least violence' in full understanding of the necessity of conceptual delimitation. The essay is in this respect indebted to Aristotelian ontology and Aristotle's notion of prudence. This chapter has spoken a lot of responsibility, political judgement and risk in terms which respond to postmodern IR's own commitments to them, developed in the previous chapter. It has in a certain sense suggested that postmodern IR gets identity and difference the wrong way round when it thinks in terms of ethically informed political decision-making: conceptual limits are a necessary condition of fostering difference, just as the possibility of singularity in the political field requires political limits. Since postmodern IR uses Derrida's philosophy to formalize the above commitments, this final section considers more closely Derrida's understanding of decision and risk and responds to it using a concrete example of supranational public policy ('circular migration'). My example allows me, finally, to circumscribe the difference in these respects between cosmopolitan and Realist judgement (see chapter 2, section 2.3).

In his essay 'Invention of the other' (1987) Derrida lays out his aporetic logic of invention. All his subsequent writings on ethico-political responsibility are inscribed within the arguments of this reflection; I therefore briefly consider it here. In the essay Derrida gives account of two logics of invention in modernity (ibid., pp. 42–6). The first, pre-modern, is one of discovery: invention brings forth what is already there (following Heidegger, art is his foremost example). The second, modern, is one of production: invention institutes what was not already there. The second modern notion of production is technico-epistemological and leads invention in terms of technical machines and programs. Derrida does not oppose these two conceptions (ibid., p. 51): for an invention to secure its status in the world, the novelty of the invention must be repeatable. All inventions are in principle programmable. However, for Derrida, the 'whole modern politics of invention' (ibid.) leads to the capture of 'the aleatory' in 'programmatic calculation', since contingency is considered 'a calculable margin' (ibid., pp. 52–3). The technologization of modern invention attempts, in other words, to master contingency and chance. A deconstructive notion of invention wishes to transcend this risk. Rather than integrating the aleatory into the 'same', Derrida proposes, the deconstructive notion of invention 'prepares itself for the coming of the other'. Invention as such would be pure singularity and alterity outside calculation. Such invention is 'impossible'. This impossibility is, as I developed in the last chapter, not negative however; it is the very condition of invention from the perspective of deconstruction. 'To let the other come . . . is precisely what does not invent itself, deconstructive inventability can only consist in opening up, unclosing, destabilizing structures of foreclusion in order to let the passage to the other come' (ibid., p. 60).

Derrida's understanding of ethico-political responsibility is understood in terms of this deconstructive 'inventability'. Thus, in his short essay 'On cosmopolitanism' (see 2001, pp. 3–29), a deconstructive invention regarding immigration policy is worked out in terms of this radical impossible invention of the other. Derrida recalls that in 'Perpetual peace', after failing to establish the interest of a world government, Kant limits cosmopolitan law to the 'right of universal hospitality' (1795/1991, p. 106; Derrida, 2001, pp. 12–15). For Kant, the right to the earth's surface is grounded in the spherical nature of the globe: 'since the earth is a globe, peoples cannot disperse over an infinite area, but must necessarily tolerate one another's company' (1795/1991, p. 106). This right serves to advance world peace and the advent of a cosmopolitan constitution (see the important article by G. W. Brown, 2010). This cosmopolitan right constitutes a right of visitation only, not of stay or residence. Such stay would, for Kant, depend on a prior agreement between the states from, and to which, the visitor is travelling. It is therefore excluded by Kant from the cosmopolitan right because it depends on political treaty between sovereign nation-states. Rather than developing a bolder cosmopolitan right of resort, Derrida emphasizes from a philosophical perspective, the aporetic logic of hospitality through which all more inclusive inventions of hospitality must necessarily pass. The argument is structurally the same as that of the aporia of democracy in which he embeds world politics in *Rogues*. On the one hand, there is an ethics of unconditional hospitality, implying 'an unconditional law, both singular and universal, which order[s] that the borders be open to each and everyone, to every other, to all who might come, without question or without their even having to identify who they are or whence they came' (Derrida, 2001, p. 18). On the other hand, there are the conditional acts of determinate hospitality: not only the specific modalities of asylum, refugee and immigration policy but also the conditional hospitality of any ethics that rules terms of entrance. Unconditional hospitality is impossible and must be determined by ethical reflection and juridical mediation; but it is this unconditional precondition of singularity alone that 'can give meaning and practical rationality to a concept of hospitality' (Derrida, 2005, p. 149). 'Less violent' inventions and decisions are therefore based on negotiating a relation between this impossible singularity and juridical practice:

> It is a question of knowing how to transform and improve the law, and of knowing if this improvement is possible within an historical space which takes place *between* the Law of an unconditional hospitality, offered *a priori* to everyone, to all newcomers, *whoever they may be*, and *the* conditional laws of a right to hospitality, without which *the* unconditional law of hospitality would be in danger of remaining pious and irresponsible. (Derrida, 2001, p. 23)

Responsibility names the risk taken to negotiate in the immeasurable gap between unconditional openness and measured requirements of exit and entry, stay and departure. My argument is that this is too general a notion of invention for one to make proper sense of the political decision. Based on a Heideggerian generalization of invention specific to the aesthetic domain, this notion overrides political specificity. Unlike artistic or technical invention, political invention takes place in a field of differently weighted, mobile forces. Both artistic and technical forms of invention have, of course, their own forces to negotiate: tradition, patrons, clients, competition, etc. But the specificity of political invention lies – as Realism emphasizes – in the immanence of this force-field to the terms of invention. Not only must one, as Derrida emphasizes, pose limits 'not to remain pious and irresponsible' (ibid.); one must accept that limits constitute the political field in the first place. The whole question of politics is the nature of this limit, of this border. In struggle with other forces delimiting more violently than less – a more restrictive politics of immigration and asylum, for example – one opens up the possibility of alterity and difference by *delimiting* less violently. Derrida would not disagree empirically. But this means, at a politico-theoretical level, that determination is the condition of the aleatory in a field of immediately contesting forces. If deconstructive 'inventability' 'can only consist in opening up, unclosing, destabilizing structures of foreclosure in order to let the passage to the other come' (1987, p. 60), deconstruction takes neither responsibility nor risk in the political field. The large paradox of deconstruction is that, in wishing to prevent mastery and domination, it runs the risk of reproducing it by *not* contesting it in determined ways (Beardsworth, 2007).[7]

Given the nature of global problems and over-delimited nation-state politics, to forge an ethos and politics of less democratic hypocrisy and greater cooperation between developed and developing nations requires the risk of more global determinations and more leadership. Focus on the singular, the local, the marginal as exceptions to the rule of modern determination and as conditions of a politics released from the programmes of modernity places the ball in the wrong court. The political game will go on regardless. The cosmopolitan project of greater inclusiveness is

necessarily vulnerable, particularly to political limitation, but this is, precisely, the risk it takes: to embody its knowledge within the limits of
politics. An ethico-political risk is not a decision in which, as Maja
Zehfuss argues, 'knowledge is of little help', and 'where the rules of
ethics do not alleviate the problem' (2009, p. 146); it is, rather, the embodiment of proactive purpose under constraint. A more Nietzschean understanding of force and embodiment than deconstruction can countenance
is therefore required in order to understand, and rehearse, contemporary
ethico-political responsibility in the field of international relations.

The European Union commends itself on its cosmopolitan normative
principles and its foregrounding of soft power (Rumford, 2007). It is a
regional institution founded on the principles of Enlightenment democratic
reason. We have seen that cosmopolitan thinkers like Jürgen Habermas
consider it an example for world politics. Let me argue why in different
terms here, terms that present another model of judgement from that of
deconstruction, but accept the limits of political community. Present EU
immigration policy contradicts the above 'cosmopolitan' aspirations.
Postmodern IR theory basically theorizes this kind of contradiction between
the normative and the empirical. Following the methodologies of Foucault
and Derrida, it has not yet, however, offered other terms of exit and entry,
focusing on the exclusions of liberal law in a critical, rather than proactive
manner. At the moment, EU immigration policy is a closely guarded
national competence despite the Schengen agreement that stipulates free
mobility of persons between member states (with the exemptions of Ireland
and the UK). A single immigration policy is a long way off, given the
present troubles of the Union, but it is likely to happen in economic terms
(Collett, 2008). 'Selected' or 'managed' immigration policy risks giving
way, as in the US and Southeast Asia, to 'chosen' terms of immigration.
This policy, with its economic criteria of selection, severely limits the right
of families to join their parent migrants in the host nation. Given present
economic reality and the relations of force, immigration policy convergence between member states is likely to centre on the economic and
criminalize non-economic migration. This would be politics of the worst
kind, which would condemn EU democracies – and democratic government is the condition of entry into the union – to the continuing charge of
Western hypocrisy and roguery.

That said, the EU interest in circular migration policy would align, in
Archibugi's (2008) terms, the 'foreign' policy of the EU more with its
'domestic' policies. 'Circular migration' is presently considered by the
European Council as an interesting avenue of invention and has been the
intent of more progressive immigration policy circles for some time. It has
been canvassed in the media as 'a win–win–win' situation for host nation,

home nation and migrant. This game-theory language smacks, in Jenny Edkins's terms, of techno-scientific *hubris*. However, the policy that migrants come to a host nation, work for a period of time, return to their home nation and then be allowed to return again is a good one under the circumstances. The two-way process allows both the host and the home countries to develop economically as their needs require, allows migrants to send remittances to their families, and may foster a broadening of cultures on the part of all actors involved. The negative risks are clear. The circle of migration is cut short (the visa of return to the host country is ignored, and the migrant becomes another temporary contract); a two track citizenship could emerge ('normal' citizens with all rights of mobility versus 'less than normal' *Gastarbeiter* with curtailed social, civil and political rights); exploitation; brain-drain from the home country; powerful lobbying from business for specific migrants, and so forth. Given the dissymmetry of globalization processes, and the consequences of climate change, migration is a long-term phenomenon of increasing complexity. Circular migration policy could help in these circumstances to foster relations of reciprocity between the developed and developing parts of the world. It targets individuals and societies, not a mass of immigrant 'naked life'. It could foster emerging policies of dual and multiple citizenship, as long as terms of reciprocity, the rule of law and the full migration circle are adhered to. A regulatory framework of migration and immigration is therefore necessary at the regional EU level. Circular migration, as embodied by EU institutions, could eventually be considered as the start to a trajectory of national, regional and global policies that end up advocating, effectively, borderless migration of labour across the world as a whole. In these terms, the policy constitutes an effective transcendence of policy convergence on economic EU needs alone.

The policy presents an example of political invention within the force-field of political limits; one that advocates the lesser violence. It does not negotiate between unconditional freedom and the risk of decision. It negotiates with a force-field of different policy options and countries, and it risks embodying, *as far as possible within these constraints*, the strong cosmopolitan principle of moral personhood. Only in this sense would I agree with Habermas that the EU could, without too much hypocrisy, form part of a progressive liberal cosmopolitan project. In contradistinction to Derrida-inspired postmodernism, cosmopolitan judgement here starts with a practical reality, not with unconditioned singularity. But, in contradistinction to Realism, its prudence has in mind, on this policy issue, the ambition and dignity of moral personality. The example of EU circular migration suggests one way of thinking a cosmopolitan judgement of the lesser violence in the short term.

5 Conclusion

My rehearsal of a cosmopolitan response to postmodernism has argued not only that we are still in modernity, but that this modernity should be affirmed and reinvented in the new historical context. We are still moderns in this sense; the 'we' here is indeterminate, but it is a historical necessity of human lives located in modernization processes and negotiating, at different levels and in different ways, with them. My response has focused on the specificity of liberal law, on a politics of the lesser violence and on cosmopolitan judgement and risk. It has emphasized that law slows down interests and dissymmetries of power in both intrastate and interstate spheres of social action. Liberal law is not a governance regime of domination that reduces difference to the same. It is a mechanism of redress of unfreedom and inequality, if pitched at the appropriate level and embodied in appropriate terms. This level and these terms must also now be global if greater symmetry, reciprocity and freedom is to be achieved. Postmodern IR critiques of technologizing reason are important in highlighting the dangers of scientific rationalism in the domain of social activity, in spotlighting the liberal constructions of otherness and exception, and the incalculable, at times lethal, consequences of 'biopolitical' intervention. The response to these liberal effects is not vigilance and particularism, however, but a larger and more encompassing ethos according to which local struggles works with international and global governance regimes, and vice versa. Democratic reason must be open to chance, but chance has more chance of happening than less through appropriate determination and calculation. This is a normative goal, with all the risks which normativity implies. Moral, normative, legal and political modalities of cosmopolitanism should be considered, therefore, more as conditions of difference than as 'global projects of closure'.

In defence of a modest progressive liberal cosmopolitanism, I have also emphasized the vital importance of minor differences in the political domain. Postmodern critique ignores these differences and vacates the political domain accordingly. Homogenizing law and decision, it reduces the possibility of political agency all the while tarnishing liberalism with the 'depoliticizing' brush. This argument is logically flawed and, in its most radical examples, ends up metaphysical. Since the 1980s, when economic neo-liberalism took a hold, and, more recently, with the inception of neo-conservatism, minor differences within liberal regimes have affected the orientation of the world. It is imprudent, I have argued, to make all cows black in this context.

The cosmopolitan project is differentiated, normative and ongoing. It is a project that is necessary for our world (the 'we' here is again indeterminate): some of its instantiations are, over this century, inevitable. But they will be messy, because messiness is the nature of political limitation. Such messiness does not excuse wrong-doing, failures and mistakes. But it suggests that good politics assumes these mistakes as its own and, in public recognition, can move on from them with broader consent. This requires global leadership at national and international levels and grass-roots activism.

The risk of any project is dogmatism, of which postmodern IR theory speaks well, but too much. It is not the purpose of a philosophically con-ceived project to rehearse prescriptions, but it is incumbent upon such a project to show how it conceives freedom in specific relation to the object studied. I hope to have done this. The fact that 'others' always emerge as political institutions are built is not a reason to affirm institutions in a persistently ambivalent manner. Politics demands ethos and decision; good politics embodies such ethos and decision through example and is ready to admit failure and loss. This is a politics of the least bad or the lesser violence, an understanding of which can best defend cosmopolitan political risk and responsibility. Vigilance is therefore necessary. Postmodern cri-tique is predicated on vigilance, questioning and problematization. But its practices go too far when it loses sight of the nature of the political sphere: delimitation and limitation of life in the context of other forces. A politics of greater *inclusion* and *agency* must invent from within these limits (as the example of 'circular migration' illustrated) and should address the necessity of its own violence. How this politics will work itself out this century is, by its very nature, unpredictable. Whatever the coming empiri-cal divisions of the world, the project offers nevertheless a framework within which problems can be addressed and judgement offered.

In an issue of *International Politics* based on 'moving beyond cosmo-politanism', the editors argued against 'a dichotomy between cosmopolitan and post-structural approaches to ethics' in world politics (Brassett and Bulley, 2007, p. 13). The task is 'rather to engage across perspectives, opening up alternatives and identifying blindspots' (ibid., p. 14). Such a conversation is itself ethical in the perspective of pluralism and in the context of existing and changing IR frameworks. In similar vein, Rob Walker argues at the end of his dense article, 'Polis, cosmopolis, politics':

> If cosmopolitanism is a name to be given to an openness to connections, to a sense that we all participate in various patterns of both commonality and diversity that are not and cannot be fixed by the lines inscribed by modern subjectivities, and that also insists on recognizing the radically uneven developments and sites in which people struggle to act in the world, then there is much to be said for it. If it is one more excuse for not thinking hard

about politics . . . then we can leave it those moralists who already know where we must be going. That kind of cosmopolitanism has precisely to be resisted. (2003, p. 285)

I cannot agree either with Brassett and Bulley or with Walker's comment. Regarding ethico-political responsibility, there is an important difference between cosmopolitan and postmodern approaches, and that difference must remain clear for any conversation to be effective. Lack of clarity about basic differences of understanding will only muddy further debate. Ethico-political responsibility in the cosmopolitan project is a framework that believes in the dignity of life (at the very least) and the dignity of the moral person (at the most), in the effectiveness of law, and in political invention according to principles of public reason, subsidiarity and the lesser violence. Such beliefs can be squarely sustained by civil actors in the field of world politics; they can be argued for by state actors, enacted by their example, and maintained by them through clear commitments to minimal cosmopolitan responsibilities. Resistance to this overall cosmo-politan disposition, in the name of 'openness to connections', would be wrong-headed. A project is a project, which can be improved. In all due modesty and firmness, the architect stands, within limits, by what the project projects, and assumes the successes and failures of his or her judge-ments. Political limits change as a result.

Until these differences are convincingly formulated, the one research agenda that I consider important for cosmopolitanism in the light of post-modern critique is examination of the relation between law, control and accountability at the frontiers of national and regional space.

Conclusion: Idealism and Realism Today

In his Realist critique of interwar liberal internationalism, *The Twenty Years' Crisis: 1919–1939*, E. H. Carr argues for a double moral responsibility of political thought. On the one hand, it is moral 'to separate ethics from politics' given 'the realities of power' and 'the inequality of actors' (2001, p. 198): in the absence of international political community, for example, international legalism immorally hides the reality of power. On the other hand, it is immoral so to separate ethics from politics that the latter is reduced to the vagaries of 'pure power and interest'; in the absence of moral leadership, for example, 'the horizon of peaceful change' in international relations recedes (ibid., p. 202). Throughout its critique of liberal 'utopianism', *The Twenty Years' Crisis* seeks thereby a relation between morality and politics that is distinct from Kant's internationalization of liberal republicanism (the subordination of political power to moral rule through law). Since law does not have coercive force at the international level, the major specificity of international politics lies in recurrently finding a 'compromise between ethics and politics' in a force-field of political uncertainty (ibid., p. 95). It is not a question of either idealism or realism alone; rather, political ethics concerns the terms of coordination between the two. Despite this critique of Kantian idealism – in the shape of Wilsonian internationalism – Carr's argument is, in theoretical gesture, profoundly Kantian. In his *Critique of Pure Reason*, Kant famously argues that without intuition 'thoughts are empty', but without concepts, 'intuitions are blind' (Kant, 1781/1929, p. 93). He continues:

> It is therefore just as necessary to make our concepts sensible, that is, to add the object to them in intuition, as to make our intuitions intelligible, that is to bring them under concepts. . . . The [faculty of] understanding can intuit nothing; the senses can think nothing. Only through their union can knowledge arise. (Ibid.)

Although this language of the faculties is obsolete, and although Kant speaks here of cognition, not of rational moral interest, the theoretical point neatly underpins, I would argue, Carr's search for coordination between idealism and realism. In the field of international relations, ethical thought is 'empty' without the addition of the concerns of power and interest; without bringing them under ethical concepts, however, power and interest are 'blind'. To seek the 'union' of idealism and realism is the responsibility of 'knowledge' in world politics.

With both this moral and this theoretical responsibility in mind, the preceding chapters have staged three debates between IR theory and contemporary cosmopolitanism. My conclusion rehearses the book's basic moves, brings together its overall arguments and rehearses some strengths and weaknesses.

The book has assumed, first, that to discuss relations between ethics and international relations, it is important to develop more systematic dialogues between contemporary cosmopolitan thought and IR theory as such. Riding on the back of normative IR theory, it takes for granted that the field of IR theory is open to such dialogues given: (a) its cognitivism (as Kant put it, 'without concepts, intuitions are blind'); and (b) its methodological pluralism (the object of international relations is so layered that different theories of the international relation are required and welcome). This book assumes, second, a necessary relationship between contemporary cosmopolitanism and liberalism. This assumption relies, in turn, on two arguments:

1 Although cosmopolitan interest in humanity as a whole transcends the particular political ideology of liberalism, in the modern field of world politics cosmopolitanism's legacy lies in the thought of the European Enlightenment (chapter 1, section 1). This legacy redounds to moral egalitarianism (understood as the moral equivalence of all individual human beings).
2 However this moral equivalence is then thought within cosmopolitan moral and political thought (dignity of individual human life versus dignity of moral personhood), contemporary cosmopolitanism basically works from out of this liberal paradigm (to keep the latter limited at the international level or to extend it beyond national borders).

With these two assumptions behind it – the necessity of theory; the entanglements of cosmopolitanism and liberalism – this book addresses three critiques of liberal universalism in field of IR: those of Realism, Marxism and postmodernism. The three schools have been chosen – as opposed to those of rational choice theory, of institutionalism or of the English school – because their critiques of liberalism are straightforwardly constitutive of their historical and intellectual parameters. All three schools of thought define themselves, that is, in critical relation to domestic and/or international liberalism and have recently extended their criticisms of either or both to contemporary cosmopolitanism. Since the 1990s, these criticisms have been most insistent in the field of IR regarding the new practices of interventionism, global governance and strategies of development. The book has accordingly staged three dialogues between, on the one hand, these schools' critiques of cosmopolitanism and, on the other, a cosmopolitan response to each critique.

Prior to their staging, the 'debates' required both clear exposition of the various modalities of contemporary cosmopolitan ideas and a sense of how I would use these modalities, as I understand them, through the debates. A brief history of the cosmopolitan disposition and a lengthy exposition of contemporary cosmopolitan ideas served these two purposes in chapter 1. There, I emphasized in particular four points for later argument: the complex status of the normative in cosmopolitan thought; the distinction between weak and strong forms of cosmopolitanism; the important differences between different modalities of cosmopolitanism; and the fact that, nevertheless, when thought within the field of IR, these different cosmopolitanisms (moral, normative, legal, institutional, political) must complement each other.

In my view, the debates also required that each cosmopolitan response fitted the schools' *respective* concerns: for Realism, the nature of reality and political ethics; for Marxism, the systemic effects of global capitalism and global liberal governance; for postmodernism, liberalism's strategies of domination and non-normative notions of freedom and responsibility. Each cosmopolitan response has met each critique of cosmopolitanism, immanently, through these concerns, rather than unilaterally offering a universalist point of view in response. The cosmopolitan response to Realist critique undermined Realist use of 'category errors' in its criticisms of universalism, and advocated, against contemporary Realist positions, a prudent cosmopolitan politics of the lesser violence. The cosmopolitan response to Marxism offered a different perspective on the strengths and weaknesses of global capitalism, a perspective that required an in-depth analysis of regulation so that post-national progressive liberal goals could be pitched appropriately. The cosmopolitan response to postmodern thought in IR rehearsed a strong understanding of liberal law (as the condition of difference and empowerment), considered ways to reinvent this understanding in a differentiated analysis of international law and emphasized the essential importance of norms, rules and limits in the political domain. The book's methodology has, as a result, spawned a wide variety of intellectual ideas and intellectual strategies as the reader moves from one set of chapters (or debate) to the next. It would be wrong to attempt to bring all these thoughts together in a conclusion, and I refer the reader back to the introduction for a summary of chapter-specific arguments. There are, however, a number of recurrent common theoretical claims, underpinned by the differences and complementarities between the various cosmopolitan positions.

The overall aim of the book has been to argue for a sophisticated contemporary cosmopolitan disposition: one that is normative – that is, principled – but also feasible and practical. Such a disposition requires flexibility and an ability to posit argument that is tailored to context. I do not argue for a comprehensive cosmopolitan position towards the world. I have suggested several times, but specifically in relation to the respective thought of Thomas Pogge and Simon Caney (chapter 1, sections 2.2 and 2.4), that such a position makes little sense in a dialogue with the field of IR. In his defence of global distributive justice, Caney argued with Samuel Black that a liberal 'distributive theory that ascribes rights and claims on the basis of certain universal attributes of persons, cannot at the same time restrict the grounds for those claims to a person's membership or status within a given society' (quoted in Caney, 2005, p. 107). This is an excellent normative claim for cosmopolitan liberalism. It argues in trenchant black-and-white terms against the restriction of the liberal subject to domestic liberal polity. International relations are not black and white, however, but grey; as I argued in the last chapter, trenchant decisions must be made on the basis of this grey (chapter 7, section 4). This means that the principles which inform these decisions must *both* respond to the emerging practical reality of interdependence (chapter 3, section 1, on the reality of interdependence) *and* work within the limits of the major agents of change (states) (chapter 3, section 2, on the wielding of international power; chapter 5, section 4, on the global collective action of climate change mitigation and minimum cosmopolitan responsibility; chapter 7, section 3, on minimum state responsibility to a state's own peoples). I have consequently not argued for a weak cosmopolitan position either. I find this position consistent in response to the comprehensive commitments of strong cosmopolitanism, but itself too limiting in response to interdependence. My overall argument has been informed, rather, by the following.

First, cosmopolitan commitments with regard to human suffering, radical inequality and specific problems that affect the world as a whole must vary according to the agent concerned. *States are*, therefore, *not exempt from cosmopolitan responsibility* under conditions of interdependence, but these transborder responsibilities are necessarily weaker and more concentrated than either those of intergovernmental organizations or private transnational organizations. Cosmopolitan analysis must, consequently, be multilayered.

Second, a multilayered analysis does not occlude the *complementary* nature of different cosmopolitan positions. A cosmopolitan moral position regarding the moral equivalence of all individuals does not translate into immediate commitments to the political lives of suffering individuals. It does suggest, however, that basic human rights must be respected across the world; that legal and institutional arrangements must be increasingly made to guarantee, at best, this respect or, at worst, response to its non-fulfilment; and that greater individual and collective freedoms can only be argued for through example and discussion. Moral, legal and institutional cosmopolitan positions are, therefore, complementary despite the difference of emphasis. A multilayered position must not occlude either political argument for upholding these rights in the context of domestic reticence or geopolitical conflict of interests. Legal and political modalities of cosmopolitanism are complementary because the *legitimacy* of cosmopolitan legality has to be constantly argued for, politically, given the radical lack of world government (legitimate global coercive force).

Third, contemporary cosmopolitanism should be understood as a differentiated form of universalism. This *differentiated universalism* not only translates the cosmopolitan pragmatism of my first point above. It translates the more general fact that the practical implementation of cosmopolitan ideas is necessarily layered. I have argued this point in several ways throughout the debates. In response to the Realist critique of cosmopolitan democracy, I emphasized, within Held and Archibugi's project of cosmopolitan democracy, the need not simply to extend, but also to reinvent democracy at post-national levels. This is the fifth moment of democratic reinvention in history (chapter 3, section 5). The principle of 'subsidiarity' suggests the right way forward for this invention, since it combines questions of efficiency with legitimacy, as the gap between governor and governed widens. In response to the Marxist critique of cosmopolitan democratism, I emphasized the need to respond to an integrated world economy in such a way that national, regional and global levels of governance are explicitly coordinated. I therefore argued *contra* contemporary Marxist particularism that, without this coordination, national macroeconomic policy for democratic ends is not possible in the first place. In this respect I loosely defended Held's over-extended concept of 'global social democracy' on strategic grounds. In response to the Realist and postmodernist critiques of cosmopolitan legal theory a nd practice, I argued (i) for a differentiated analysis of law that articulated the differences between law, force and interest according to the level concerned; (ii) for the legal requirements of basic and more advanced freedoms under conditions of social complexity; and (iii) for political argument and leadership to complement legal proceduralism. I also argued from a historico-sociological perspective that, under conditions of interdependence, increasing differentiation of function across the world will inevitably result in increasing universal coordination; and that this coordination will be more or less centralized according to the issue at hand. The differentiated universalism of the principle of subsidiarity and the differentiated universalisms of re-embedding capitalism and international legal practice obviously work together.

Fourth, this understanding of universalism means that one can consistently argue for a larger sense of political community and of social justice than that of the nation *without* advocating a strong cosmopolitanism as such. Cosmopolitan realism (minimal cosmopolitan state responsibility) and a modest progressive liberal cosmopolitanism (concerns with radical inequality, basic individual freedoms, social justice at the appropriate level of self-determination) are compatible within a theoretical framework of different agents, different levels of analysis and different outcomes. This theoretical framework is, I have argued, neither abstract nor inflated; it responds to the material reality of increasing interdependence in a flexible and practical manner.

Fifth, the book argues for cosmopolitan political judgement. While a comprehensive liberal cosmopolitanism has no concrete meaning in the field of world politics, judgements, informed to a greater or lesser extent by cosmopolitan principle, do. The reach of the judgement depends on what actor is concerned and what the circumstances are. Judgement involves how one relates norm to experience in the empirical world. In response to the postmodernist critique of cosmopolitan norms (chapter 7, section 4), I argued that the act of judgement is a risk precisely because it takes place within a force-field of other actors at play. *Contra* postmodernist temperament, I claim that this risk requires drawing intellectual and institutional limits in order to achieve productive ends. At the level of the state and intergovernmental organizations (the UNSC), judgement should be made, I therefore argued, in the name of a cosmopolitan politics of the lesser violence. At the level of transnational civil actors or international organizations as a whole, judgement is more easily made in the name of progressive social goals that should redound, according to the principle of subsidiarity, to *endogenous* development.

Through exposition of the spectrum of cosmopolitanism and three debates on the nature of universalism in the field of international relations, this book has, in sum, defended: a tiered analysis of cosmopolitan responsibility; a responsibility that depends on the complementarity between different modalities of contemporary cosmopolitanism; a responsibility that advocates a differentiated universalism; and one that is accompanied, at the moment of political decision-making, by bold, but prudent political judgement.

What are the strengths and weaknesses of these overall arguments with regard to the field of IR theory?

Regarding strengths, it seems to me that these general claims of the book address the practical reality of interdependence and its effects, but do so without falling into the respective 'traps' of a formal or unrealistic universalism (a universal criterion of justice, world government, substantial UN reform) or an unfeasible particularism (national sovereignty). They call, accordingly, for ways of thinking about both theoretical and institutional responses to interdependence that assume *both* the given nature of the state-system *and* the slowly evolving nature of normative behaviour and political community. A particular strength of these arguments lies, I am arguing, in the fact that they remain focused on the practical necessity of feasibility and construction within a larger horizon of incremental change. The simultaneous argument for cosmopolitan realism (chapter 3, section 4; chapter 5, section, 4; chapter 7, section 3) and long-term qualitative changes in the nature of normative behaviour (chapter 3, section 1), in the nature of international power and national interest (chapter 3, section 2), and in the nature of regulatory global capitalism (chapter 5, sections 2 and 3) are particularly important in this respect.

The major weakness in these arguments accompanies these very strengths. Realist and Marxist critiques of cosmopolitanism concern the irreducible nature of political and economic power in the field of world politics. However flexible my theoretical framework may be in response to interdependence, it is, therefore, power that has to be demarcated appropriately. In the field of international relations there is no enforcement of global rules; the only level at which enforcement is effective remains that of the state. On global questions like climate change mitigation, global financial regulation, denuclearization, both Realism and Marxism look, therefore, to the state as the only effective agent of change at this historical moment. Not until national sovereignty is ceded to supranational authority will there by a systemic change in power relations that will allow one to practise the supranational. For Realism, this requires world government; for Marxism this requires a level playing field of social and political agents. However much I have argued, therefore, for incremental changes in state behaviour under conditions of interdependence, the bottom line remains the monopoly of power; my arguments have not addressed this bottom line enough. Until that monopoly is effectively curtailed or reinvented, analyses of differentiated universalism are theoretically consistent, but practically rhetorical.

In all three debates, I have circumvented this potential criticism by turning the argument against itself. I have claimed that, under conditions of interdependence, leading states should now assume minimum cosmopolitan responsibilities. In other words, the Realist and Marxist focus on the state as the major agent in international relations should be effectively transformed into a focus on the state as the major agent of change for minimal cosmopolitan commitments so that global collective action problems are properly addressed. It is, in other words, only through state-led global leadership that state sovereignty will be ceded on specific global concerns. Since this has been a recurrent proposal within my overall argument, I must, in turn, consider its strengths and weaknesses.

The strengths of the argument are several. As I suggested in my response to Realism, it displaces opposition between the goal of states and that of moral cosmopolitanism (collective interest of a bounded community on the one hand; concern with the dignity of individual life on the other). Since this opposition informs much Realist and cosmopolitan literature, it would be useful to go beyond it, for both theoretical and practical reasons. It would allow one, theoretically, no longer to conceive of the relation between states and individuals as an opposition at the international level; it would allow one, practically, to work at the resolution of global collective action problems in traditional Realist and rational choice terms, but under the assumption of widening national interest. The argument is also consistent; it fits well with my earlier points: the practical reality of interdependence, the expanding nature of national interest in the context of global problems, the changing nature of international power under conditions of interdependence, the responsibility of states to set example rather than impose principle. Most importantly, the focus on the state *as* the agent of change at the global level meets directly the Realist and Marxist counterargument of power.

What are the inherent weaknesses of this argument? From a cosmopolitan perspective, this focus on the state as the agent of change appears to underestimate the role of transnational civil society. It is this actor that, after all, has advanced the cause of humanity and put constituent pressure on states to meet more cosmopolitan commitments (Patrick Hayden's *Cosmopolitan Global Politics* (2005) presents a very good summary of this position). In a multi-actor environment, to refuse this point would be churlish.

However, the pertinent question here is how change of power is possible at the global level. For lack of a global social actor, refocusing on the powers and responsibilities of the nation-state would appear correct. Another approach would be an institutionalist one: it looks not to the state but to the relation *between* states, and its institutionalization, to seek the motivation of effective change in state behaviour at the global level (Baldwin, 1993; Keohane, 1988; most recently, Mattli and Woods, 2009, pp. 1–43). A current example of this institutionalization would be the emergence of the G20 and its gradual replacement of the G8. Given the canvas of players within it, it is more rather than less likely that some form of global tax regulation is instituted and that transfer of funds from the developed world towards the developing countries, to offset the outcomes of climate change, takes place (G. Brown, 2010). That said, global leadership is still needed on these issues, and it will not be the G20 as a whole but leading states *within* the G20 that assume this leadership – until there is a transfer of sovereign power from states to international authorities. At this moment of transfer only would these authorities become supranational bodies. The paradox is clear: the shift from the international to the supranational can only be made by states (albeit states in close relation with each other). My argument for a cosmopolitan politics of the lesser violence still stands because responsible states are its major vehicle. The argument may however be weak as a result less of the paradoxes of structural change than of the direction of historical change.

I have spoken several times of the shift of economic power to Asia, especially in the chapters on Marxism devoted to the world economy and economic power. This shift is not a direct subject of concern to this book; it is pointed more towards the period since the 1990s and its arguments, concerned to untie current conflations between cosmopolitanism, on the one hand, and neo-conservatism and neo-liberalism on the other. As I put it in my Introduction, this book has aimed to clear some theoretical air. That said, I have indicated several times that the rise of the autocratic state of China to global power may well undermine contemporary cosmopolitan commitments. The 1990s may be seen, retrospectively, as the decade of the re-emergence of these commitments following the end of the Cold War; the first decade of the twenty-first century may be seen either as their entanglement with, or their replacement by, a nationalist universalism in the US; the second decade of the twenty-first century may concretize the retreat of cosmopolitan global rules as a new balance of power comes into place (C. Brown, 2010). Following this narrative, international relations will reconfigure, and cosmopolitan commitments will remain regional and/ or normative. This is neither the moment nor the place to pursue this objection properly. Suffice it to say the following with respect to my argument on state-led global leadership.

Western alarm among some academics, policy-makers and politicians concerning China's growing political power appears focused, for the moment, on the African continent. According to the OECD, China's investment in sub-Saharan Africa still ranked eighth in the world in 2005, well below both the US and old European colonial powers (OECD, 2009). This share is nevertheless rising fast relatively. When the US placed financial sanctions on the Sudanese government in 2006, accusing it of genocide in the region of Darfur, Chinese firms immediately replaced US investment in Sudanese oilfields (Shaxson, 2007). By 2007, it became Sudan's first economic partner, taking 70 per cent of its exports (of which the majority is oil) (Fontrier, 2009). China's exploitation of the legacy of European colonialism and of American Cold War politics on the African continent is evident (Eisenmann and Shinn, 2008). Its lack of concern for the fulfilment of basic human rights in authoritarian countries like Nigeria, Sudan and Zimbabwe, while cynical (adhering to the principle of non-interference), mirrors the behaviour of previous Western regimes and is attractive to semi-democratic and non-democratic countries after the years of neo-liberal conditionality (Halper, 2010; Jacques, 2010). It has even been argued that China aspires to remove the IMF and the WB from the African continent as its private and public investment strategies increase (Hilsum, 2005).[1] Together with its forceful behaviour at the UN Copenhagen summit, all this would tend to suggest that China will refuse to play by the global rules of the 'international community' and that, as I put it in chapter 2, cosmopolitanism constitutes a discourse of the declining powers.

This argument against a modest cosmopolitan politics seems precipitate and too secure. Too many variables are at play for one to predict with any certainty what both the international and domestic futures of China hold. For example, the quasi-contract between the Chinese state and the Chinese middle class that economics and politics remain separate is steeped in Chinese Confucian tradition. Following my historically embedded normative arguments in response to the Realist and Marxist critiques (chapter 1, section 2.3; chapter 3, section 1; chapter 5, section 1), this situation may well change with increasing modernization. As is well established in political science literature, modernization processes (industrialization, urbanization, wealth, health and education) are necessary, but not sufficient conditions of democratization (Lipset, 1959; Huntington, 1968). Their outcomes are, however, not politically static either. Internationally, on specific global policy issues like climate change mitigation, China could well consider it in its own interest to assume global rules in order to assert its own leadership role at the global level. Such assumption would necessarily have effects on Chinese domestic rule. These are not demonstrable statements, but the point is simply the following.

Under conditions of interdependence, the futures of domestic order and world order are politically all the more *uncertain*. Within this uncertainty,

China is by no means bound to become a new world leader that returns the international community to the principles of equality of states and non-interference. It is precisely because of this uncertainty that state example and state leadership at the global level will be crucial in the coming years. As a result, the relations between value and power at the global level are bound to become a major issue.[2] Therefore, rather than the emerging future world order undermining cosmopolitan engagement in world politics, I would argue that this engagement could hold a strong place in coming academic and political debates. And it will hold an important place all the more if it argues for its positions with political courage and works from out of the practical reality at hand: the need for threshold consensus on global rules concerning global governance issues. For all these reasons, one major claim of this book – leading states with minimal cosmopolitan commitments must seek to resolve global collective action problems and thereby institute supranational authority on concentrated issues of global governance – remains in fact strong.

I think, then, that my five overall claims, when contested on the strict criterion of present relations of power, offer a clear theoretical and practical way forward: leading states' commitments to a minimum set of cosmopolitan values to resolve the paradoxes of global governance. This book therefore advocates in general terms: (i) a modest progressive liberal cosmopolitanism; (ii) a cosmopolitan realism; (iii) cosmopolitan political judgement.

Through these three debates and my general arguments, I consider four research agendas of particular import. These research agendas work within and between international political theory, international politics, and international economics: (i) exposition of the responsibilities of global leadership and of the role of a responsible state in a globalized world; (ii) the reinvention (rather than extension) of democracy for a globalized world; (iii) a detailed exposition of the world economy and of the possibility of coordination on global governance issues from a cosmopolitan realist perspective; (iv) an analysis of global liberal governance that holds strategies of empowerment and control together and offers legal and political remedy.

On the basis of the preceding arguments and these research futures, I believe that cosmopolitanism merits a strong place in IR theory, one that is already more than that of normative political theory and that holds purchase on present and future equivocations between the international and the supranational.

Notes

Introduction

1 Following standard practice, IR will henceforth designate the discipline of International Relations as a sub-category of political science. The uncapitalized 'international relations' will refer to the field of relations between nation-states. In this book 'world politics' will refer to political activity, whatever its source (national, regional, international), that has global implications. 'Global politics' will refer to the domain of post-national politics that require international institutions and supranational coordination. Terms like 'regional politics' will follow commonsense definition.

2 The fairly recent term 'international political theory' consolidates this growth, as seen in the new interdisciplinary journals *International Political Theory* (Edinburgh University Press) and *International Theory* (Cambridge University Press).

3 My thanks to two anonymous reviewers for asking me to clarify my theoretical perspective.

4 My use of the terms 'weak' and 'strong' varies in this book according to context. Following precedent in analytical philosophy, I predominantly use the term 'weak' when defining a minimalist cosmopolitan position (belief, for example, in the generalization of basic human rights or a basic common culture for humanity) and 'strong' when defining the more comprehensive cosmopolitan outlook that looks to supranational civil and political rights and duties. I also use the term 'weak' when describing an argument that is loose by choice. 'Weak' and 'strong' do not connote respectively poor and good (arguments), except when the context makes it clear.

5 Throughout the book I capitalize Realism and Marxism as schools of thought within IR theory. I do not capitalize postmodernism given its resistance to being considered a school of thought. There are nevertheless enough common tenets within its diverse thinking practices that it be determined as a loose school within IR thinking.

6 I understand 'political ethics' throughout the book in a Weberian sense: the thought and practice of ethical responsibility in the force-field of politics (Weber, 1968).

7 The concerns of 'global justice' obviously emerge here, although Marxist thought tends, as I will argue in chapter 4, to avoid this 'liberal' term.

8 I use the terms 'progressive liberal cosmopolitanism' and 'cosmopolitan progressive liberalism' interchangeably in this book. The distinction is one of emphasis: a cosmopolitanism that is liberal progressive (a liberal cosmopolitanism concerned with general questions of equality and equity); a progressive liberalism that is cosmopolitan (a social liberalism that has some form of a global outlook). In analogy with domestic concerns with social justice, both are concerned with global articulations of economic and social justice. Weak cosmopolitans like John Rawls, Thomas Nagel and David Miller would straightforwardly refuse these inversions since, as mentioned, progressive political goals like social justice can only be achieved within political order (Nagel, 2005) or community (Miller, 1998 and 2007a, 2007b, 2007c; Rawls, 1999). As chapter 1, section 2.2 makes clear, I find these distinctions between the domestic and the global important, but too categorical given the emergence of both post-national orders and communities and an integrated world economy that structures domestic order and community. My understanding of 'progressive liberal cosmopolitanism' is, accordingly, a modest one: it seeks to frame global capitalism at a supranational level such that local forms of self-determination and social justice are possible *in the first place*.

9 My cosmopolitan response to Marxism is, therefore, both normative and concerned, more empirically, with the grounds of policy prescription. Some readers may find this theoretical shift difficult. I am concerned to show, in the context of the Marxist critique of liberalism and cosmopolitanism, how contemporary cosmopolitan ideas can work, or not, in relation to global capitalism. I am grateful to an anonymous reviewer for responding to the difference of theoretical modalities in chapter 5.

10 While George W. Bush's universalism was nationalist (a neo-conservative understanding of American exceptionalism), the fates of this universalism and those of cosmopolitan humanitarian interventionism are often compared in Realist and postmodern IR theory (see chapters 2 and 6): hence my comparison.

Chapter 1: The Spectrum of Cosmopolitanism

1 I am grateful to an anonymous reviewer for asking me to emphasize this point.

2 Beck understands by 'globalism' political affirmation of neo-liberal globalization.

3 As I mentioned in the Introduction, the work of Andrew Linklater is increasingly concerned with developing a cosmopolitan ethic in these terms (Linklater 2002, 2007a, 2007b).

4 This use of the concept of 'normative impossibility' is not theorized by Habermas (it would work against his linguistic transcendentalism). It is also distinct from Derrida's deconstruction of normativity, which I expounded with regard to the Kantian idea in *Derrida and the Political* (Beardsworth, 1996, pp. 61–9), since I consider the normative horizon a space of political invention. I return to, and critique Derrida's understanding of the relation between norm, impossibility and invention in chapter 7.

5 Institutional cosmopolitanism necessarily takes Pogge to the formation of *global public policy*. There is increasing convergence here between neo-liberal institutionalism in IR theory and cosmopolitanism, although their initial assumptions are different. Compare my chapter 5, section 3 ('The cosmopolitan logic of re-embedded liberalism').

6 China at present exploits this legacy of Western colonialism and hypocrisy in its relations with semi-democratic and autocratic African governments. It is argued that the one conditionality China poses for its international loans and infrastructure-building is refusal to recognize Taiwan (Eisenmann and Shinn, 2008). I address the rise of China in the Conclusion.

Chapter 2: The Realist Critique of Cosmopolitanism

1 Under liberal universalism I include 'liberal internationalism' that dates back, for the American Realist school, to the US presidency of Woodrow Wilson and his Fourteen Points announced in January 1918 (particularly his help in setting up the League of Nations and promoting national 'self-determination'). The US Congress failed to pass the Versailles peace treaty in 1919, and 'Wilsonian internationalism became a synonym for utopianism in the study of international relations for the next seventy years' (Griffiths, 1999, p. 99).

2 Classical realists like Niebuhr and Morgenthau use the term 'lesser evil' in this context (Morgenthau, 1946, pp. 204–5; Niebuhr, 2008, pp. 154–5). The concept of 'lesser evil' is predicated on Christian anthropology: humanity's sinful lust for power. In my cosmopolitan responses to both Realism and postmodernism, I prefer the non-essentialist terms 'lesser violence', 'lesser bad' or 'least bad', specifically given the contemporary incursion of religion into world politics. I nevertheless affirm, with classical Realism, the fundamental notion of limits that informs political ethics (see also Ignatieff, 2005).

3 I place this argument specifically in the context of American democracy promotion later in this section.

4 My reading of Tony Smith's recent argument on the debt of neo-conservative nationalist universalism to the Wilsonian tradition of liberal internationalism came too late for me to include it properly in this chapter. I hope to address the present debate in the US between contemporary Wilsonians and Realists in another place (see Ikenberry et al., 2009).

5 Williams stresses the ambivalence of neo-conservatism with regard to liberal-ism: on the one hand, neo-conservatism criticizes liberal rationalism for theo-reticism and legalism; on the other, its own roots are to be found in the classical liberal republican subject. Despite this ambivalence, I consider that Williams places liberalism and neo-conservatism together in the specific context of interventionism and that this conflation is unmediated and precipitate. I am indebted to Michael Williams for useful discussion and disagreement on this point.

Chapter 3: A Cosmopolitan Response to Realism

1 My thanks to Ariel Colonomos for asking for clarification on this point in response to a lecture based on this chapter's arguments at Sci Po, Paris, February 2010.
2 This example ignores the implications of Richard Goldstone's UN report on the Gaza War in 2009 as well as continuing resistance on the part of the Israeli government to effective policy change in the Middle East. It is difficult to imagine, however, how the inequality of power between the two negotiating partners can remain a legitimate domestic issue for the US. For this reason I hold to my example of Israel, even though it is not itself the global power-wielder. I thank Michael Williams for seeking clarification on this point.
3 Chapter 5 returns to the collective action problem of climate change in the context of the cosmopolitan response to Marxism.
4 Despite the difficulty of defining an armed conflict, the following statistics from the Uppsala Conflict Data program indicate the highpoints of regional conflict after World War II: 1950 = 20; 1966 = 33; 1990 = 52; 2008 = 36: see http://www.prio.no/CSCWD/Datasets/Armed-Conflict/UCDP-PRIO/2009. From a historical perspective, the last figure is not huge. I am grateful to Tyler Shenk-Boright for researching this information and for that of note 5.
5 This is to one side of comparative analysis of different countries' judicial judgement, which is obviously increasing. US Supreme Court justices have referred to comparative foreign experience in several recent opinions, although the percentage of cases with foreign law citations remains very low (1%): see http://www.supremecourtus.gov/publicinfo/speeches.
6 Compare William Smith's (2007) call for context-sensitive judgements regard-ing humanitarian intervention.
7 I return to the question of decision and risk when considering postmodern IR theory.

Chapter 4: The Marxist Critique of Cosmopolitanism

1 Following common usage, I define 'neo-Marxism' as a body of thought that works with basic Marxist tenets, but supplements them with other epistemo-logical theories of subjectivity to make Marxism relevant to contemporary

modern society. I understand by 'post-Marxism' thought that holds to the basic materialist tenets of Marxism, but rejects emphasis on the economic determination of power. These distinctions are, that said, not crucial to the debate here.

2 On this point I am grateful to an anonymous reviewer's request for clarity.

3 I thank my friend and colleague Peter Hägel for stressing the importance of this last point to me and for pointing me to political science literature on international capital mobility.

Chapter 5: The Cosmopolitan Response to Marxism

1 I am again grateful to an anonymous reviewer for seeking clarification on my use of basic economic theory in this chapter.

2 The defeat of the Labour Party in May 2010 in the UK general election suggests that 'Third Way' thinking is now closed. How to strike a balance between efficiency and equity remains, nevertheless, a major political question.

3 It is here that cosmopolitan argument clearly dovetails with that of institutionalism and regime-analysis in IR theory, while remaining focused on its own principles of legitimacy. In the domain of international political economy, see Drezner, 2006.

4 One shortcoming of this chapter is that it does not analyse more the mediating role of regional organizations between nation-states and global institutions. This is an important research agenda for expounding differentiated universalism. I thank Michael Dorsch for discussion on this point.

5 My thanks to Peter Hägel for discussions on the cession of national sovereignty in the world economy.

6 On the eve of the G8 summit, July 2009, the Indian Prime Minister attributed, for example, the 'historical responsibility' of global warming to Western industrialization and materialism and led demands for a resource-fund of $120 billion, paid for by the West, that would help developing countries combat climate change. This 'Green fund' was promised at Copenhagen, but has not yet begun to materialize. See http://www.imf.org/external/pubs/ft/spn/2010/spn1006.pdf.

7 On the difficulty of negotiations between Europe, the US and China at Copenhagen, see, particularly, http://www.spiegel.de/international/world/0,1518,692861,00.html. My thanks to Elke Schwarz for the reference.

Chapter 6: The Postmodern Critique of Cosmopolitanism

1 Because of lack of space, I leave out of account here Der Derian's use of the French theorist Paul Virilio.

2 Source: http://www.ushistory.org/Declaration/document/index.htm.

3 Dillon and Reid's argument that without reference to God, the modern subject is a 'burnt-out' political horizon is therefore incorrect from a Derridean perspective. The impossibility of the norm of modern subjectivity (individual or

national) does not make this norm 'burnt-out'; it problematizes the conceptual horizon of the norm, making it immediately vulnerable to perversion (not simply vulnerable over time). The first reading discards the norm; the second supplements it with judgement (see Beardsworth, 1996). My own critique of the Derridean understanding of 'normative impossibility' is to be found in chapter 7.

Chapter 7: A Cosmopolitan Response to Postmodernism

1 Source: http://www.hrcr.org/docs/frenchdec.html.
2 For the Heideggerian interpretation of reason as an 'enframing' that challenges forth the world as 'standing-reserve', see Heidegger, 1977. This interpretation underwrites Agamben's understanding of political modern rationality.
3 See the discussion documents on the Global Centre for Responsibility to Protect: http://globalr2p.org/resources/generalassembly.php.
4 Kofi Annan's wish was well publicized in December 2004. For a history of the High-Level Panel and its report, see http://www.un-globalsecurity.org/panel.htm.
5 'Position paper of the People's Republic of China on United Nations reform', 8 June 2005. At http://www.fmprc.gov.cn/eng/zxxx/t199318.htm.
6 For an aporetic reading of a politics of the lesser violence, in distinction to mine, see Michael Dillon's instructive essay 'Violences of the messianic' (2010), an essay to which, on other accounts, I am indebted.
7 Deconstructive responses to me are found in the same volume (Fagan et al., 2007). For Alex Thomson, for example, my argument underestimates Derrida's double strategy of responsibility, in search of a 'militant' cosmopolitan programme (ibid., pp. 75–8). Thomson underestimates the specificity of the political field under circumstances of social complexity. In this space one accepts the difficult responsibility of a project: to do so is not militancy, but ambitious prudence.

Conclusion

1 My thanks to Jacob Lewis's research on Nigerian underdevelopment for this reference.
2 I am grateful to Anne-Marie Le Gloannec for discussion on the importance of this question for IR.

References

Agamben, G. (1998) *Homo Sacer: Sovereign Power and Bare Life*. Stanford, CA: Stanford University Press.

Annan, K. (1999) Annual Report of the General Secretary to the General Assembly, 20 September.

Appiah, K. (1997) Cosmopolitan patriots. *Critical Inquiry*, 23 (3).

Appiah, K. (2006) *Cosmopolitanism: Ethics in a World of Strangers*. London and New York: Penguin.

Aradau, C. (2007) Law transformed: Guantánamo and the 'other' exception. *Third World Quarterly*, 28 (3).

Aradau, C. (2008) Forget equality? Security and liberty in the 'War on Terror'. *Alternatives*, 33.

Archibugi, D. (1995) From the United Nations to cosmopolitan democracy. In D. Archibugi and D. Held (eds), *Cosmopolitan Democracy: An Agenda for a New World Order*. Cambridge: Polity.

Archibugi, D. (1998) Principles of cosmopolitan democracy. In D. Archibugi, D. Held and M. Köhler (eds), *Re-imagining Political Community: Studies in Cosmopolitan Democracy*. Stanford, CA: Stanford University Press.

Archibugi, D. (ed.) (2003) *Debating Cosmopolitics*. London: Verso.

Archibugi, D. (2008) *The Global Commonwealth of Citizens: Towards Cosmopolitan Democracy*. Princeton and Oxford: Princeton University Press.

Archibugi, D. and Held, D. (eds) (1995) *Cosmopolitan Democracy: An Agenda for a New World Order*. Cambridge: Polity.

Arendt, H. (1968) *The Origins of Totalitarianism*. Orlando, FL: Harcourt, Inc.

Aristotle. (1984a) *Nicomachean Ethics*. In J. Barnes (ed.), *The Complete Works of Aristotle* (vol. 2). Princeton, NJ: Princeton University Press.

Aristotle. (1984b) *Politics*. In J. Barnes (ed.), *The Complete Works of Aristotle* (vol. 2). Princeton, NJ: Princeton University Press.

Artus, P. and Virard, M.-P. (2008) *Globalisation: le pire est à venir*. Paris: La découverte.

Ashley, R. and Walker, R. (1990) Conclusion. Reading dissidence/writing the discipline: crisis and the question of sovereignty in international relations. *International Studies Quarterly*, 34.

Augustine. (1972) *City of God*. Harmondsworth: Penguin.

Bacevich, A. (2008) *The Limits of Power: The End of American Exceptionalism*. New York: Metropolitan Books.

Baldwin, D. A. (1993) *Neorealism and Neoliberalism: The Contemporary Debate*. New York: Columbia University Press.

Ball, P. et al. (2002) *Killings and Refugee Flow in Kosovo March–June 1999: A Report to the International Criminal Court for the Former Yugoslavia*. Washington, DC: AAAS.

Bannon, A. (2006) The responsibility to protect: the UN World Summit and question of unilateralism. *Yale Law Journal*, 115 (5).

Baran, P. (1976) *The Political Economy of Growth*. Harmondsworth: Penguin.

Barnett, M. and Finnemore, M. (2004) *Rules for the World: International Organizations in Global Politics*. Ithaca and London: Cornell University Press.

Barry, B. and Hardin, R. (1983) *Rational Man and Irrational Society?* London: Sage.

Beardsworth, R. (1996) *Derrida and the Political*. London and New York: Routledge.

Beardsworth, R. (2004) Futures of spirit: Hegel, Nietzsche and beyond. In T. Rajan and A. Plotnitsky (eds), *Idealism Without Absolutes: Philosophy and Romantic Culture*. Albany, NY: SUNY Press.

Beardsworth, R. (2007) The future of critical theory and world politics. In M. Fagan et al. (eds), *Derrida: Negotiating the Legacy*. Edinburgh: Edinburgh University Press.

Beardsworth, R. (2008) Cosmopolitanism and realism: towards a theoretical convergence? *Millennium: Journal of International Studies*, 37 (1).

Beardsworth, R. (2009) Postmodernism and international relations. *Sage Political Science Encyclopedia* (online).

Beardsworth, R. (2010a) Tragedy, world politics and ethical community. In T. Erskine and N. Lebow (eds), *Tragedy and International Relations*. London: Palgrave.

Beardsworth, R. (2010b). For a cosmopolitan politics of the lesser violence. Paper presented at the International Studies Association Annual Conference, New Orleans, February 2010.

Beck, U. (1992) *The Risk Society: Towards a New Modernity*. London: Sage.

Beck, U. (1997) *The Reinvention of Politics: Rethinking Modernity in the Global Order*. Cambridge: Polity.

Beck, U. (1999) *World Risk Society*. Cambridge: Polity.

Beck, U. (2005) *Power in the Global Age*. Cambridge: Polity.

Beck, U. (2006) *The Cosmopolitan Vision*. Cambridge: Polity.

Beitz, C. (1999a) *Political Theory and International Relations*. Princeton, NJ: Princeton University Press. Revised Edition with Afterword.

Beitz, C. (1999b) International liberalism and distributive justice. *World Politics*, 51.

Beitz, C. (1999c) Social and cosmopolitan liberalism. *International Affairs*, 75.

Bellamy, A. (2005) The responsibility to protect or a Trojan horse? The crisis in Dafur and humanitarian intervention after Iraq. *Ethics and International Affairs*, 19 (2).

Bellamy, A. (2008) The responsibility to protect and the problem of military intervention. *International Affairs*, 84 (4).

Benhabib, S. (2004) *The Rights of Others: Aliens, Residents and Citizens*. Cambridge: Cambridge University Press.

Benhabib, S. (2006) *Another Cosmopolitanism*. Oxford: Oxford University Press.

Benhabib, S. (2009) Cosmopolitan norms, human rights and democratic iterations. Unpublished paper.

Berger, S. (2003) *Notre première mondialisation*. Paris: Seuil.

Bernstein, J. (1991) Right, revolution and community: Marx's 'On the Jewish Question'. In P. Osborne (ed.), *Socialism and the Limits of Liberalism*. London: Verso.

Bhagwati, J. (2004) *In Defense of Globalization*. Oxford: Oxford University Press.

Bigo, D. (2004) Global (in)security: the field of the professionals of unease management and the banopticon. *Traces*, 4.

Bigo, D. and Tsoukala, A. (2008) *Terror, Insecurity, and Liberty: Illiberal Practices of Liberal Regimes after 9/11*. London and New York: Routledge.

Blake, M. (2001) Distributive justice, state coercion, and autonomy. *Philosophy and Public Affairs*, 30.

Brassett, J. and Bulley, D. (2007) Ethics in world politics: cosmopolitanism and beyond? *International Politics*, 44.

Braudel, F. (1993) *Grammaire des civilisations*. Paris: Flammarion.

Brennan, T. (2003) Cosmopolitanism and internationalism. In D. Archibugi (ed.), *Debating Cosmopolitics*. London: Verso.

Brenner, R. (2002) *The Boom and the Bubble: The US in the World Economy*. London and New York: Verso.

Brenner, R. (2006) *The Economics of Global Turbulence*. London and New York: Verso.

British Petroleum. (2008/9) Distribution of oil and natural gas reserves. At http://www.bp.com/productlanding.do.

Brock, G. and Brighouse, H. (2005) *The Political Philosophy of Cosmopolitanism*. Cambridge: Cambridge University Press.

Brown, C. (1992) *International Relations Theory: New Normative Approaches*. London: Harvester Wheatsheaf.

Brown, C. (1997) Theories of international justice. *British Journal of Political Science*, 27 (2).

Brown, C. (2002) *Sovereignty, Rights and Justice: International Political Theory Today*. Cambridge: Polity.

Brown, C. (2005) *Understanding International Relations*. 3rd edn. Basingstoke: Palgrave Macmillan.

Brown, C. (2010) Response to Charles Beitz (Human Rights in Theory and Practice). International Studies Association Annual Conference, New Orleans, February 2010.

Brown, C., Hardin, T. and Rengger, N. (2004) *International Relations in Political Thought*. Cambridge: Cambridge University Press.

Brown, G. (2009) *Newsweek*. September.

Brown, G. (2010) A clear agenda for reform in 2010. At *Huffington Post*: www. huffingtonpost.com/. . .brown/a-clear-agenda-for-reform_b_401291.html.

Brown, G. W. (2008) Moving from cosmopolitan legal theory to legal practice: Models of cosmopolitan law. *Legal Studies*, 28/3.

Brown, G. W. (2009) *Grounding Cosmopolitanism: From Kant to the Idea of a Cosmopolitan Constitution*. Edinburgh: Edinburgh University Press.

Brown, G. W. (2010) The Laws of hospitality, asylum seekers and cosmopolitan right: A Kantian response to Jacques Derrida. *European Journal of Political Theory*, 9/3.

Brown, G. W. and Held, D. (eds) (2010) *The Cosmopolitan Reader*. Cambridge: Polity.

Bryant, R. (2003) *Turbulent Waters: Cross-border Finance and International Governance*. Washington, DC: Brookings Institution.

Buchanan, A. (2003) *Justice, Legitimacy and Self-determination: Moral Foundations for International Law*. Oxford: Oxford University Press.

Bull, H. (1977) *The Anarchical Society: A Study of Order in World Politics*. New York: Columbia University Press.

Burke, A. (2008) Postmodernism. In C. Reus-Smit and D. Snidal (eds), *The Oxford Handbook of International Relations*. Oxford: Oxford University Press.

Cabrera, L. (2004) *Political Theory of Global Justice*. London and New York: Routledge.

Cabrera, L. (2005) The cosmopolitan imperative: global justice through accountable integration. *Journal of Ethics*, 9 (1/2).

Calhoun, C. (2003) The class-consciousness of frequent travelers: towards a critique of actually existing cosmopolitanism. In D. Archibugi (ed.), *Debating Cosmopolitics*. London: Verso.

Cammack, P. (2008) Why are some people better off than others? In J. Edkins and M. Zehfuss (eds), *Global Politics: A New Introduction*. London and New York: Routledge.

Campbell, D. (1992) *Writing Security: United States Foreign Policy and the Politics of Identity*. Minneapolis: University of Minnesota Press.

Campbell, D. (1998) *National Deconstruction: Violence, Identity, and Justice in Bosnia*. Minneapolis: University of Minnesota Press.

Caney, S. (2005) *Justice Beyond Borders*. Oxford: Oxford University Press.

Caney, S. (2009a) Climate change, human rights and moral thresholds. In S. Humphreys (ed.), *Human Rights and Climate Change*. Cambridge: Cambridge University Press.

Caney, S. (2009b) Climate change and the future: discounting for time, wealth and risk. *Journal of Social Philosophy*, 40 (2).

Caney, S. (2009c) Justice and the distribution of greenhouse gas emissions. *Journal of Global Ethics*, 5 (2).

Carr, E. H. (2001) *The Twenty Years' Crisis 1919–1939*. London: Palgrave.

Cassese, A. (2005) *International Law*. 2nd edn. Oxford: Oxford University Press.

Castells, M. (1996) *The Rise of the Network Society*. Oxford: Blackwell.

Cerny, P. (2008) Embedded neoliberalism: the evolution of a hegemonic paradigm. *Journal of International Trade and Diplomacy*, 2 (1).

Chandler, D. (2003) 'International Justice'. In D. Archibugi (ed.), *Debating Cosmopolitics*. London: Verso.

Chang, H.-J. (2002) *Kicking Away the Ladder: Development Strategy in Historical Perspective*. London: Anthem Press.

Chang, H.-J. (2007) *Bad Samaritans: The Guilty Secrets of Rich Nations and the Threat to Global Prosperity*. London: Random House.

Chevalier, J.-M. (2009) *The New Energy Crisis: Climate, Economics and Geopolitics*. London: Palgrave Macmillan.

Chevalier, J.-M. and Meritet, S. (2009) la Politique énérgétique. *Encyclopaedia Universalis*.

Clark, I. (2005) *Legitimacy in International Society*. Oxford: Oxford University Press.

Clark, W. (2001) *Waging Modern War*. Cambridge, MA: Perseus Group Books.

Clinton, W. (1999) Statement by the President to the Nation, 24 March.

Cohen, B. (1995) The triad and the unholy trinity: problems of international monetary relations. In J. Frieden and D. Lake (eds), *International Political Economy: Perspectives on Global Power and Wealth*, New York: St Martin's Press.

Cohen, B. (2008) *International Political Economy: An Intellectual History*. Princeton, NJ: Princeton University Press.

Cohen, D. (2009) *la Prospérité du vice. Une introduction (inquiète) à l'économie*. Paris: Albin Michel.

Cohen, J. (2004) Whose sovereignty? Empire versus international law. *Ethics and International Affairs*, 18 (3).

Cohen, J. (2005) Sovereign equality versus imperial right: the battle over the 'the new world order'. *Constellations*, 13 (4).

Cohen, J. (2008) A global state of emergency of the further constitutionalization of international law: a pluralist perspective. *Constellations*, 15 (4).

Collett, E. (2008) The EU immigration pact – from Hague to Stockholm, via Paris. European Policy Centre papers.

Connelly, W. (1988) *Political Theory and Modernity*. Oxford: Blackwell.

Constantin, S. (2008) Rethinking subsidiarity and the balance of powers in the EU in the light of the Lisbon Treaty and beyond. *Croatian Yearbook of European Law and Policy*, 4.

Cox, R. (1981) Social forces, states and world orders. *Millennium: Journal of International Studies*, 10 (2).

Cox, R. (1987) *Production, Power and World Order*. New York: Columbia University Press.

Crouch, C. (2009) Privatised Keynesianism: an unacknowledged policy regime. *The British Journal of Politics and International Relations*, 11.

Dallmayr, F. (1996) *Beyond Orientalism: Essays on Cross-cultural Encounter*. Albany, NY: SUNY Press.

Dallmayr, F. (2002) *Dialogue Among Civilizations*. London: Palgrave Macmillan.

Dallmayr, F. (2004) *Peace Talks: Who Will Listen?* Notre Dame, IN: University of Notre Dame Press.

Dallmayr, F. (2010) *The Promise of Democracy.* Albany, NY: SUNY Press.

De Perthius, C. (2009) *Et pour quelques degrés de plus. . . . Nos choix économiques face au risque climatique.* Paris: Pearson Education Forum.

Deeg, R. and O'Sullivan, M. (2009) Review: the political economy of global finance capital, *World Politics*, 61 (4).

Defarges, P. (1997) *la Mondialisation.* Paris: PUF.

Delanty, G. and Rumford, C. (2005) *Rethinking Europe: Social Theory and the Implications of Europeanization.* London: Routledge.

Der Derian, J. (1997) Post-theory: The eternal return of ethics in international relations. In M. Doyle (ed.), *New Thinking in International Relations Theory.* Boulder, CO: Westview Press.

Derrida, J. (1967) The violence of metaphysics. In J. Derrida, *Writing and Difference.* Chicago: Chicago University Press, 1978.

Derrida, J. (1974) *Glas.* Paris: Daniel/Gonthier.

Derrida, J. (1986) Declarations of independence. *New Political Science*, 15.

Derrida, J. (1987) Invention of the other. In L. Waters and W. Godzich (eds), *Reading de Man Reading.* Minneapolis: University of Minnesota Press.

Derrida, J. (1990) Force of law: the 'mystical foundation of authority'. *Cardoza Law Review*, 11 (919).

Derrida, J. (1994) *Specters of Marx.* London and New York: Routledge.

Derrida, J. (2000) *On Hospitality.* Stanford, CA: Stanford University Press.

Derrida, J. (2001) *On Cosmopolitanism and Forgiveness.* London and New York: Routledge.

Derrida, J. (2005) *Rogues. Two Essays on Reason.* Stanford, CA: Stanford University Press.

Derrida, J. and Habermas, J. (2003) *Philosophy in a Time of Terror.* Chicago: Chicago University Press.

Desai, M. (2002) *Marx's Revenge: The Resurgence of Capitalism and the Death of Statist Capitalism.* London: Verso.

Desch, M. (2007) America's liberal illiberalism: the ideological origins of over-reaction in US foreign policy. *International Security*, 32 (3).

Devetak, R. (2008) Postmodernism. In S. Burchill et al. (eds), *Theories of International Relations.* London: Palgrave Macmillan.

Dillon, M. (2010) Violences of the messianic. In A. Bradley and P. Fletcher (eds), *The Politics to Come: Power, Modernity and the Messianic.* London: Continuum.

Dillon, M. and Reid, J. (2009) *The Liberal Way of War: Killing to Make Life Live.* London and New York: Routledge.

Dollar, D. (2007) Globalization, poverty and inequality since 1980. In D. Held and A. Kaye (eds), *Global Inequality.* Cambridge: Polity.

Donnelly, J. (1989) *Universal Human Rights in Theory and Practice.* Ithaca, NY: Cornell University Press.

Donnelly, J. (2008) The ethics of Realism. In C. Reus-Smit and D. Snidal (eds), *The Oxford Handbook of International Relations.* Oxford: Oxford University Press.

Doyle, M. (1986) Liberalism and world politics, *American Political Science Review*, 80.

Drezner, D. (2006) *All Politics is Global: Explaining International Regulatory Regimes*. Princeton, NJ: Princeton University Press.

Edkins, J. (2000) *Whose Hunger? Concepts of Famine, Practices of Aid*. Minneapolis: University of Minnesota Press.

Edkins, J. and Vaughan-Williams, N. (2009) *Critical Theorists and International Relations*. London and New York: Routledge.

Edkins, J. and Zehfuss, M. (2008) *Global Politics: A New Introduction*. London and New York: Routledge.

Edkins, J., Persram, N. and Pin-Fat, V. (eds) (1999) *Sovereignty and Subjectivity*. Boulder, CO: Lynne Rienner.

Edkins, J., Pin-Fat, V. and Shapiro, M. (2004) *Sovereign Lives: Power in Global Politics*. New York: Routledge.

Eichengreen, B. (2008) *Globalizing Capital: A History of the International Monetary System*. 2nd edn. Princeton, NJ: Princeton University Press.

Eichengreen, B., Tobin, J. and Wypslosz, C. (1995) Two cases for sand in the wheels of international finance. *Economic Journal*, 105 (428).

Eisenmann, S. and Shinn, D. (2008) Responding to China in Africa. *American Foreign Policy Council*, June. At http://www.afpc.org/publication_listings/viewPolicyPaper/236.

Elias, N. (1982) *The Civilizing Process*. 2 vols. Oxford: Blackwell.

Ellis, E. (2005) *Kant's Politics: Provisional Theory for an Uncertain World*. New Haven, CT: Yale University Press.

Elshtain, J. (2004) *Just War against Terror: The Burden of American Power in a Violent World*. New York: Basic Books.

Erskine, T. (2001) Assigning responsibilities to institutional moral agents: the case of states and quasi-states. *Ethics and International Affairs*, 15 (2).

Erskine, T. (2008a) *Embedded Cosmopolitanism: Duties to Strangers and Enemies in a World of 'Dislocated Communities'*. Oxford: Oxford University Press.

Erskine, T. (2008b) Locating responsibility: the problem of moral agency in international relations. In C. Reus-Smit and D. Snidal (eds), *The Oxford Handbook of International Relations*. Oxford: Oxford University Press.

Erskine, T. (2010) Kicking bodies and damning souls: the danger of harming 'innocent' individuals while punishing 'delinquent' states. *Ethics and International Affairs,* 24 (3).

Fagan, M., Glorieux, L., Hasimbegovic, I. and Suetsugu, M. (eds) (2007) *Derrida: Negotiating the Legacy*. Edinburgh: Edinburgh University Press.

Falk, R. (2004) *The Declining World Order: America's Imperial Politics*. New York and London: Routledge.

Fine, R. (2007) *Cosmopolitanism*. London: Routledge.

Finnis, J. (1992) Natural law and legal reasoning. In R. George (ed.), *Natural Law Theory: Contemporary Essays*. Oxford: Oxford University Press.

Follesdal, A. (2000) Subsidiarity and democratic deliberation. In E. Eriksen and J. Fossum (eds), *Democracy in the European Union: Integration through Deliberation?* London: Routledge.

Fontrier, M. (2009) *Le Darfour*. Paris: L'Harmattan.

Foucault, M. (1965) *Madness and Civilization: A History of Insanity in the Age of Reason*. New York: Random House.

Foucault, M. (1973) *The Birth of the Clinic. An Archaeology of Medical Perception*. London: Tavistock Publications.

Foucault, M. (1977) *Discipline and Punish: The Birth of the Prison*. London: Penguin.

Foucault, M. (1980) *Power/Knowledge*. Brighton: Harvester Press.

Foucault, M. (1984) What is Enlightenment? In P. Rabinow (ed.), *The Foucault Reader*. New York: Random House.

Foucault, M. (1988–90) *History of Sexuality*. 3 vols. London: Penguin.

Foucault, M. (2000) *Power: Essential Works of Foucault* (vol 3). New York: New Press.

Foucault, M. (2007) *Security, Territory, Population*. London and New York: Palgrave Macmillan.

Foucault, M. (2008) *The Birth of Biopolitics*. London and New York: Palgrave Macmillan.

Franco, P. (1999) *Hegel's Philosophy of Freedom*. New Haven and London: Yale University Press.

Frank, A. (1971) *Capitalism and Underdevelopment: Historical Studies of Chile and Brazil*. Harmondsworth: Penguin.

Freedman, L. (2000) Victim and victor: reflections on the Kosovo war. *Review of International Studies*, 26 (3).

Frieden, J. et al. (2009) *International Political Economy: Perspectives on Global Power and Wealth*. 5th edn. Bedford: St Martins.

Friedman, T. (2002) *The Lexus and the Olive Tree: Understanding Globalisation*. New York: Random House.

Friedman, T. (2005) *The World Is Flat: The Globalized World in the Twenty-First Century*. London and New York: Penguin.

Frost, M. (1996) *Ethics in International Relations: A Constitutive Theory*. Cambridge: Cambridge University Press.

Fukuyama, F. (1992) *The End of History and the Last Man*. New York: Avon Books, Inc.

Fukuyama, F. (2007) *After the Neocons: America at the Crossroads*. London: Profile Books.

Gamble, P. (2009). *The Spectre at the Feast: Capitalist Crisis and the Politics of Recession*. Basingstoke: Palgrave Macmillan.

Giddens, A. (1990) *The Consequences of Modernity*. Cambridge: Polity.

Giddens, A. (1998) *The Third Way: The Renewal of Social Democracy*. Cambridge: Polity.

Gill, S. (1990) *American Hegemony and the Trilateral Commission*. Cambridge and New York: Cambridge University Press.

Gill, S. (2003) *Power and Resistance in the New World Order*. Basingstoke: Palgrave Macmillan.

Gilpin, R. (2001) *Global Political Economy*. Princeton, NJ: Princeton University Press.

Goldgeier, J. (2010) Barack Obama and the war in Afghanistan. Paper presented at the International Studies Association Annual Conference, New Orleans, February 2010.

Goldsmith, J. and Posner, E. (2005) *The Limits of International Law*. Oxford: Oxford University Press.

Gowan, P. (1999) *The Global Gamble: Washington's Faustian Bid for World Dominance*. London and New York: Verso.

Gowan, P. (2003a) The new liberal cosmopolitanism. In D. Archibugi (ed.), *Debating Cosmopolitics*. London: Verso.

Gowan, P. (2003b) US hegemony today. *Monthly Review*, Jul–Aug.

Gowan, P. (2009) Crisis in the heartland: consequences of the New Wall Street system. *Left Review*, 55, Jan–Feb.

Gramsci, A. (1971) *Selections from Prison Notebooks*. London: Lawrence and Wishart.

Gregory, P. and Stuart, R. (1995) *Comparative Economic Systems*. 5th edn. Boston, MA: Houghton Mifflin.

Griffiths, M. (1999) *Fifty Key Thinkers in International Relations*. Abingdon: Routledge.

Habermas, J. (1984) *The Theory of Communicative Action* (vol. 1). Boston, MA: Beacon Press.

Habermas, J. (1987) *The Philosophical Discourse of Modernity*. Cambridge, MA: MIT Press.

Habermas, J. (1991) *The Structural Transformation of the Public Sphere: An Inquiry into the Category of Bourgeois Society*. Cambridge, MA: MIT Press.

Habermas, J. (1996) *Between Facts and Norms: Contributions to a Discourse Theory of Law and Democracy*. Cambridge: Polity.

Habermas, J. (1997) Kant's idea of perpetual peace, with the benefit of two hundred years' hindsight. In J. Bohman and M. Lutz-Bachmann (eds), *Perpetual Peace: Essays on Kant's Cosmopolitan Ideal*. Cambridge, MA: The MIT Press.

Habermas, J. (2000) Bestiality and humanity: A war on the border between law and morality. In W. Buckley (ed.), *Kosovo: Contending Voices on Balkan Interventions*. Grand Rapids, MI: Eerdmans Publishing.

Habermas, J. (2001) The postnational constellation and the future of democracy. In J. Habermas, *The Postnational Constellation and Other Essays*. Cambridge: Polity.

Habermas, J. (2006) *The Divided West*. Cambridge: Polity.

Halper, S. (2010) *The Beijing Consensus*. New York: Basic Books.

Harrison, A. (2007) Globalization and poverty: introduction. In A. Harrison (ed.), *Globalization and Poverty*. Cambridge, MA: National Bureau of Economic Research.

Harvey, D. (1982) *The Limits to Capital*. London: Verso.

Harvey, D. (2007) *A Brief History of Neoliberalism*. Oxford: Oxford University Press.

Harvey, D. (2010) *The Enigma of Capital and the Crises of Capitalism*. London: Profile Books.

Hawthorn, G. (2003) Running the world through windows. In D. Archibugi (ed.), *Debating Cosmopolitics*. London: Verso Press.

Hayden, P. (2005) *Cosmopolitan Global Politics*. Aldershot: Ashgate.

Hayden, P. (2008) *Political Evil in a Global Age*. Abingdon: Routledge.

Heater, D. (1996) *World Citizenship and Government: Cosmopolitan Ideas in the History of Western Political Thought*. Basingstoke: Macmillan.

Heater, D. (2002) *World Citizenship*. New York and London: Continuum.

Hegel, G. W. F. (1807/1977) *Phenomenology of Spirit*. Oxford: Oxford University Press.

Hegel, G. W. F. (1831/1952) *Philosophy of Right*. Oxford: Oxford University Press.

Heidegger, M. (1977) The question concerning technology. In *Basic Writings*. San Francisco: Harper and Row.

Held, D. (1995a) *Democracy and the Global Order: From the Modern State to Cosmopolitan Governance*. Cambridge: Polity.

Held, D. (1995b) Democracy and the new international order. In D. Archibugi and D. Held (eds), *Cosmopolitan Democracy: An Agenda for a New World Order*. Cambridge: Polity.

Held, D. (2003) From executive to cosmopolitan multilateralism. In D. Held and M. Koenig-Archibugi (eds), *Taming Globalization: Frontiers of Governance*. Cambridge: Polity.

Held, D. (2004) *Global Covenant: The Social Democratic Alternative to the Washington Consensus*. Cambridge: Polity.

Held, D. (2005a) Principles of cosmopolitan order. In G. Brock and H. Brighouse (eds), *The Political Philosophy of Cosmopolitanism*. Cambridge: Cambridge University Press.

Held, D. (2005b) What are the dangers and the answers? Clashes over globalization. In D. Held et al. (eds) *Debating Globalization*. Cambridge: Polity.

Held, D. et al. (eds) (1999) *Global Transformations*. Cambridge: Polity.

Held, D. et al. (eds) (2005) *Debating Globalization*. Cambridge: Polity.

Held, D. and Kaya, A. (eds) (2007) *Global Inequality: Patterns and Explanations*. Cambridge: Polity.

Held, D. and Koenig-Archibugi, M. (2003) *Taming Globalization: Frontiers of Governance*. Cambridge: Polity.

Held, D. and McGrew, A. (eds) (2000) *The Global Transformations Reader*. Cambridge: Polity.

Held, D. and McGrew, A. (eds) (2002) *Governing Globalization*. Cambridge: Polity.

Held, D. and Moore, H. L. (eds) (2008) *Cultural Politics in a Global Age*. Oxford: Oneworld.

Helleiner, E. (2005) The evolution of the international monetary and financial system. In J. Ravenhill (ed.), *Global Political Economy*. Oxford: Oxford University Press.

Helm, D. (2007) *The New Energy Paradigm*. Oxford: Oxford University Press.

Herz, J. (1950) Idealist internationalism and the security dilemma. *World Politics*, 2.

Hilsum, L. (2005) Re-enter the dragon: China's new mission in Africa. *Review of African Political Economy*, 32 (104/5).

Hirst, P. and Thompson, G. (1998) *Globalization in Question*. Cambridge: Polity.

Hiscox, M. (2005) The domestic sources of foreign economic policies. In J. Ravenhill (ed.), *Global Political Economy*. Oxford: Oxford University Press.

Hobbes, T. (1651/1982) *Leviathan*. Harmondsworth: Penguin.

Human Rights Watch. (2000) Civilian deaths in the NATO air campaign. At http://www.hrw.org/legacy/reports/2000/nato/Natbm200.htm.

Human Rights Watch. (2001) Under orders: war crimes in Kosovo. At http://www.hrw.org/legacy/reports/2001/kosovo/undwood.htm.

Hume, D. (1777/1985) On the balance of trade. In D. Hume, *Essays: Moral, Political and Literary*. Indianapolis, IN: Liberty Classics.

Huntington, S. (1968) *Political Order in Changing Societies*. New Haven, CT: Yale University Press.

Huntington, S. (1996) *The Clash of Civilizations and the Reworking of World Order*. New York: Touchstone.

Ignatieff, M. (2005) *The Lesser Evil: Political Ethics in an Age of Terror*. Edinburgh: Edinburgh University Press.

Ikenberry, G. J. (2006) *Liberal Order and Imperial Ambition*. Cambridge: Polity.

Ikenberry, G. J. et al. (eds) (2009) *The Crisis of American Foreign Policy: 'Wilsonianism' in the Twenty-First Century*. Princeton, NJ: Princeton University Press.

International Commission on Intervention and State Sovereignty. (2001) Responsibility to Protect. At http://www.iciss.ca/report2-en.asp.

International Criminal Court. (1998) Rome Statute of the International Criminal Court. At http://www.icccpi.int/Menus/ICC/Legal+Texts/Rome+Statute.htm.

International Energy Agency. (2007) *World Energy Outlook*. Paris: IEA Publications.

International Energy Agency. (2008) *World Energy Outlook*. Paris: IEA Publications.

International Panel on Climate Change (IPCC). (2007) *Fourth Assessment Report*. At http://www. Ipcc.ch/pdf/assessment-report/ar4/syr/ar4_syr.pdf.

Itoh, S. (2007) Sino-Russian energy partnership: dilemma of cooperation and mutual distrust. In G. Austin and M.-A. Shellekens-Gaiffe (eds), *Energy and Conflict Prevention*. Stockholm: Instant Book AB.

Jacques, M. (2010) *When China Rules the World: The End of the Western World and the Birth of a New Global Order.* New York: Penguin.

Jervis, R. (1998) Realism in the study of world politics. *International Organization*, 52/4.

Jervis, R. (1999) Realism, neoliberalism, and cooperation: understanding the debate. *International Security*, 24/1.

Johnson, S. (2010) *13 Bankers: The Wall Street Takeover and the Next Financial Meltdown*. New York: Pantheon.

Joppke, C. (2010) *Citizenship and Immigration*. Cambridge: Polity.

Kagan, R. (2003) *Of Paradise and Power: America and Europe in the New World Order*. New York: Knopf.

Kagan, R. (2008) *The Return of History and the End of Dreams*. New York: Knopf.

Kahler, M. and Lake, D. (eds) (2003) *Governance in a Global Economy: Political Authority in Transition*. Princeton, NJ: Princeton University Press.

Kant, I. (1781/1929) *Critique of Pure Reason*. London: Macmillan.

Kant, I. (1784/1991) Idea for a universal history with a cosmopolitan purpose. In H. Reiss (ed.), *Kant: Political Writings*. Cambridge: Cambridge University Press.

Kant, I. (1785/1987) *Fundamental Principles of the Metaphysics of Morals*. New York: Prometheus Books.

Kant, I. (1788/1956) *Critique of Practical Reason*. New York: Macmillan.

Kant. I. (1791/1998) *Religion within the Boundaries of Reason Alone*. Cambridge: Cambridge University Press.

Kant, I. (1793/1991) On the common saying: 'This may be true in theory but it does not apply in practice'. In H. Reiss (ed.), *Kant: Political Writings*. Cambridge: Cambridge University Press.

Kant, I. (1795/1991) Perpetual peace: a philosophical sketch. In H. Reiss (ed.), *Kant: Political Writings*. Cambridge: Cambridge University Press.

Kant, I. (1797/1991) The theory of right. In H. Reiss (ed.), *Kant: Political Writings*. Cambridge: Cambridge University Press.

Kant, I. (1798/1991) A renewed attempt to answer the question: 'Is the human race continually improving?'. In H. Reiss (ed.), *Kant: Political Writings*. Cambridge: Cambridge University Press.

Katzenstein, P., Keohane, R. and Krasner, S. (1998) International organization and the study of world politics. *International Organization*, 52.

Kaul, I. et al. (eds) (1999) *Global Public Goods: International Cooperation in the Twenty-first Century*. New York and Oxford: Oxford University Press.

Kaul, I. et al. (eds) (2003) *Providing Global Public Goods: Managing Globalization*. New York and Oxford: Oxford University Press.

Kennan, G. F. (1984) *American Diplomacy*. Expanded edn. Chicago: Chicago University Press.

Keohane, R. (ed.) (1986) *Neorealism and its Critics*. New York: Columbia University Press.

Keohane, R. (1988) International institutions. Two approaches. *International Studies Quarterly*, 32.

Keohane, R. and Nye, J. (1977) *Power and Interdependence*. New York: Longman.

Keohane, R. and Nye, J. (2003) Redefining accountability for global governance. In M. Kahler and D. Lake (eds), *Governance in a Global Economy: Political Authority in Transition*. Princeton, NJ: Princeton University Press.

Keppler, J. (2009) Climate change, security of supply and competitiveness: does Europe have the means to implement its ambitious energy vision? In J.-M. Chevalier, *The New Energy Crisis: Climate, Economics and Geopolitics*. London: Palgrave Macmillan.

Keukeleire, S. and MacNaughtan, J. (2008) *The Foreign Policy of the European Union*. London: Palgrave Macmillan.

Kissinger, H. (1994) *Diplomacy*. New York: Simon and Schuster.

Koenig-Archibugi, M. (2003) Globalization and the challenge to governance. In D. Held and M. Koenig-Archibugi (eds), *Taming Globalization: Frontiers of Governance*. Cambridge: Polity.

Kornai, J. (1992) *The Socialist System: the Political Economy of Communism*. Princeton, NJ: Princeton University Press.

Krasner, S. (ed.) (1983) *International Regimes*. Ithaca, NY: Cornell University Press.

Krasner, S. (1992) Realism, imperialism and democracy: a response to Gilbert. *Political Theory*, 20/1.

Krugman, P. (2008) *The Return of Depression Economics and the Crisis of 2008*. 2nd edn. London and New York: Penguin.

Kupchan, C. (2005) Independence for Kosovo: yielding to Balkan reality. *Foreign Affairs*, 84 (6).

Kymlicka, W. (2001) *Politics in the Vernacular: Nationalism, Multiculturalism and Citizenship*. Oxford: Oxford University Press.

Kymlicka, W. (2005) *Contemporary Political Philosophy: An Introduction*. 2nd edn. Oxford: Oxford University Press.

Laertius, D. (n.d.) Life of Diogenes the Cynic. *Lives and Opinions of Eminent Philosophers*, VI. At http://classicpersuasion.org/pw/diogenes/dldiogenes.htm.

Lakatos, I. (1970) Falsification and the methodology of scientific research programmes. In I. Lakatos and A. Musgrave (eds), *Criticism and the Growth of Knowledge*. Cambridge: Cambridge University Press.

Lampton, D. (2008) *The Three Faces of Chinese Power: Might, Money and Minds*. Berkeley: California University Press.

Lawler, P. (2008) The ethics of postmodernism. In C. Reus-Smit and D. Snidal (eds), *The Oxford Handbook of International Relations*. Oxford: Oxford University Press.

Lebow, N. (2003) *The Tragic Vision of Politics. Ethics, Interests and Orders*. Cambridge: Cambridge University Press.

Lenin, I. (1917/1997) Imperialism: the highest stage of capitalism. In I. Lenin, *The Essential Writings of* Lenin. New York: Dover Publications Inc.

Levinas, E. (1969) *Totality and Infinity*. Pittsburgh, PA: Duquesne University Press.

Lieven, A. and Hulsman, J. (2006) *Ethical Realism: A Vision for America's Role in the World*. New York: Pantheon Books.

Linklater, A. (1998) *Transformation of Political Community: Ethical Foundations of the Post-Westphalian Era*. Cambridge: Polity.

Linklater, A. (1999) The evolving spheres of international justice. *International Affairs*, 75 (1).

Linklater, A. (2002) The problems of harm in world politics. *International Affairs*, 78.

Linklater, A. (2007a) Towards a sociology of global morals. *Review of International Studies*, 33 (special issue on Critical International Relations).

Linklater, A. (2007b) Public spheres and civilizing processes. *Theory, Culture and Society*, 24 (4).

Lipset, S. (1959) Some social requisites of democracy: economic development and political legitimacy. *American Political Science Review*, 53 (1).

Lukes, S. (1987) *Marxism and Morality*. Oxford: Oxford Paperbacks.

Machiavelli, N. (1531/2005) *The Prince*. Oxford: Oxford University Press.

Machiavelli, N. (1532/1983) *Discourses on the Ten Books of Titus Livy*. London: Penguin.

Mamdani, M. (2009) *Saviours and Survivors: Dafur, Politics and the War on Terror*. New York: Pantheon Books.

Mandela, N. (1994) *Long Walk to Freedom*. London: Abacus Books.

Mandelbaum, M. (2002) *The Ideas that Conquered the World: Peace, Democracy, and Free Markets in the Twenty-first Century*. New York: Public Affairs.

Manin, B. (1996) *Principes du gouvernement représentatif*. Paris: Flammarion.

Marx, K. (1843/1992) 'On the Jewish Question'. In K. Marx, *Early Writings*. London and New York: Penguin.

Marx, K. (1844/1992) Economic and philosophical manuscripts. In K. Marx, *Early Writings*. London and New York: Penguin.

Marx, K. (1867/1990) *Capital: A Critique of Political Economy* (vol. 1). London and New York: Penguin.

Marx, K. (1894/1991) *Capital: A Critique of Political Economy* (vol. 3). London and New York: Penguin.

Marx, K. (1939/1973) *Grundrisse*. Harmondsworth: Penguin.

Marx, K. and Engels, F. (1848/2005) *The Communist Manifesto*. London: Penguin.

Mattli, W. and Woods, N. (2009) In whose benefit? Explaining regulatory change in world politics. In W. Mattli and N. Woods (eds), *The Politics of Global Regulation*. Princeton, NJ: Princeton University Press.

McCormick, J. (2002) *Understanding the European Union*. 2nd edn. Basingstoke: Palgrave Macmillan.

Mearsheimer, J. (2001) *The Tragedy of Great Power Politics*. New York and London: W.W. Norton & Co.

Mearsheimer, J. and Walt, S. (2008) *The Israel Lobby and US Foreign Policy*. London: Penguin.

Meritet, S. (2009) What can be expected today from the United States in energy-environment discussions? *Enérgie et société*. Special issue. Fall.

Mészáros, I. (1975) *Marx's Theory of Alienation*. London: Merlin Press.

Mészáros, I. and Foster, J. (2010) *The Stuctural Crisis of Capital*. New York: Monthly Review Press.

Miller, D. (1998) The limits of cosmopolitan justice. In D. Mapel and T. Nardin (eds.), *International Society: Diverse Ethical Perspectives*, Princeton, NJ: Princeton University Press.

Miller, D. (2002) Cosmopolitanism: a critique. *Critical Review of International Social and Political Philosophy*, 5 (3).

Miller, D. (2007a) *National Responsibility and Global Justice*. Oxford: Oxford University Press.

Miller, D. (2007b) Human rights, basic needs, and scarcity. At www.politics.ox.ac. uk/research/working_papers/SJ007.

Miller, D. (2007c) The responsibility to protect human rights. At www.politics.ox.ac.uk/research/working_papers/SJ007.

Milner, H. (1993) The assumption of anarchy in International Relations theory: a critique. In D. Baldwin (ed.), *Neorealism and Neoliberalism: The Contemporary Debate*. New York: Columbia University Press.

Mold, A. (2007) Policy ownership and aid conditionality in the light of the financial crisis: a critical review. OECD Development Center Studies.

Molloy, S. (2006) *The Hidden History of Realism: A Genealogy of Power Politics*. New York and Basingstoke: Palgrave Macmillan.

Molloy, S. (2009) Aristotle, Epicurus, Morgenthau: the politics of the lesser evil. *Journal of International Political Theory*, 5 (1).

Morgenthau, H. (1946) *Scientific Man versus Power Politics*. Chicago: Chicago University Press.

Morgenthau, H. (1952) *In Defense of the National Interest: A Critical Examination of American Foreign Policy*. New York: Knopf.

Morgenthau, H. (1971) *Politics in the Twentieth Century*. Chicago and London: Chicago University Press (original publication in 3 volumes, 1962).

Morgenthau, H. (2004) *Political Theory and International Affairs: Hans Morgenthau on Aristotle's The Politics*. Ed. A. Lang. Westport, CT: Praeger Publishers.

Morgenthau, H. (2005) *Politics Among Nations: The Struggle for Power and Peace*. 7th edn. Columbus, OH: McGraw-Hill.

Mouffe, C. (2000) *The Democratic Paradox*. London: Verso.

Nagel, T. (2005) The problem of global justice. *Philosophy and Public Affairs*, 33 (2).

Neal, A. (2009) 'Foucault'. In J. Edkins and N. Vaughan-Williams (eds), *Critical Theorists and International Relations*. London and New York: Routledge.

Niebuhr, R. (2002) *Moral Man and Immoral Society. A Study in Ethics and Politics*. Louisville, KY: Westminster John Knox Press.

Niebuhr, R. (2008) *The Irony of American History*. Chicago: Chicago University Press.

Nietzsche, F. (1887/1994) Guilt, bad conscience and related matters. In F. Nietzsche, *On the Genealogy of Morality*. Cambridge: Cambridge University Press.

Nietzsche, F. (1888/1988) The four great errors. In F. Nietzsche, *Twilight of the Idols/The Anti-Christ*. London: Penguin.

Nussbaum, M. (1994) Cosmopolitanism and patriotism. *The Boston Review*, 19 (5).

Nussbaum, M. (1997) Kant and cosmopolitanism. In J. Bohman and M. Lutz-Bahmann (eds), *Perpetual Peace: Essays on Kant's Cosmopolitan Ideal*. Cambridge, MA: The MIT Press.

Nussbaum, M. (1998) *Cultivating Humanity: A Classical Defense of Reform in Liberal Education*. Cambridge, MA: Harvard University Press.

Nussbaum, M. (2001) *Women and Human Development: The Capabilities Approach*. Cambridge: Cambridge University Press.

Nye, J. (2004) *Soft Power: The Means to Success in World Politics*. New York: Public Affairs.

Obama, B. (2009a). *Remarks to the Nation on the Way Forward in Afghanistan and Pakistan*. White House Press.

Obama, B. (2009b) Obama's Nobel peace prize speech. White House Press.

OECD. (2009) *OECD Investment News*. June, issue 10.

Olson, M. (1965) *The Logic of Collective Action*. Cambridge, MA: Harvard University Press.

O'Neill, O. (1975/1999) Lifeboat earth. In M. Rosen and J. Wolff (eds), *Political Thought*. Oxford: Oxford University Press.

Owens, P. (2007) *Between War and Politics: International Relations and the Thought of Hannah Arendt*. Oxford: Oxford University Press.

Owens, P. (2009a) Walking corpses: Arendt on the limits and possibilities of cosmopolitan politics. In C. Moore and C. Farrands (eds), *International Relations Theory and Philosophy: Interpretive Dialogues*. London: Routledge.

Owens, P. (2009b) Reclaiming the 'bare life' of refugees. Unpublished manuscript.

Palan, R. (2003) *The Offshore World: Sovereign Markets, Virtual Places, and Nomad Millionaires*. Ithaca, NY: Cornell University Press.

Patomäki, H. (2001) *Democratising Globalisation: The Leverage of the Tobin Tax*. London and New York: Zed Books.

Peterson, P. and Schackleton, M. (2002) *The Institutions of the European Union*. Oxford: Oxford University Press.

Pettit, P. (1997) *Republicanism: A Theory of Freedom and Government*. Oxford: Oxford University Press.

Pew Global Attitudes Project. (2003) *Views of a Changing World June 2003*. Summary at http://pewglobal.org/2003/06/03/views-of-a-changing-world-2003.

Pierson, C. (1991) *Beyond the Welfare State: New Political Economy of Welfare*. Cambridge: Polity.

Pinder, J. (2001) *The European Union: A Very Short Introduction*. Oxford: Oxford University Press.

Pinto, H. (2010) Energy and environment in Brazil. Working-paper. At http://www.aup.edu/main/academics/wpseries.htm.

Plihon, D. (2001) *Le nouveau capitalisme*. Paris: Flammarion.

Pogge, T. (1992) Cosmopolitanism and sovereignty. *Ethics*, 103 (1).

Pogge, T. (2005) A cosmopolitan perspective on the global economic order. In G. Brock and H. Brighouse (eds), *The Political Philosophy of Cosmopolitanism*. Cambridge: Cambridge University Press.

Pogge, T. (2008) *World Poverty and Human Rights*. 2nd edn. Cambridge: Polity.

Polanyi, K. (1944/2001) *The Great Transformation*. Boston, MA: Beacon Press.

Population Reference Bureau. (2010) *2010 World Population Data Sheet*. At http://www.prb.org/pdf10/10wpds_eng.pdf.

Poulantzas, N. (1978) *State, Power, Socialism*. London: New Left Review.

Power, S. (2002) *A Problem of Hell: America and the Age of Genocide*. London: Flamingo.

Prasad, E. et al. (2007) Effects of financial globalisation on developing countries: some empirical evidence. In A. Harrison (ed.), *Globalization and Poverty*. Cambridge, MA: National Bureau of Economic Research.

Ramonet, I. (2009) *Le Krach parfait: crise du siècle et refondation de l'avenir.* Paris: Galilée.

Rashid, A. (2001) *Taliban.* New Haven, CT: Yale University Press.

Rashid, A. (2008) *Descent into Chaos: The US and the Disaster in Afghanistan, Pakistan and Central Asia.* New York and London: Penguin.

Rawls, J. (1971) *A Theory of Justice.* Oxford: Oxford University Press.

Rawls, J. (1993) The law of peoples. *Critical Inquiry,* 20 (1).

Rawls, J. (1999) *The Law of Peoples.* Cambridge, MA: Harvard University Press.

Reilly, J. (2009) Obama foreign policy: a new beginning or Bush II. Lecture at the American University of Paris, 15 September.

Rengger, N. (1995) *Political Theory, Modernity and Postmodernity.* Oxford: Blackwell.

Risse, M. (2005) What do we owe to the global poor? *The Journal of Ethics,* 9 (1/2).

Robertson, G. (2002) *Crimes against Humanity: The Struggle for Global Justice.* 2nd edn. New York: New Press.

Rodrik, D. (1997) *Has Globalization Gone Too Far?* Washington, DC: Institute for International Economics.

Roemer, J. (1994) *Futures of Socialism.* Cambridge, MA: Harvard University Press.

Rosanvallon, P. (2006) *la Contre-démocratie.* Paris: Seuil.

Rosanvallon, P. (2008) *la Légitimité démocratique: impartialité, réflexivité, proximité.* Paris: Seuil.

Rose, G. (1981) *Hegel Contra Sociology.* London: Athlone Press.

Rosen, M. and Wolff, R. (1999) *Political Thought.* Oxford: Oxford University Press.

Rousseau, J-J. (1762) *The Social Contract.* At http://www.constitution.org/jjr/socon.htm.

Ruggie, J. (1982) International regimes, transactions, and change: embedded liberalism in postwar economic order. *International Organization,* 36 (2).

Ruggie, J. (1993) Territoriality and beyond: problematizing modernity in international relations. *International Organization,* 47 (1).

Ruggie, J. (2003) Taking embedded liberalism global: the corporate connection. In D. Held and M. Koenig-Archibugi (eds), *Taming Globalization: Frontiers of Governance.* Cambridge: Polity.

Rumford, C. (2007) *Cosmopolitanism and Europe.* Liverpool: Liverpool University Press.

Sachs, J. (2005) *The End of Poverty: Economic Possibilities for Our Time.* New York: Penguin.

Salvatore, D. (1999) *International Economics.* New York: John Wiley and Sons.

Sandler, T. (1997) *Global Challenges: An Approach to Environmental, Political and Economic Problems.* Cambridge: Cambridge University Press.

Sandler, T. (2004) *Global Collective Action.* Cambridge: Cambridge University Press.

Sands, P. (2005) *The Lawless World.* London: Penguin.

Scheuer, M. (2008) *Marching Toward Hell: America and Islam after Iraq*. New York: Free Press.

Schmidt, B. (1999) *The Political Discourse of Anarchy: A Disciplinary History of International Relations*. Albany, NY: SUNY Press.

Schmitt, C. (1927/2007) *The Concept of the Political*. Chicago: Chicago University Press.

Schofield, M. (1991) *The Stoic Idea of the City*. Cambridge: Cambridge University Press.

Sciolino, E. and Bronner, E. (1999) The road to war: a special report. *New York Times*, 18 April.

Shaw, J. (2000) *The Law of the European Union*. 3rd edn. Basingstoke: Palgrave.

Shaxson, N. (2007) *Poisoned Wells: The Dirty Politics of African Oil*. New York and London: Palgrave Macmillan.

Shepsle, K. A. and Bonchek, M. S. (1997) *Analyzing Politics: Rationality, Behaviour and Institutions*. New York and London: W.W. Norton & Co.

Simmons, B. (1999) The internationalization of capital. In J. Stephens et al. (eds), *Change and Continuity in Contemporary Capitalism*. Cambridge: Cambridge University Press.

Simmons, B. (2006) The future of central bank cooperation. Working-paper #200. Basel: Bank for International Settlements.

Singer, P. (1972) Famine, affluence, and morality. *Philosophy and Public Affairs*, 1 (3).

Skidelsky, R. and Ignatieff, M. (1999) Is military intervention over Kosovo justified? *Prospect*, June 1.

Slaughter, A.-M. (2004) *A New World Order*. Princeton and Oxford: Princeton University Press.

Smith, D. (2008) *The State of the World Atlas*. Brighton: Earthscan editions.

Smith, K. (2008). *European Union Foreign Policy in a Changing World*. Oxford: Blackwell.

Smith, T. (2009) The end of liberal internationalism? In G. J. Ikenberry et al. (eds), *The Crisis of American Foreign Policy: 'Wilsonianism' in the Twenty-First Century*. Princeton, NJ: Princeton University Press.

Smith, T. (2010) From 'fortunate vagueness' to 'democratic globalism': American democracy promotion as imperialism. Paper presented at the International Studies Association Annual Conference, New Orleans, February 2010.

Smith, W. (2007) Anticipating a cosmopolitan future: the case of humanitarian military intervention. *International Politics*, 44/1.

Snyder, J. (1991) *Myths of Empire: Domestic Politics and International Ambition*. Ithaca, NY: Cornell University Press.

Soros, G. (2002) *On Globalization*. New York: Perseus Group Books.

Steger, M. (2003) *Globalisation. A Very Short Introduction*. Oxford: Oxford University Press.

Stiegler, B. (2009) *Pour une nouvelle critique de l'économie politique*. Paris: Galilée.

Stiglitz, J. (2002) *Globalization and Its Discontents*. New York: W.W. Norton and Co.

Strange, S. (1986) *Casino Capitalism*. Oxford: Blackwell.

Strange, S. (1996) *The Retreat of the State: The Diffusion of Power in the World Economy*. Cambridge: Cambridge University Press.

Strange, S. (1998) *Mad Money: When Markets Outgrow Governments*. Ann Arbor: University of Michigan Press.

Suganami, H. (2007) Understanding sovereignty through Kelsen/Schmitt. *Review of International Studies*, 33 (3).

Swift, A. (2006) *Political Philosophy: A Beginner's Guide for Students and Politicians*. 2nd edn. Cambridge: Polity.

Thompson, G. (2007) Global inequality, the 'Great Divergence' and supranational regionalization. In D. Held and A. Kaye (eds), *Global Inequality*. Cambridge: Polity.

Thomson, A. (2007) *Deconstruction and Democracy*. London: Continuum.

Thucydides. (1954) *History of the Peloponnesian War*. London: Penguin.

Tilly, C. (1990) *Coercion, Capital and European States: AD 890–1990*. Oxford: Blackwell.

Tucker, R. (1969) *Marx's Revolutionary Idea*. Princeton, NJ: Princeton University Press.

UN. (2004) A more secure world: our shared responsibility. Report of the UN High-Level Panel on Threats, Challenges and Change. At http://www.un.org/secureworld/.

United Nations Population Division. (2008) *2008 World Population Prospects*. At http://esa.un.org/unpp/

Vaughan-Williams, N. (2007) Beyond a cosmopolitan ideal: the politics of singularity. *International Politics*, 44.

Vidal, C. (1998) Le génocide des Rwandais tutsi et l'usage public de l'histoire. *Cahiers des Etudes Africaines*, 38 (150/152).

Wade, R. (2003) The disturbing rise in poverty and inequality: is it all a 'Big Lie'? In D. Held and M. Koenig-Archibugi (eds), *Taming Globalization: Frontiers of Governance*. Cambridge: Polity.

Wade, R. (2007) Should we worry about income inequality? In D. Held and A. Kaye (eds), *Global Inequality*. Cambridge: Polity.

Walker, R. B. J. (1993) *Inside/Outside: International Relations as Political Theory*. Cambridge: Cambridge University Press.

Walker, R. B. J. (2003) Polis, cosmopolis, politics. *Alternatives*, 28.

Walker, R. B. J. (2010) *After the Globe, Before the World*. Abingdon: Routledge.

Wallerstein, I. (1980–1) *The Modern-World System* (vols 1 & 2). Academic Press.

Wallerstein, I. (2003) *The Decline of American Power*. New York: The New Press.

Waltz, K. (1954) *Man, the State and War: A Theoretical Analysis*. New York: Columbia University Press.

Waltz, K. (1979) *Theory of International Politics*. California: Addison-Wesley Publishing Co.

Walzer, M. (1977) *Just and Unjust Wars*. New York: Basic Books.

Weber, M. (1968) Politics as a vocation. In H. H. Gerth and C. Wright Mills (eds), *From Max Weber*. Oxford: Oxford University Press.

Weber, M. (1978) *Economy and Society*. 2 vols. Berkeley: University of California Press.

Weller, M. (1999) The Rambouillet conference. *International Affairs*, 75 (2).

Wendt, A. (1999) *Social Theory of International Relations*. Cambridge: Cambridge University Press.

Williams, M. (2005) *The Realist Tradition and the Limits of International Relations*. Cambridge: Cambridge University Press.

Williams, M. (2007) *Culture and Security: Symbolic Power and the Politics of International Security*. London and New York: Routledge.

Williamson, J. (1993) Democracy and the 'Washington Consensus'. *World Development*, 21 (8).

Wohlforth, W. (2008) Realism. In C. Reus-Smit and D. Snidal (eds), *The Oxford Handbook of International Relations*. Oxford: Oxford University Press.

Wolf, M. (2004) *Why Globalization Works*. New Haven and London: Yale University Press.

Wolf, M. (2008) *Fixing Global Finance*. Baltimore, MD: Johns Hopkins University Press.

Wood, A. (1972) The Marxian critique of justice. *Philosophy and Public Affairs*, 1 (3).

Wood, A. (1979) Marx on right and justice: a reply to Husami. *Philosophy and Public Affairs*, 8 (3).

Wood, A. (1986) Marx and equality. In J. Roemer (ed.), *Analytical Marxism*. Cambridge: Cambridge University Press.

World Bank. (2007) *World Development Report 2007*. At www.worldbank.org/wdr2007.

World Bank. (2009) *World Development Indicators*. Washington, DC: World Bank.

Ypi, L. (2008) Statist cosmopolitanism. *The Journal of Political Philosophy*, 16 (1).

Zehfuss, M. (2002) *Constructivism in International Relations: The Politics of Reality*. Cambridge: Cambridge University Press.

Zehfuss, M. (2009) Derrida. In J. Edkins and N. Vaughan-Williams (eds), *Critical Theorists and International Relations*. London and New York: Routledge.

Zhao, H. (2007) Some thoughts on Sino-US energy cooperation. In G. Austin and M.-A. Schellekens-Gaiffe, *Energy and Conflict Prevention*. New York: East West Institute.

Zolo, D. (1997) *Cosmopolis: Prospects for World Government*. Cambridge: Polity.

Index